in search *of* teaching style

Abraham Shumsky
Brooklyn College
The City University of New York

in search *of* teaching style

with the participation of
Adaia Shumsky
The Great Neck School System, New York

 New York

Appleton-Century-Crofts

Division of Meredith Corporation

to Mendel

Son of man, stand upon thy feet and
I will speak unto thee

—*Ezekiel*

preface

Recently, I had the interesting experience of meeting a group of European teachers visiting educational institutions in this country. In discussing their impressions of American education, their first reactions were very complimentary.

I wish that people in my country would be as interested in education as the people here.

Education is a central concern of your mass media. I found out that some of the best-seller books deal with school problems.

I admire the amount of experimentation going on. In many schools the greeting was "Let me tell you about the experiment we are conducting."

As the discussion continued, however, the European educators started to raise questions.

In my country, we are in the process of changing our 8:4:4 school structure to a 6:3:3 system. I have just found out that in some American cities the plan is to abandon this approach. Why?

As part of our educational reform we have decided to adopt the policy of "continuous promotion." This was the advice of our American consultants. Why did you go back to a "non-promotion" policy?

I understand that the More Effective Schools experiment showed no significant progress in reading; the nationwide survey of compensatory education by Coleman reached similar conclusions. What are the reasons for the lack of success?

In essence, the European educators are making two observations. One is that American education is inconsistent and is swinging like a pendulum. And the second is that despite all the fervent energy and experimentation, real progress is limited.

The critique of the European teachers and their observations of the American educational scene are valid to a great extent. For instance, examine how the pendulum swung with regard to the school-promotion controversy. In the midst of the progressive education era the detrimental effect of the non-promotion policy on children had become a main concern. Educators awakened to the reality that a 10 per cent average of non-promotion meant that out of one hundred children entering the first grade, only fifty-four graduated after six years of schooling. In other words, 46 per cent were defeated in their educational progress. Especially in lower-class communities, non-promotion symbolized defeat, despair, and alienation.

As a result of this awareness, many schools "solved" the failure problem by a simple administrative device. They abolished non-promotion and inaugurated a "social progress" policy by which all children are promoted. Did they solve the school failure problem?

The postprogressive education era in which we live perceives the social-progress policy of school promotion as the source of almost all evil. As one mother from a disadvantaged community puts it:

My boy, he passed the fifth grade this year and he can't hardly read at all. That just not right. Why they pass him when he don't know how to read? That school, it just not doing the job it ought.

Social promotion is criticized as one of the expressions of the teachers' lack of confidence in the ability of lower-class children to achieve academically: "Don't expect too much of these kids, just keep them moving along as best you can." So, the pendulum is swinging back. Continuous progress and social promotion have become "bad words." The trend is back to the non-promotion policy. Will this trend help resolve the apathy and alienation of disadvantaged children? . . .

One may ask: What is right and what is wrong—non-promotion or social promotion? Which policy is better for our population-at-large and the disadvantaged community in particular? Underlying this question is an assumption that the *administrative decision* with regard to promotion has a crucial impact on academic achievement and school climate; that one policy, versus another, will raise achievement and decrease alienation. This assumption is an oversimplification of the main issues involved in learning. The identification of the problem as social versus non-promotion stems from a skewed and imbalanced value system of education. It stems from the belief that administrative matters *per se* are the panacea to educational problems and the main avenue to school reform.

The experience of the last generation has definitely shown that *administrative solutions* are insufficient when real change is sought.

Several studies published recently indicate only limited success with compensatory-education efforts to help the disadvantaged learner. Why do we fail to make faster progress? It seems that compensatory education is based on the belief in the healing effects of quantitative, additive, and administrative solutions: more teachers, more services, more materials. The school day is extended; the school week and school year are lengthened. This formula of *"Let's have more of the same"* is quantitative rather than qualitative in nature, and increased quantity cannot compensate for deficiencies in quality.

The resolution of the problem of cultural deprivation does not lie merely in increasing school services, but rather in raising the professional competencies of the present teachers as they try to work with lower-class children. The main problem underlying educational change is lack of focus on the *quality* of the teaching-learning experience. Therefore, it is the qualitative examination of the teaching style in the classroom which is the center of discussion in this book.

Whether the school systems of the big cities will be centralized or decentralized; whether we should work toward school integration (advocated by "moderate" leaders) or community control of schools (advocated by the Black Power movement) are very important issues. They may prove secondary, however, in terms of their effect on what really happens to children. The main problem of schooling, potentially more influential than the above hotly debated issues is the quality of teaching behavior in the classroom. What are the dimensions and variations of the teaching style? Why do teachers teach the way they teach? What is the threat and challenge teachers perceive in various teaching styles? What is the impact of specific styles on children? How can teaching style be improved and what is blocking this improvement? Progress on these questions, I believe, will result in higher academic achievement and better intellectual, social, and emotional functioning of children.

The cartoonist observing the present educational scene may give it an exciting title: "The Spank-the-Teacher Era." All over the country the cry is heard: "The teacher is to blame!" One of the most powerful discussions on the damaging impact of teachers on children is a book written by Jonathan Kozol: *Death At an Early Age* (Houghton Mifflin, 1967). The author describes his experience as a substitute teacher and portrays the "destruction of the heart and minds of Negro children in the Boston Public Schools." The main villain responsible for this destruction is the classroom teacher.

Kozol is powerful in describing the meanness and squalor of the schools, the destructive resentment of the teachers, and the smell of urine in the basement. He has a great compassion for deprived children. He lacks, however, any *compassion for teachers*. With great empathy and feeling, he depicts the children as people. The teacher, however, is not portrayed as a person; he is rather a malicious and irrational monster.

I am not going to join the bandwagon and become a member of the "spank-the-teacher club." Underlying my work is the belief that the teacher is a person. He does not love *or* hate; he rather loves *and* hates. He is not good *or* bad; he is rather good *and* bad. He is not only threatened by change; he is also challenged by the need to change!

The title of this book is *In Search of Teaching Style*. The title implies two themes: teaching style and the experience of the teacher who searches to improve his teaching style. To suggest ideas about better ways of teaching is not enough. It is important to explore what happens to the teacher in the process of "the search," to examine his ambivalent feelings and conflicts, and to analyze the reasons for his success or failure. It is not correct to say that teachers do not want to grow. *In Search of Teaching Style* suggests that they are afraid to grow and that they want to grow!

The book is based on my experience in working with novice teachers in the City of New York. It draws on my previous work *Creative Teaching in the Elementary School*, published by Appleton-Century-Crofts, and on a comprehensive study entitled *Personal Assertive Orientation and Intellectual Functioning* (mimeographed). The latter study was conducted with my wife, Dr. Adaia Shumsky, in our sabbatical year.

My deepest appreciation goes to my wife who joined me in writing several sections of this book and whose rich experience as a school psychologist contributed to a more insightful discussion of the teaching-learning process.

A. S.

contents

one

in search of teaching style

1

the climate of repetition

What would be the reactions of beginning teachers to a teaching behavior characterized by emphasis on recall, identification and specificity of facts? Would they recognize the teacher-centeredness, controlling behavior, or lack of emphasis on productive thinking in this way of teaching? Or would they perceive this teaching orientation as democratic, stimulating, and creative? If the last question is answered in the affirmative, what are the factors responsible for the subversion of the good judgment of the novice teacher, causing him to confuse repetitive and controlling instruction with democratic teaching behavior?

To answer the above questions, a group of novice teachers were advised:

I am going to role-play a lesson illustrating a way of teaching. To avoid any value judgment on my part, I'll call this teaching behavior teacher *A*.

On the completion of the demonstration, please write your reactions to teacher *A*, emphasizing his characteristics, the way he would be expected to teach other subject areas, and the motivation underlying his teaching behavior.

The subject matter taught was a reading lesson based on a simple story taken from a second grade basal reader, *The New Friends and Neighbors*[G7]. The story is called "Long-Tail."

It describes Dick, Jane, and Sally finding a baby squirrel and thinking that is a long-tailed kitten.

The following is a brief summary of the role-playing of teacher *A*.

Motivation: A brief discussion of children's experiences with pets.

New Words: Puts the new words, such as *mewing, bigger,* and *long-tail,* on the blackboard. The class discusses the meaning and structure of the new words.

Objective: Announces the objective—reading "Long-Tail."

Reading and Discussion: A brief paragraph is orally read by a pupil. The teacher tests comprehension by asking questions emphasizing specificity: What did Dick hear? (Funny noise.) Where? (In the playhouse.) What did he open? (The door.) A second brief paragraph is read by another child and the testing of comprehension continues in the same pattern: What was the cat's color? How many kittens? Children take turns in reading aloud brief paragraphs. The teacher continues to test the comprehension of the specific and detailed facts. From time to time she emphasizes the spelling and structure of words.

Analysis of Picture: The teacher sensitizes the children to the detailed elements of the pictures: Who is in the picture? What does the boy wear? What does the girl wear?

Dramatization: Children are assigned roles (Dick, Sally, Father, etc.). Each child reads his part from the text. The teacher pays special attention to correct pronunciation.

Seat Work: The teacher distributes mimeographed work and instructs the children to draw a line under the correct word:

    Father saw Long-Tail (during, before, after) dinner.

    (Mother, Father, Dick) said: "Well, well."

    Dick found (a squirrel, a kitten, a duck).

    Draw a picture of Puff and the kittens.

In their reaction to the role-playing, the observers felt that the demonstration was a portrayal of a teacher familiar to them in their experience as pupils and as student teachers. They differed, however, in their evaluation of teacher *A*, assessing the behavior as varying from democratic and modern to authoritarian and traditional. A substantial majority of the group had a positive evaluation of model *A*.

the imparter of information

Both positive and negative responses viewed teacher A as an imparter of knowledge. They differed, however, in their evaluation of the quality of this behavior.

the positive group

As perceived by the "positive group," model A is a portrayal of a teacher who stresses knowledge. To them this is the fundamental and most important function of the teacher. Teacher A is seen as one who is thorough, comprehensive, and systematic. He covers the subject matter of the story, as well as the rest of the course of study prescribed by the Board of Education. Whether teaching reading, arithmetic, or science, he is going to pay attention to the facts, develop the basic skills, and establish a sound foundation for future education.

Bloom states in the *Taxonomy of Educational Objectives*[B8] that the most common educational objective in American education is the acquisition of "knowledge." For the taxonomy purposes, he defines "knowledge" mainly as remembering the idea or phenomenon in a form very close to the way in which it was originally encountered. Or to use Guilford's terminology,[G8] this type of objective emphasizes primarily the psychological processes of cognition and memory, as distinguished from a broader conception of knowledge which includes processes of convergent thinking, divergent thinking, and evaluation.

Those young teachers favorably inclined toward model A do not sense the narrowness of his conception of knowledge, but rather, perceive his behavior as one which promotes thinking, culture, and the necessary fundamentals of a sound education. For example,

Children are young. They have little experience. They know so little about the world. You have to give them facts and information. This is especially correct with regard to the children we new teachers work with—lower-class children. They come from deprived homes. Their parents do not tell them much. We have to start from the beginning to teach them about the world, so that they will know something.

Remember that the emphasis of teacher A on specific skills and facts is basic to all the other ends of education. The broader objectives of problem-solving and thinking cannot be carried on in a vacuum. The teaching of the specifics is a prerequisite to any other learning. You should have your groundwork before you are ready to spread your wings.

Model *A* is perceived as an energetic teacher who works relentlessly to sensitize his pupils to facts and information. He is dedicated to the promotion of the reverence for knowledge. The data collected in this study shows that this knowledge is justified not only because of its importance to children, but also because of the important emotional role it plays in the life of the teachers themselves.

Teacher A is me and my friends studying in your class. We grew up in middle-class families where it was so important to gather information and know things. I see how my older sister treats her children. She wants the young one to look at a book and to name the animals. "This is not a horse, this is a giraffe. Say *giraffe*." She wants the older one to watch the informative educational programs on television. The children watch a trip to the Treasury Department and then are asked questions: "Do you know what counterfeit money means?" "What do they call the police who track counterfeiters?" This type of information is important in my family.

Level *A* of knowledge may often express the fundamental dynamics of a parent-child relationship. Many of the hopes, aspirations, and sense of fulfillment of parents is expressed in their involvement with their child's learning. Much anxiety, guilt, and even sense of defeat is aroused when the child is slow or fails to learn. Subtle or even direct pressure is applied in order that the child will make progress in absorbing knowledge and in being *interested* in knowledge.

For the middle-class child groping for knowledge, knowing

how to read and spell, learning the meaning of words, etc., has a definite emotional connotation. It must be seen as an integral part of the deepest possible matrix, namely, reaching for parental approval.

In reacting to the demonstration of model A, many teachers spoke about the nature of knowledge emphasized in their own schooling and its resemblance to the knowledge communicated by teacher A. Their reactions reveal the tremendous weight which factual information played in their own education. It was the basic way they knew how to succeed at school. Much of their respect for model A can be explained in terms of this identification and sense of continuation. Some teachers feel that teacher A is an extension of their identity.

I belong to a group of people who were always successful in school. We knew the answers on the short-answer tests, or multiple-choice quizzes. We had status with our peers and our teachers. Many of us graduated with honors and were admitted to the college with very high grades in high school. May I put it this way; I believe this teacher A went to school together with us. She got the same education and had the same success. I guess most of us are going to teach like her.

the negative group

The negative reactions to model A criticized his conception of knowledge as narrow and limited. They questioned the intellectual level on which teacher A functioned.

I found it both dull and meaningless to stop and evaluate each short sentence. The questions were of a rote nature. How unexciting for young children this person would be, with his emphasis on repetition and mechanical questions. He provoked no thought in the minds of pupils.

He is interested in comprehension but this to him ends with noticing the specific elements and details in the story or the pictures. His questions require mere identification, rather than any thinking or creativity on the part of children. . . .

The assumption underlying the A way of teaching is that

the mere summation of details will, by itself, create the total
idea—the *Gestalt*. Aware that a total idea is greater than the
composite of its parts, this group suggested that pupils exposed to Model *A* may master the detailed information but
miss the basic message. They may learn the importance of
memorization but might fail to learn the importance of productive thinking. They may learn that Dick heard a funny
noise in the playhouse (rather than in the backyard) but may
fail to comprehend the main idea—the confusing of a squirrel
with a little kitten.

Any appraisal of the quality of the educational process
must start with the fundamental question of whether the intellectual development of children is facilitated or hindered by
the teacher's behavior. With this question in mind, examine
the following not atypical illustrations of classroom practices.
The first is an assignment given to an average third grade.

The answers to these questions are on the blackboard. You must
think and look carefully in order to find them.

1. Who were the first settlers in the "new land?"
2. What does their name mean?
3. Where did they first go before coming to America?
4. What boat did they come to America on?
5. What ocean did they cross?
6. Where was the very first place they settled?
7. Who was their leader?
8. Who were the Indians that made peace with them?
9. What did the Indians teach them to grow?
10. Who brought about the first Thanksgiving day?

All these questions can be answered with a one-word factual response. The mental process required is exclusively that
of memory and identification. No opportunity is offered to explore, to put facts together, or to elaborate an idea. No attempt
is made, for instance, to ask children to state the main problems with which the Pilgrims were faced.

Social studies, a discipline whose main function is to develop critical thinking and social awareness, has too often become methodology which merely attempts to cover subject

matter and impart an aggregation of factual information. For instance, in studying the export-import balance of a given country the main emphasis often becomes the naming of the export items, instead of opening this study to the relationship between import and export, or its impact on the way the people make their living.

limited conception of comprehension

This narrow conception of knowledge, with its emphasis on specificity and recall, is a central and dominant feature of the reading comprehension test.

Two scientists "camped" for a week on the bottom of the sea. Their underwater home was a cabin shaped like a barrel. The shelter was anchored to the sea floor.

1. For how long did the scientists "camp"?
2. Where did the scientists "camp" for a week?
3. What kept the shelter from floating away?

To answer such questions, children do not have to think, to ask why, or to create a generalization. They were not asked to demonstrate *comprehension* by stating, for example, why the scientists were "camped" on the bottom of the sea, or why their shelter was anchored to the sea floor. They were asked only to *repeat*.

A case reported by Nila Smith will illustrate the negative impact of the limited conception of comprehension on teachers.[S11:286] A boy was sent to Dr. Smith for diagnosis. He was considered at school a *good reader* but was failing in other subjects. The boy was asked by the examiner to read the story of Johnny Appleseed and then was asked questions which could be answered by restating what had been said directly in the text. He was asked such questions as these: "How long ago did Johnny Appleseed live?" "What was his real name?" "How did he spend his time?" The boy answered all these questions correctly.

The consensus of the education students who observed

the testing of the boy had been that his comprehension was perfect. However, when the boy was asked a question calling for the interpretation of meaning conveyed but not stated directly in the text, his lack of real comprehension was discovered.

Why did Johnny choose to plant his trees deep in the wilderness when the settlers had not yet come?
He wanted to be alone while he was working.

The boy missed the main implication that the motivation for planting the trees was to prepare the ground for the future settlers.
This case was presented in some detail to illustrate how a limited conception of comprehension subverts the good judgment of teachers. It interferes with their ability to recognize difficulties children may have in comprehension, and furthermore, it teaches them to develop a reading curriculum which aims primarily at these low-level comprehension skills.
The pervasiveness of this type of "literal comprehension" of the paragraph can be found in every reading workbook. In too many classrooms reading becomes a process of reaction to "easy-to-score" objective-type questions, factual items, true-false statements, or multiple-choice questions.
Comprehension is the heart of the reading program, because reading is a thinking process. There is, however, over-emphasis on the low-level literal comprehension, without at least equal stress on the higher dimensions of reading comprehension—namely, creative reading. This criticism does not question the need for literal comprehension, but rather the lack of balance.

suggested observations

The reader is urged to examine the climate of the classroom by raising questions like the following:
What is the nature of the verbal interchange between the teacher and the pupils? Do the teacher's questions elicit primarily recall-type responses or foster productive thinking?

In discussing subject matter, is the emphasis primarily on "covering" the content, or rather on the understanding of the major issues? To what extent are children encouraged to come forward with their own ideas or react to divergent questions? ("What do you think may happen because of the St. Lawrence Seaway?" "What do you think should be done?" Or, "How would you feel if you were there?")

In reading children's compositions, is the emphasis merely on the "correction" of the specifics of spelling mistakes, or does the teacher attempt to react to the main thoughts the writer wanted to convey? What is the time allotment for teaching spelling versus the time spent on writing compositions?

Is the science lesson centered on the transmission of factual information, or are the facts utilized to develop a generalization?

Is the stress in arithmetic on the "how-to-do-it" skill ("do arithmetic"), or is the emphasis on the understanding of the rationale ("think arithmetic")?

friendly or controlling?

The positive reactions viewed model A as friendly, supportive, warm, nice, and a rewarding teacher. The negative responses perceived him as controlling and constricting. Is teacher A friendly or controlling? The attempt to answer this question will lead us to an analysis of the meaning of control, a characteristic of teaching behavior seen by some observers as a dominant and destructive educational factor.[H15]

Positive reactions state:

Teacher A is not punitive. He is nice, friendly and rewarding. I remember his expressions: "How smart this class is today!" Or, "Oh, this class has all the answers."

The atmosphere was lots of fun. Children enjoyed answering the questions. You saw on their faces the satisfaction of giving the right answer . . . The teacher showed interest in what they had to say.

Teachers live in a culture which is other-directed. As stressed by Riesman,[R3] the concern is less with the *quality* of production than with smooth group relationships. What matters is not so much depth of learning but rather "participation" and external manifestations of satisfaction. When asked why they want to be teachers, the majority answered, "I like children." As a group, they come from child-centered homes where parents always sacrificed and gave. As college students, they live in an educational culture which idealizes the child, his needs, and interests, and speaks more than on anything else about the dynamics of human relations. They live in an educational culture which believes that there are three levels of "nastiness"—nasty, very nasty, and authoritarian. Therefore, is it possible to call a seemingly friendly, praising, and smiling teacher by the terrible name "controlling and authoritarian?"

In the fairy tales there is a sharp polarization into "good" and "bad." It would have been easy to do the same with model *A*. It would have been possible to portray a teacher who is hostile and punitive. This path was not followed deliberately. On the contrary, every effort was made to present a teacher who moves through the motions of being friendly and "nice."

The equation of authoritarian and constricting with punitive and harsh is an extreme oversimplification of the problem. The majority of teachers are friendly rather than hostile. The overwhelming majority of their "acts" toward children are pleasant and supportive rather than punitive. Nevertheless, the majority of elementary school teachers tend to be at least somewhat overcontrolling in their teaching behavior.

overstructured teaching style

The major means of *control* in the classroom is not the threat of punishment, but rather the way the teacher *structures* the learning process. Model *A* overstructures the learning process and therefore he is an overcontrolling teacher.

Observing model *A*, one of my colleagues had a picturesque reaction: "A mother hen controls the peeping of the chicks through her feathers." What are the elements in the behavior of teacher *A* which engender control? Again and again, teachers say:

In following teacher *A*'s behavior, I know what to ask. I follow the text and I don't have to worry what will come next.

The following of the text means *structure*. It alleviates a major problem of the novice teacher—what to say, what to do, or where to go next. As new teachers say: "There is something to hang on to." The end result is security in following the text—the authority.

A second element which contributes to control and security is the *fixed answer problem-solving*. The problems teacher *A* asks have fixed answers. The exact answer to be regurgitated by the student can be found in the text. One has only to parrot back the text's words. For instance,

1. The first settlers in the "new land were the (Pilgrims).
2. Before coming to America they went to (Holland).
3. The boat they came to America on was (the Mayflower).

Whether the child responds orally or in writing, it is very easy to control and direct this kind of learning behavior. Teaching becomes so routinized that hardly anything unexpected happens. The learner's responses are fixed and predetermined. The degree of routinization of learning is well illustrated by Dewey's story in which he asked a class "What would you find if you dug a hole in the earth?" Getting no response, he repeated the question with no results. The teacher chided Dewey, "You are asking the wrong questions." Turning to the class, she asked, "What is the state of the center of the earth?" The class replied in unsion, "Igneous fusion."[D8]

A third element in teacher *A*'s behavior which enhances the sense of control and security is the impression of *success*. So-called success is easy to achieve under teacher *A*'s pattern of leadership. The easy questions which call for reproduction rather than production, mean quick response and almost complete "participation" on the part of children. Participation is equated with "interest"; if everyone participates, then everyone is interested.

Immediate and predetermined responses to narrow stimuli (questions) give the impression of quick and smooth movement from one question to another. The reason is simple. What can one say in response to the question: "Where did Dick see the cat?" The text says: "Dick saw the cat in the playhouse." There is not much that the learner can add to this point of information. The only thing to do is to progress to the next question: "How many kittens did the cat have?" Smooth progress from one point or part to another gives the illusion of success. And the feeling of success in turn enhances the sense of security and achievement which the teacher is craving for. He feels he is in complete *control*.

The reader may ask: "What is wrong with this control? Do you want children to run wild in the classroom? Do you advocate a theory of teaching behavior of the nature of 'Children, what do you want to do today?' "

These are real and down-to-earth questions. This book is not written from a child-centered point of view; it definitely believes that the teacher has to play a directive and even controlling function. It is a controlling behavior which is *constricting* that is criticized here, rather than the control itself. Young teachers who perceived the *A* model negatively wrote:

It is one-way communication . . . Preconceived ideas of what should be said or done.

The predetermined response does not provide freedom for children to think and create. If you are exposed to this teacher, it affects your own sense of being a person.

The last sentence stresses that the *A* climate "affects your own sense of being a person." An attitude is conveyed by the overcontrolling teacher that the child himself lacks power and strength. The only thing the child can do is move when the teacher tells him how, where, and when to move. The pupil is not supposed to make a movement on his own.

curricular illustrations of overstructured style

A second grade is discussing the safety problem in crossing the street.

Teacher: Let's play it. Who has something red? [A child raises her red pen.] O.K. Come and stand here. You are the red light. Who has something green? [A girl points to her scarf.] Very good, stand near the "red." You are . . . [the girl completes: "green light."] Now, who wants to be a person who crosses the street? [Children raise their hands with excitement.] Sue, you were very nice today, come and join the play. What are you? [Sue: "I'll try to cross the street."] Oh, I forgot—we need a truck. Who wants to be a truck? [Children raise their hands with excitement.] Come Harry, you will be the truck. [Takes a piece of chalk and makes a line.] What is this? [Looks playfully at the children and waits until everyone raises his hand. A child answers: "A street."] Yes, you are very smart today. Now, we are ready. Show red light! Show green light! Sue, quick, cross the street. Red light; Now, Harry the truck, it is your turn to pass.

The children are happy. The teacher is happy. Everyone is happy. They had "lots of fun," and what can be a greater achievement in our culture, which is fun-oriented? Despite the overt enjoyment, psychologically speaking, the example illustrates a process of diminution conducted with disarming sweetness. Without verbalizing it the child learns, as one of the negative reactions states, that "Only what the teacher has in mind is important. I have no power to think on my own." If the teacher were harsh then the children could rebel, or at least hate. The A model is "nice and sweet." It is difficult to reject or resist her.

It is possible in trying to demonstrate the scene of crossing the street, to ask: "Children, how are we going to play it?" It is possible to appoint a small group to play and demonstrate the scene. An approach of this nature means that the learner has to mobilize his resources, think through the needs of the situation, and come out with a plan of his own.

The following is an illustration from the methodology of arithmetic, demonstrating the contention that the constricting behavior of the A model does not provide children with *freedom* to think. A first grade is studying numbers.

The teacher puts on the blackboard $1 + 4 =$. The children raise their hands. The teacher calls on a boy to go to the blackboard and write the answer. The boy looks for a piece of chalk and climbs on a chair to reach the correct spot. He finds it difficult to write with chalk, but finally he has it—number 5. The class waits patiently. The teacher puts on the blackboard $2 + 3 =$ and again a child writes 5. The same procedure is repeated with $3 + 2 =$, $4 + 1 =$. No one makes a mistake. Everyone has the correct answer. The class is very orderly. The teacher is satisfied and happy with the achievement.

In situations like this, I am very tempted to walk to the blackboard and write $2 + 4 =$; $1 + 5 =$. My guess is that at least some children, operating on the assumption that the expected answer is 5, will "give" out of habit the expected answer.

It is possible in teaching number 5 to call on several children and ask them to go to the blackboard and put down all the combinations of two groups which make number 5. Let them have *freedom* to figure out a *variety* of combinations, rather than limiting their role to repeating the correct responses. Let several people work on the blackboard simultaneously so that the classroom climate will not be dominated by waiting for one's turn. It may be pretty deadly to wait. . . .

suggested observations

The reader is urged to observe the classroom in terms of the overcontrolling problem. How do teachers give instructions? How do they regulate the learner's responses and behavior? What is the degree of *freedom to think* that pupils have? How can it be increased? Do children raise questions? Do they have an opportunity to make plans and suggest directions to be followed?

conclusions

Model *A* was developed as a stereotype to illustrate an extreme accentuation of specificity and recall. It is correct to suggest that very few teachers are as extreme as he is. However, it is also correct to observe that the style of his teaching behavior plays a too prevalent role in the present school curriculum. The traditional conception of the teacher's role as being predominantly a purveyor of information and a checker of learned facts is a major deterrent to the intellectual development of children.

The *A* orientation is overstructured and overcontrolling. It is not conducive to the experiencing of the "power to think." Especially today, when the powerlessness of the disadvantaged child and community are the center of the educational concern, the point cannot be overemphasized that the accentuation of the *A* climate of teaching is damaging. It tends to enhance passivity rather than encourage assertiveness; to stress concreteness rather than develop abstract thinking. It looks at the learner as an object to be moved, rather than as a subject that has the potential to fly.

the fear of confusion

In reacting to curricular proposals of this nature, some teachers feel that the end result will be confusion or even failure: "The children would not know what to do. You must give them step-by-step instructions." In addition to an underestimation of the ability of children to think and organize on their own, there is in these comments a misconception of the role of confusion and failure in learning. It often seems that teaching in the elementary school is on a level which is too easy for children. Teachers deliberately try to present the learning content in small chewable portions so that the children will not get confused.

What is wrong with running into difficulty, experiencing confusion, or even failing? It is wrong when (1) the confusion does not lead to increased efforts and mastery and (2) when failure is looked down upon and is punished by a poor grade. With these exceptions, a certain level of confusion and even some failure is a very educative experience for children. As Chapter 4 will demonstrate, a prerequisite to the development of creative thinking is tolerance for ambiguity and confusion.

The overprotective teacher tends to underestimate both the child's ability to take frustration and the importance of

this characteristic for growing into maturity. As suggested by
Heil in a research study on the characteristics of teacher behavior,[H7] many teachers tend to feel most secure when things
run smoothly. It seems that the internal need for control and
smooth functioning interferes with a sound estimation of the
pupil's ability and his level of frustration.

This chapter does not suggest that the mastery of facts
is not important, nor that the teacher should not play a directive role. The criticism is, to use Huxley's language, "that
those who refuse to go beyond facts rarely get as far as facts."
The criticism is that the overcontrolling behavior of model *A*
is *constricting* in nature.

The present-day elementary school teacher tends to be
friendly and warm. His means of control is not punitive action, but rather overstructuring of the learning climate
through overemphasis of memory and recall of specifics to
the detriment of the processes of productive thinking.

Havighurst and Neugarten say:[H4:390]

It is in the role of mediator of learning that the teacher tends to
be most sure of himself. What is to be taught and how it is to be
taught are the teacher's main stock in the trade . . . It is also within
this role, as contrasted with others, that the teacher's behavior is
the most *highly ritualized* and *formalized*.

Marie Hughes concludes an intensive investigation into
the behavior of the elementary school teacher by saying:[H15:186]

The furniture in the classroom, the color on the walls, the illustration in books . . . have all changed, as has the appearance and groom-
ing of the teacher. But the basic pattern of teacher-child relation
[control] has not changed.

Although this conclusion is perhaps somewhat extreme,
it would seem that a major function of the elementary school
teacher is to break away from a repetitive and controlling way
of teaching, toward a behavior which aims at *productive
thinking*. Toward this direction models *B* and *C* are going to
move in the next two chapters.

selected bibliography

BURTON, WILLIAM H., *The Guidance of Learning Activities.* New York: Appleton-Century-Crofts, 1962. Chapter 5 criticizes the overemphasis on memorizing of isolated facts.

HEIL, M. LOUIS, POWELL, MARION, and FEIFER, IRWIN, *Characteristics of Teacher Behavior Related to the Achievement of Children in Several Elementary Grades.* New York: Brooklyn College, 1960. An investigation into the relationship between teacher personality, teacher behavior, and pupils' achievement. Teacher *B* has important implications to my discussion of model *A*.

HUGHES, MARIE, *Assessment of the Quality of Teaching in Elementary Schools.* Salt Lake City, Utah: The University of Utah Press, 1959. Chapter 5 is a discussion of the controlling teacher.

2

the climate of thinking

A demonstration was presented before the same group of novice teachers, illustrating how the *same lesson* (the story called "Long-Tail") could be taught emphasizing the *B* orientation. It was followed by written reactions and interviews. The following is a sketch of the role-playing of teacher *B*.

Motivation: Discussion of children's experiences with identifying animals.

Objective: The main idea in the story.

Reading: The class is asked to read the story silently from the beginning to the end.

Discussion and Reading: The teacher raises questions attempting to tap and develop the pupil's comprehension of the basic theme of the total story: What happened? What are the main points? What is the main idea? *Why* did they make a mistake in calling a squirrel a long-tailed kitten? Would you make a mistake like this? Much of the emphasis is on the *why*. Pupils read orally the parts they like best, explain these parts, and speak about favorite words and expressions.

Picture Analysis: Emphasis is placed on the basic message of the pictures: What does the picture say? What else? How does it help to understand the story?

Dramatization: The group decides on the major scenes in the story, (work which calls for organizing the major parts). They select one scene for dramatization. Children volunteer for roles. The children play one scene spontaneously, sticking to the content of the story but without reading from the book. The teacher emphasizes spontaneous and logical oral expression.

Seat work: Draw a picture of the part that you like best and write the story in your own words.

Whereas the group's perception of model *A* was polarized, the perceptions of model *B* were very favorable. While there were some teachers who perceived weaknesses in the *B* approach, or predicted some dangers in its application, the overall response was—"I want to be like teacher *B*."

The following are some illustrations of the favorable written reactions to model *B*.

Teacher *B* strives to teach the child to look for the general meaning. What is the main idea? The child reads with meaning and pleasure.

What does the picture say? This emphasis on a central meaningful question gives the student a chance to think for himself, rather than being almost told the answer in teacher *A*'s way of questioning— Is the cat big or small?

It was the feeling of the group that the emphasis of teacher *B* on the meaning of basic ideas, his encouragement of productive thinking, and his provisions for freedom constituted a higher level of teaching than the stress of model *A* on specificity and overstructured behavior.

the main idea

The group realized that the major characteristics underlying the *B* approach was the emphasis on the main idea—the Gestalt. Perhaps all the other characteristics are a product of this emphasis. The search for the development of a main idea, the producing of a generalization and a structure, permeates the various steps taken by teacher *B*, such as reading, discussion, and picture analysis. This teacher continuously asks himself: "What are the key concepts which are central? What are the principles to be developed?"

There has been within the last several years a renewed

interest in American education in the meaning of knowledge. The study of the structure of the various disciplines of subject matter is becoming a major endeavor of the postprogressive education era. Bruner's book, *The Process of Education,* is a landmark signifying the great interest in the meaning of *structure,* that is, the learning of how things are related and the understanding of the fundamental principles "ordering" a discipline.[B12]

The objective of teacher *B* is to help the learner distinguish between data and structure and move as quickly as possible from the first to the second. In contrast to *A,* he is a *constructionist,* who attempts to organize the encountered data in a manner which is conductive to discovery of regularity and relatedness. To quote from the reactions of teachers:

In teaching about housing she will stress major concepts. For example, the relationship between types of housing and climate, or the relations between housing and safety . . . A typical question will be: "Why are the houses in the European farms arranged in villages, whereas the farms in America are far from each other?"

I see teacher *B,* teaching science and arithmetic. In teaching science, she will try to show what various scientific facts and observations mean in terms of a major principle, such as, "air takes space." She will always ask for the why, the reason and explanation. In teaching arithmetic, she will not be satisfied with drill, or the knowledge of accurate computation. Teacher *B* will rather emphasize arithmetical relationship and the main concepts.

To the extent that the learner is less mature in terms of his thought processes, or less versed in the specific discipline which he is studying, he will tend to have difficulty in grasping the uniting structure. His thinking will be characterized by *empiricism* rather than *constructionism.*

In playing the game of Twenty Questions, the immature child tends to ask specific questions: "Is it an apple, an orange, a banana?" He is concrete and empirical in his thinking. The mature child attempts to identify constraints in the problem: "Do we eat it? Is it fruit? Is it round?" This child is a constructionist. In contrast to the first, he is able to organize and utilize the learned information and therefore will tend to be faster in finding the solution.[B11]

Model *B* attempts to develop the capacity of children to move from empiricism to constructionism. For him it is not sufficient that the child knows the correct answer to an arithmetical computation. The pupil must, rather, understand the rationale underlying the principle. For teacher *B*, arithmetic is a system of ideas rather than merely an aggregation of correct responses. Likewise, he is not satisfied with the child's knowing the correct answers to level *A* questions on a reading comprehension test. To him, real comprehension calls for the grasp of the main ideas communicated by the reading matter. In brief, in contrast to *A*, *B* is not interested in *covering* the subject matter; his interest is, rather, in the uniting structure emerging from the factual data.

To develop theory and structure means to grasp the relatedness of knowledge. Without structure, arithmetic becomes an aggregation of computation skills, history becomes merely reporting of events, and science is identical with the observation of discrete facts. The emphasis on structure means the potential to apply knowledge. As Bruner says: "It bestows the gift of intellectual travel beyond the information given."[B12:109]

A teaching style which helps the child think in terms of constructs and grasp the structure of subject matter is conducive to growth toward intellectual mobility.

main ideas: difficulties

The tendency of many teachers is to select concepts that are too easy in terms of children's comprehension and too trivial in terms of social significance. Stendler[S14] makes the point that knowing that Bolivian women wear many petticoats may be an interesting fact, but is hardly socially significant; knowing that firemen slide down a pole from their upstairs quarters to answer an alarm is insignificant in relation to the concept that fire departments are maintained by local taxes. In a study of dairying it is more important for children to know that the quantity of milk can be improved by providing proper grazing and food for cows, than to know that the four breeds of cows most commonly found in the U.S.A. are Jerseys, Holsteins, Guernseys, and Swiss.

What are the factors that stop teachers from following the *B* orientation, which emphasizes significant concepts and generalizations? A partial answer to this question was given in the discussion of model *A*. The factors include a limited conception of knowledge, home and school experience, and the need for security and control. Additional answers are found in an analysis of the reactions to teacher *B*. These include confusion with regard to the role of formulating objectives and its impact on the reality of teaching. An interviewee says:

Teacher *B* is the one who emphasizes the main ideas. I think in my teaching, I resemble teacher *B*. When I plan a unit or a lesson, I decide on my objectives. These objectives are the major concepts I want children to learn.

In planning a unit or a lesson, the teacher is expected to think first about her objectives, that is, the key concepts she wants to communicate. In doing this, the teacher follows one aspect of the *B* orientation. It seems, however, that a continuity between the objectives (key concepts) and the specific subject matter is too often lacking. To put it in extreme terms, one often has the feeling that the objectives were written by one person and the subject matter by another. Teachers revealed, during our interviews, that planning of objectives was not sufficiently meaningful when it came to actual teaching behavior. For instance,

Statement of objectives is found only in the Board of Education materials, or in the lesson plans presented to the college professor who supervises student teachers. The classroom teacher, who has to teach the whole day, does not bother with "objectives." Perhaps she puts some in the planbook to be inspected by the assistant principal. But anyhow, she does not follow her planbook.

These critical remarks are honest. The formulation of key concepts expressed in the language of objectives is often perceived as dictated by an authority—an assignment by the college instructor or an expectation of the principal. The

teacher is not always convinced of the educational value of
this step and its helpfulness to him as a practitioner. He often
tends to emphasize specific elements of subject matter, questions, materials, and activities, rather than the totality (so
central in the *B* orientation) that has to emerge.

What one witnesses here is not an uncommon phenomenon.
The basic idea which is the primary reason for the development of an educational activity loses its central role and is
pushed to the periphery, to a secondary position. A major
reason is the preoccupation of an anxious practitioner with
the minutes of teaching. The emphasis is on a smooth and
organized presentation of minute subject matter and activities,
without sufficient thinking through of the final concepts to
emerge.

Another difficulty which some teachers mention is a conflict between the desire to develop the major idea and the
sense of obligation to "cover" the subject matter. An interviewee says:

I wanted to teach a poem which conveyed a feeling of loneliness.
The plan was to ask children to describe the mood and explain the
clues which give the impression of loneliness. As the lesson pro-
ceeded, however, the center of discussion became the analysis of
the difficult words and the attempt to put them in sentences.

The above teacher cuts her emphasis on the *B* orientation
with a lengthy discussion of word study. In this process the *B*
orientation is undermined and the emergence of the key concept—the mood of loneliness—is lost. The *A* orientation is so
strong and ingrained that in too many cases it permits mainly
the coverage of factual information. Observations of curricular practices show that this is especially true in the areas
of language arts and social studies. It appears to a lesser extent in the areas of science and arithmetic.

main ideas: language arts

In the area of language arts, the skills of reading and
writing (in the narrow sense of the word "skill") often become dominant. In this process, the ideas and values com-

municated in the reading and writing matter often become irrelevant, or at least secondary. In social studies the factual information of dates, names, events, and numbers, receives a dominant role. In this process the development of the Gestalt, so central in the B orientation, is relegated to secondary position. The development of significant key concepts is often not reached, and sometimes not even attempted.

Interestingly enough, it is in two disciplines of the curriculum considered difficult to teach by so many teachers, where the B orientation proved to be most successful. These areas are arithmetic and science. In arithmetic the emphasis is on developmental and gradual emergence of concepts through the use of firsthand experiences and representative materials. The emphasis is on logic and relationships rather than solely on the mechanics of accurate computation. Many teachers are working hard on following the teaching of developmental arithmetic with its emphasis on structure and Gestalt—the major characteristics of the B orientation.

In the area of reading, however, the experiencing of the intellectual, emotional, and aesthetic ramifications of the reading content assumes a secondary place, while words rather than ideas become a central focus. The following observations may illustrate this point.

A teacher often starts a reading activity by putting the new words on the blackboard and devoting a significant part of the lesson to the study of the "new words." In essence, this type of teaching behavior implies that what counts is word knowledge, rather than the content and the adventure of ideas. Too many children read to study words, rather than to be nourished by ideas.

In oral reading the child is corrected or helped when he mispronounces a word or does not know the meaning of a word, but lacking here is an equal emphasis on oral reading which expresses the child's identification with the characters or his understanding of the mood.

Similarly, the most dominant aspect of the teaching of writing is the "spelling program," emphasizing the correct spelling of discrete words. There is lacking an equal emphasis on the communication of ideas and feelings through the media of writing.

In discussing stories or poems, the teacher often tends to rush into the analysis of the particulars, the difficult words, rather than delve into the message or meaning of the content. An example will illustrate this aspect of word-centeredness.

"The Star-Spangled Banner" is taught to a group of sixth graders. The novice teacher tells the group the story of Francis Scott Key, who was inspired to write the poem by the sight of the American flag flying over Fort McHenry during its bombardment by the British frigate *Surprise*. She tells them that he, himself, was a captive on the boat. When the story is finished, the children read the poem orally. The lesson is culminated by looking for the meaning of the difficult words with the help of a dictionary. What is the impact of the experience of the poet on the message of the poem? Why was the poem selected to become the national anthem? How do the children feel when they sing it? No attempt is made to delve into questions of this nature. The novice, rather, rushes to find refuge in the safety of vocabulary development and dictionary skills.

People equally facile in language will vary in the wealth of their verbal expression depending on the extent of their contact and familiarity with the life situation they are describing. The intellectual, emotional, and aesthetic experience of an idea is the *father of the word* and is the most productive source for language development.

However, it should be noticed that a novice teacher may be somewhat blocked in recognizing the rich potentials of this approach. His experience as a student tells him that the way to pass some of the examinations he has to take is to cram from a book on "increasing your word vocabulary." Before some examinations, he does not read a novel or become immersed in an intellectual endeavor, but rather memorizes a dictionary list.

The novice was told by his friends that the recent Board of Education examination for teachers asked for the definition of tachistoscope. Therefore, he is not interested in the impact

of this "reading machine" on children or the rationale underlying its use; his primary interest is only to learn the *word*.

The novice opens a textbook on the English language,
written for third graders.[S:15] He finds a chapter entitled "En-
joying Poetry" to be full of exciting poems. Then he looks
at the end of the chapter and finds that the *only* suggestions
for testing are "word-centered":

1. The child is asked to choose a word from a list of sounds
   and picture words and to write a sentence using the word.
2. The text presents a list of poem titles, and the child is asked
   to use capital letters where they belong.
3. Two lists of words are presented, and the child is asked to
   match the words which rhyme.

When the novice is introduced to the basal reader (the
book dominating the reading program), he finds out that the
major rationale underlying the construction of this book is
the science of words as expressed in formulas of controlled
vocabulary. He hears much about the science of words, but
hears little about the science of ideas, or the literary quality
of the reader.

main ideas: social studies

In social studies the factual information of dates, names,
events, and numbers receives a dominant role. In this process,
the development of the Gestalt, so central in the *B* orientation,
is relegated to secondary position. The development of significant key concepts is often not reached and sometimes not even
attempted.

In a discussion of the lack of balance in the social studies
program, Sanders observes that textbooks in this field provide
ample information on the nature and use of maps, globes,
charts, and graphs; and that there is adequate stress on the
use of the library. The deficiency is primarily in the area of
productive thinking, such as forming generalizations, comparing and contrasting points of view, separating relevant
from irrelevant information, or formulating the basic issues.[S1:27]

Perhaps more than any other curriculum area, social studies tends to operate on level *A* of knowledge. As Foshay says:[F3:7]

We have taught places in the name of geography, thus almost losing this vitally important and interesting field to our schools. We have taught facts in the name of history, thus as I say, betraying a basic discipline.

It seems that in too many cases, teaching materials continue to deal with the level of enumeration rather than productive thinking. In a book calling for a strong intellectual orientation in programs for young children, Wann criticizes the elaboration of the obvious.[W1:5]

We develop units of study in which we devote considerable time to identifying and enumerating the community helpers and landmarks in the community. On the other hand, when we listen to young children we find that most of their questions are "how and why" questions, indicating a desire for more penetrating understanding than simply being content with identification of "what is."

Torrance reports two studies relevant to the emphasis on thinking in social studies teaching. A questionnaire was sent to elementary school teachers in which they were asked to name a subject they taught in social studies and to list what they considered to be the three most important objectives of this subject. A classification of the objectives suggests that around 80 per cent deal with memory.[T4:4-5]

In another study Torrance reports that "even the least effective mathematics teachers appear to be more concerned about stimulating their pupils to leap the barrier between learning and thinking" than their social studies counterpart.[T4:6]

In reacting to the incomplete sentence "The most important thing about social studies is . . ." the novice teachers under discussion stressed group work and human relations. When they reacted to the same item with regard to science, the emphasis was on experimentation and the development of generalizations. It seems that especially in comparison to science the goal of productive thinking does not appear to be as central in the *practice* of the methodology of social studies.

Novice teachers often speak about the "elusiveness" of the social studies concepts (government, ancient times) and compare them with science concepts. In teaching science the concept, such as vibration, is developed from the concrete to the abstract. It is possible to sense it, see it, touch it. Even if one does not see with his own eyes that sound travels or that it travels in all directions, he can infer it from simple experimentation. The same can be said about arithmetic. For instance, the concept of multiplication can be introduced through representative materials and developed as a shortcut to addition. In social studies the relationship between the concrete and the abstract, the development through firsthand experience, or the testing of the idea within the four walls of the classroom is more difficult to attain. To quote from an interview:

How do you explain to primary children the meaning of the Pledge of Allegiance? How do you reduce this idea into a simple concept?

main ideas: arithmetic

In his article, "After John Dewey, What"[B11:121], Bruner says that

Mathematics, like any other subject, must begin with experience; but progress toward abstraction and understanding requires precisely that there be a weaning away from the obviousness of superficial experience.

Progressive education enriched the teaching of arithmetic by stressing its experiential and social aspect. The emphasis was on making teaching functional (for instance, learning addition and subtraction in the context of a store, run by the class) and on representative materials. Observation of primary grades illustrates especially well the vitalizing impact of the modern educational ideas—movement from drill and exercises toward operation in problem and action-centered situations.

Progressive education is being criticized, however, for

its stresses on the child's experience and its neglect of the structure of subject matter. As seen by the mathematician, progressive education has been preoccupied with the social experiential origin of arithmetic. Such emphasis on the pragmatic aspects has brought about a delineation of arithmetic as a skill, emphasis on "do arithmetic" rather than "think arithmetic." Learning failed to move sufficiently from the experiential to the abstract. Under the impact of the "mathematic revolution" teachers are in the process of learning to view and teach arithmetic as a system of ideas, to stress discovery and productive thinking.

The new concept suggested by the "mathematic revolution" implemented "progress toward abstraction" but has often failed to pay due attention to the springboard—the experience. As a result, some of the new programs communicate a sense of verbalism and formalism. Especially today when the education of the deprived child is a central issue, neglect of the concrete experience and excessive formalism are highly questionable.

A basic theme of this book is movement from the concrete to the abstract. This movement can be made only by using the concrete data to develop abstraction. It cannot be attained by neglect of the first and the mere centering on the latter.

main ideas: science

The major factor responsible for the relatively successful implementation of the *B* approach in the teaching of science is the emphasis on experimentation. The method of scientific investigation, with its emphasis on the one hand on experimentation and observation, and on the other hand on inductive and deductive thinking, is a common approach which many teachers take in teaching science. The end result is often the emergence of a Gestalt—the basic concept.

In discussing science methodology, novice teachers tend to stress the potential significance of this discipline in concept formation and intellectual development of children. This attitude is in marked contrast to attitudes concerning other disciplines. In teaching reading, the obvious need of mastering the skill of reading correctly and fluently tends to prevent the teacher from giving equal attention to the intellectual message of the reading matter. In arithmetic the emphasis on the correct stimulus response of computation and the memorization of rules interferes with paying equal attention to the process of arrival, or the rationale. In social studies, the preoccupation with facts, dates, and names of places and products interferes with the novice's ability to develop generalizations and critical thinking.

It is mainly in the area of science that the methodology is commonly viewed as experimentation. Movement from the concrete to the abstract and concept formation are viewed as being as significant as the factual subject matter itself.

A group of novice teachers were asked to record in detail a science lesson they had taught. An examination of these records illustrates the dominant role of the *B* orientation of concept formation in science teaching. For instance, a lesson on sound, planned for a second grade, aims at developing the following concepts:

1. A sound is made when something vibrates.
2. A sound stops when the vibration stops.
3. There are many ways to set an object into vibration.
4. The harder the object is struck the louder the sound.
5. Large objects make lower tones than smaller objects made of the same matter.
6. Different materials produce different sounds.

A comparison of the records of science lessons with the records of language arts or social studies lessons given by the same group of teachers shows that the concept-formation goal is stronger in science teaching than in any other area of the curriculum. For instance, a typical reading lesson states that an aim is "to understand the story," or a typical social studies lesson may aim at "learning about the problems which confronted Washington." The concepts of social studies or language arts to be developed are *vague* in the teacher's own mind, in comparison to the relative clarity of the science concepts.

The examination of the records of science lessons shows that the typical lesson taught by the novice is a systematic development of the concept through observation and manipulation of materials. Despite this valuable emphasis on productive thinking and level B of knowledge, the methodology of the novice tends to be overstructured and too often constricting in nature. It is characterized by a relative lack of *freedom* for exploration as it moves the child step-by-step toward a predetermined goal.

The expression of the repetitive orientation in science teaching is not in the emphasis on the first aspect of repetitiveness—level A of knowledge—but rather on the second aspect of this model—overstructured behavior.

productive thinking

The teaching behavior of model B is composed of two basic elements: (1) the level of knowledge he wants to communicate and (2) the process by which he wants to reach this level of knowledge. These two factors are interrelated. Teaching often centers on the conclusion of an intellectual inquiry without giving equal emphasis to the process of inquiry itself. On many occasions I have heard first graders argue about Columbus.

He said that the world is flat.
No, he said that the world is round. The teacher said so.

A generalization which is transmitted by the teacher rather than developed by the learner himself may lead to verbal glibness and superficiality. This danger requires further examination of the B orientation in terms of the *process of arriving* at a major idea and its educational implications.

A teacher writes:

I call teacher B creative because she does not stick to the information in the text. She asks children to look at facts and create a new idea . . . The idea is not stated explicitly in the subject matter and therefore I call it newly produced and created.

The full-blown term—"creative," for teacher B, will be questioned in the next chapter; however, in terms of the discussion here, the above reaction stresses the aspect of production and creation in the B orientation. In other words, the A approach is denoted by reproductive and the B by productive thinking.

Perhaps it is extreme to call the process of reproductive thinking a passive way of learning. There is some degree of activity on the part of the learner in the A emphasis on identification and recall. However, productive thinking calls for a much higher degree of activity, participation, and creation on the part of the learner. He has to put much more of himself into the productive thinking process. He has to perceive the essential in a specific phenomenon or constellation, to limit and organize the infinite variety of reality phenomena, and finally to form a new concept or reach a conclusion.

Psychologists are unanimous in ascribing paramount importance to the process of productive thinking in that complex which is called "intelligence." The ability to think productively and abstractly is a primary factor for the higher levels of intelligence. Typical illustrations of the interest of the test builder in this primary factor of intelligence are test items such as: "How are a plum and a peach alike?"

One child may answer: "They are fruits." Another child may answer: "They have pits." The first child is able to see relationships on a higher level than the second and abstract a new concept—fruits. The latter has a low-level response. He reacts to one characteristic (the pit) rather than to the whole concept.

Another typical illustration of the interest of the testologist in productive thinking is the following test item taken from the revised Stanford-Binet Form L:[T3]

My neighbor has been having queer visitors. First a doctor came to the house, then a lawyer, then a minister. What happened there?

Nowhere in the story is the word "death" mentioned. The subject has to put together not only the basic facts in the story, but also some of the information about customs in our

culture that are known to him, and reach the conclusion—
"Someone was dying." Some subjects may think this way:
"The facts are that the doctor came first, the lawyer second,
and the minister last. What is the work of these people? In
my knowledge, when do they come in this order to visit a
family? The answer is—"Someone was dying."

The process of productive thinking which is described here
in a somewhat logical and sequential way may be too orderly.
Perhaps what takes place during the process of productive
thinking is what the Gestalists call "insight." The intelligent
individual toys with the factors presented in the problem
situation and with the factors known to him in his previous
experience and suddenly "sees the relationships" and "arrives
at closure," as if, metaphorically speaking, the discrete elements
in the problem situation are isolated and are therefore "open."
Only by the act of "insight" does the learner "unite" the important parts and reach "closure."

As said earlier, forming concepts is more than just receiv-
ing information. The learner must be able to organize his information into major generalizations. For instance, in reading,
the pupil looks for the major idea conveyed by the data; in
science, for the explanation of the observed phenomenon, or
in arithmetic, for the reasoning underlying the specific al-
gorithm. Forming concepts and generalizations must be viewed
as an *active process of search* on the part of the learner. Some
of the typical questions he may be thinking about during this
process of search are: What is the main idea? How can it be
explained? Why? What does it mean? What is the conclusion
or solution? What are the similarities or differences? In brief,
productive thinking is a process of discovery which culminates
in a structure of a generalization or an answer.

The underestimation of the importance of the *process* of
productive thinking generally results in two forms of teaching
behavior. One is the teacher who "gives" children the "answers," or transmits the main idea to pupils rather than allow-
ing them to discover it. A typical illustration is the memorization of a rule of grammar or of arithmetic without an inductive process which leads to the formulation of the rule. And
second, teachers who are anxious to get the "expected answer"

may tend to rush prematurely toward structuring of the discovery process.

Observation of classroom practices demonstrates that the second is a more common practice. For example, a teacher wants to develop the concept that vibration causes sound. She utilizes a tuning fork but the children do not feel that it vibrates. They look with dismay at the teacher. A girl who sits near the teacher says, "The fork vibrates." The teacher immediately *approves* the correct answer by putting it on the blackboard, and the class repeats, "Sound is vibration." Most of these second graders learned the new word "vibration," but its relation to sound is still not clear. The teacher had to wait with the final structuring of the generalization and let more children touch and feel the vibrating fork. Most of them would not express their discovery by the scientific word "vibration," but would instead say: "I feel it is shaking," or "It is moving and moving." Then other instruments, such as drums, should have been used to illustrate vibration. The vibration of an instrument should be slowed down or stopped to show its impact on sound. The end result of an indicative process of this nature is not a glib repetition of the word "vibration," but rather a meaningful conceptualization.

programmed instruction

The emphasis on the importance of the process of thinking which leads to the structuring of a new generalization underlies the *programmed instruction* approach. The limitations of these materials will be presented in other chapters. Here the interest is only in the extent to which they illustrate the process of conceptualization under discussion. Programmed instruction reflects two central interests in modern educational thinking. One is the organization of subject matter, and the other, the process of learning. The concept, or generalization to be mastered, is reduced into small steps generally called "frames." These frames are arranged in sequential order moving gradually from the simple to the complex and from the concrete to the abstract. In terms of teacher education, a major contribution of programming is sensitizing the teacher to the importance of the relationships between the part and the whole. The position is that teaching is not the transmission of discrete facts, but rather a planned and developmental approach to concept formation.

In terms of the process of learning, the programmer believes that optimum learning occurs when the learner progresses on his own without having to slow down or speed up because of group norms. The response of the learner are immediately reinforced. He knows whether he is right or wrong and can correct his mistakes. In brief, programmed instruction is based on the assumption that the *process* of conceptualization is of crucial importance, and not only the final concept itself.[T8]

productive thinking: difficulties

The process of productive thinking, denoting the *B* orientation, is more demanding and energy-consuming than the process of reproductive thinking characteristic of the *A* approach. When teacher *B* asks, "Why did the children call the squirrel a long-tailed kitten?" the pupils have to work on putting together facts presented in the subject matter and facts known to them in their previous experience, and reach insight. This is much more difficult than responding to the question of teacher *A*, "Who said, 'Well, well'?" which calls only for identification and recall. (The answer is written in the text implicitly.)

It is often suggested that there is a need for de-emphasizing "what, where, and when" questions and emphasizing "why", and "how" questions. This suggestion is somewhat misleading. The "why" and "how" questions do not necessarily demand productive thinking any more than memory. Says Sanders:[S1:9]

The question: Why did the United States enter a depression in 1929? is only a memory question if the student is expected to give back the same neat little package of answers provided in the text or in the teacher's lecture. "Why" and "how" questions are excellent when they are presented in a way that leads students to figure out the answers—not simply to remember them.

Questionnaire data show that the level of difficulty of the productive thinking required by the *B* approach troubles many teachers. A typical reaction is:

The emphasis of teacher *B* on thinking is very good for bright students. But I work with Puerto Rican children. They are practical and concrete-minded. I wouldn't try teacher *B*'s approach with them. They will not understand.

On the one hand the teachers under discussion identify with teacher *B* as a professional ego ideal, but on the other hand, at least one-half of the group questions whether this approach "will work with ethnic and lower-class children." As some say:

It is better to start teaching on the primary grades like teacher *A*, and only when they have the foundations of facts and information, to move to the thinking emphasis of teacher *B*.

The difficulty which these teachers are speaking about is very real. There is a higher incidence of concrete thinking and low ability to abstract and generalize among certain segments of the population. More children in a lower-class than in a middle-class community react in a concrete way to a test which calls for generalizing and conceptualizing.[P9] As a later chapter on the disadvantaged learner will stress, the psychological impact of poverty is a sense of powerlessness and passivity, the feeling that "this is the way it is, and I cannot change it." In terms of learning, the impact is concreteness, rigidity, and boundedness. Productive thinking, on the other hand, is an integral part of a personal behavior denoted by hopefulness and assertiveness.

However, the fact that a child or a group of children have difficulty in thinking productively on the ideational level does not mean that this process has to be dispensed with. In our western civilization the individual whose ability to think productively and abstractly is weak would tend to lag behind those in whom this ability is better developed. Therefore, the problem is not that of postponing the *B* emphasis on thinking in working with the relatively concrete-minded lower-class and ethnic child. The problem is rather that of discovering more efficient ways of helping him look at firsthand experience and factual information and see their essential interrelations.

leadership climate

The interview data show that in addition to the perception of the *B* emphasis on productive thinking as being "too difficult for many children to comprehend," many teachers feel that the *B* approach is not conducive to good control. The stress on productive thinking, in contrast to the emphasis on specificity, permits much more *freedom* to the learner. It seems that this freedom constitutes a threat to some novice teachers.

When model *B* asks children to read the whole story, or to look at a picture and suggest the main idea, the pupils are free to work on their own until they develop the answer. When teacher *B* asks children to observe a series of scientific facts and produce a generalization, or to explain the logic of a division computation in arithmetic, the students must take time to work on their own and think. The search for the answer is not so intensely structured as it is in the *A* emphasis on detailed information.

We witness here two different patterns of leadership. Teacher *A* employs short-range objectives, and teacher *B* more long-range goals. Teacher *A* must continuously ask more and more questions, or give more and more instructions in order to move the children from the accomplishment of one goal to another. Teacher *B* can limit his instructions to a few basic questions. The children are much more on their own.

The power that drives and continuously moves class *A* is the teacher. If he stops, there is no movement. The pattern of discussion is teacher-centered. The teacher asks a question; a child gives an answer; teacher questions, child answers, etc. There is very little room for interaction among pupils. The reason is simple— there is no content and process of thinking which calls for give-and-take among the learners.

These patterns are much less typical of class *B*. The teacher is less dominant and the children more active. The pattern of discussion is less teacher-centered. There is more room for pupils' interaction, pooling ideas together, reacting to each other, and arguing with the positions others take.

The essence of productive thinking, denoting the process of work of the *B* model, makes him much less authoritarian and controlling than the *A* teacher. It seems, however, that this lack of controlling structure threatens some novice teachers. As one of them said in an interview:

My cooperating teacher asked them (the children) a stimulating question. There was silence, no answer. He waited and waited. A few minutes passed and he sat waiting. I would not be able to take it, and would ask a simpler question. Finally the children figured it out and had interesting answers. I have a lot of respect for him.

This student teacher is able to recognize a sound and educative approach; however, she admits that this approach threatens her need for control. Or, as another beginning teacher puts it:

In spite of everything said in favor of teacher *B*, let's admit it, teacher *A* knows exactly what her children are doing every minute of the day. I would not say the same thing about teacher *B*.

The need for control is very acute in the educational orientation of many anxious beginners. This factor tends to contribute towards an idealization of *B*, but an acceptance of the reality and practicality of *A*.

conclusion

The last interview question was: "What do you think teacher *C* will be?" The replies were interesting. The overwhelming majority felt that teacher *C* was going to be a merger between patterns *A* and *B*. They looked for a balance between the secure but rigid emphasis on specificity, identification, and recall, and the potentially richer but less safe stress on the totality of the basic idea and its corollary—productive thinking.

   With almost no exceptions, the teachers failed to sense
the need for a more creative model, one whose conception of
knowledge and way of teaching emphasize interaction between
the individual and the subject matter and encourage divergency and creativity. These ideas will be elaborated in the next
chapter.

selected bibliography

BRUNER, JEROME, S. *The Process of Education.* Cambridge: Harvard
    University Press, 1960. Emphasis on the importance of under-
    standing the structure of the discipline.
FLEMING, ROBERT S. (Editor) *Curriculum for Today's Boys and
    Girls.* Columbus, Ohio: Charles E. Merrill Books, Inc., 1963.
    Chapters 8 and 9 deal with the problem of thinking in terms of
    its curricular applications.
SANDERS, NORRIS, *Classroom Questions.* New York: Harper & Row,
    Publishers. A rationale for developing a varied intellectual
    climate in the classroom through questions.

3

the climate of creative thinking

When the collection of the reactions to the *B* orientation was completed, the *C* model was presented before the same group of teachers. It was followed by written reactions and interviews. The following is a sketch of the role-playing.

Motivation: A discussion of a popular television program, *Lassie*, leads to the observation that Timmie's (the child hero) parents sometimes don't believe his stories, such as his seeing a wild horse. The discussion attempts to explore the feelings of both Timmie and his parents in situations like this.

Objective: To read a story where parents don't believe what their children see and to understand the feelings of the people involved.

Reading and Discussion: Silent reading of the whole story. Discussion of the main ideas with emphasis on the misunderstanding in calling a squirrel a long-tailed kitten. Selection of parts best liked by children. Reading and discussion of these parts in terms of content and style. An attempt to encourage children to read between the lines and analyze the feelings of Dick and his sisters when father is sarcastic and does not believe their observation of a long-tailed kitten. These feelings are not reported in the story and call for putting one's own feelings into the story. Some children suggest that Dick felt angry and bitter; others suggest that he was not sure of himself any more, and so on. All interpretations of possible reactions are accepted and encouraged. The point is emphasized that one cannot judge these different reactions by the criterion of correct or incorrect. All of them are logically possible.

Dramatization: Rather than repeating and sticking to the notes of the story in dramatization, the class creates a scene where Dick is going to Long-Tail to complain about his nontrusting parents. This scene is not presented by the text and constitutes a product of the children's imagination. The children are encouraged to develop the new scene by a discussion of Dick's possible reaction to his parents' disbelief, the impact of his feelings on his behavior, his way of speaking, gestures, etc., and a detailed description of the scenery.

A scene where Dick speaks with Long-Tail is played by several pairs of students. Each team has an opportunity to plan its own presentation in terms of its own interpetation. Each scene is followed by class discussion and an analysis of the character which the team attempted to portray.

Picture Analysis: An attempt to develop empathy and imagination. Typical questions are: How do the characters in the pictures feel? What happened before? What will happen later? The teacher encourages different and even opposing interpretations of the situation. Some children disagree and discuss their disagreement.

Seat Work: In contrast to those of teachers A and B, the assignment does not include a review of the story, but rather moves a step ahead. Children are asked to suggest topics for writing different endings to the story. For instance, one suggestion is: "One day the cat felt that Long-Tail acted strangely. What happened?" The children write stories of different endings and illustrate with pictures.

On the continuum from repetitive to creative teaching, the majority of the teachers perceived the A and B orientations as representing the opposing extremes. They expected model C to represent the middle point on the continuum; that is, an integration of the educative and practical qualities in the two so-called extreme teachers.

The presentation of teacher C as one who extends the continuum, rather than constitutes a balance point, and as one who pushes the horizons of teaching even further than the B orientation, was a genuine surprise to the group. The impact on the majority of the teachers was a change in the professional ego ideal: from B to C. Typical written reactions were:

If I hadn't seen teacher C, I might want to be like teacher B. But after seeing teacher C, I know that my vision was limited.

Teacher C is the ideal teacher . . . He believes in children and he believes in education . . . As young teachers, we now have a new goal.

The demonstration of teacher C also served as a strong emotional stimulus. Many teachers looked at the new professional ego ideal and asked themselves the searching question —what does it mean in terms of me as a teacher, and most important, as a person.[*]

The C demonstration was a stimulus to the teachers to speak about their unfulfilled hopes and aspirations, and especially about their struggle to reach others, and in this process to reach their own self. It encouraged the young teachers to speak about their desire of reaching their potentialities, give of themselves, and in this process grow professionally.

In the group's perception, the major characteristics of the C model were emphasis on (1) the teacher's subjective meaning of subject matter; (2) movement from the known to the unknown; (3) divergent thinking; (4) democratic teaching.

the personal meaning
of subject matter to the teacher

Perhaps the most important single characteristic of the C approach to the promotion of creativity is the fact that he himself is a creative person. In contrast to teacher A who approaches the teaching matter with the question, "What are the specifics?" and in contrast to teacher B who looks for the

*The data analysis shows that the C presentation was strongest in terms of its *personal* impact, A was second, and B was last. The reason may be that the A and C orientations constitute two extremes, while the B model has some elements of both.

main ideas inherent in the subject matter, model *C* approaches knowledge with the question, "What does the subject matter mean to me as a person?" The emphasis is on the teacher himself experiencing his own interpretation of the subject matter —in this case, a story. Teachers write:

The story, "Long-Tail," is simple and somewhat dull, like most stories in the primary readers. Even in a story like this, teacher *C* is able to read between the lines and get insight into the dynamics of family relations.

Teacher *A* starts by asking factual questions and teacher *B* by asking children to read the story as a whole. They themselves are not in the story. Teacher *C* is involved. He relates the story to his own personal life. He sees in it something new.

A teacher can communicate a rich experience to children only if he experiences it himself as an adult person. How do teachers feel about the subject matter or experience to be taught? What is the message it communicates to them as people? An answer to this question will give us better insight into the dynamics of creative teaching. A teacher writes:

I wanted to teach about inventions. I read about it and then I started to think about how to introduce it to children. I knew that if I would ask them, "What are you going to invent?" their imaginations would run wild and the end result would be a household (especially the kitchen) where Mama had to do nothing but push a button. However, for me inventions are much more than kitchen gadgets. It is satisfying man's more basic needs, such as food and health.

This teacher is able to look at the subject matter of "inventions" and ask herself, "What does it mean to *me*?" She is afraid that the limited experiences of children and their concrete thinking will result in a "gadget-centered" lesson. Therefore, she decides to move in the direction of inventions in the area of food and medicine. The involvement with subject matter, the experiencing of one's individual interpretation of an idea, is a rewarding experience for the teacher who can reach it. To quote from an interview:

The rewards in developing your own ideas and approach to the problem are thrilling. And you know all the time that the children will get "charged-up" and excited about learning. I felt "gung-ho." I did not feel fatigue that night. I could stay and work.

the impact on the teacher's behavior

The following discussion is reported here to demonstrate the impact of the ability to experience the subjective meaning of subject matter on the teacher's behavior in the classroom.

On Columbus Day, another group of teachers was asked to react in writing to three questions. The second question was announced only after the reactions to the first were completed. The third question was announced only after the reactions to the second were completed.

1. Suppose a group of Japanese teachers comes to our room and asks, "What is Columbus Day?" Jot down a brief speech answering this question.
2. How would you teach children about Columbus?
   Illustrate by one brief lesson plan.
3. What does Columbus Day mean to you?

The analysis of the responses to the first question (the "speech") revealed that most answers were factual and prosaic. The emphasis was on the historical facts of Columbus' birth, port of embarkation, names of the queen and the three boats, the year of the discovery of America, and on the statement that the world was round rather than flat. The writing of the speeches was trite. They did not convey a sense of emotion and drama, but were rather matter-of-fact. In brief, emphasis was primarily on level *A* of knowledge.

The same can be said about the majority of the responses to the second question—the lesson plans. In essence, they were a digest of the previous factual speech with some additions of arts and crafts activities. It is interesting to note that while working on the speech and on the lesson plan, some participants said to the instructor: "I don't think I can do it. I am not up-to-date on the facts."

A *minority* of the group members, however, both in the

writing of the speech and the planning of the lesson, attempted to identify with the struggle experienced by Columbus, struggle against man, convention, and nature. They looked for the symbolic meaning of the life of the explorer, that is—level C of knowledge. For instance, one teacher wanted to ask children to describe Columbus' childhood. Another wanted to put on a debate of the merit of the trip to be presented in the Queen's council. One lesson plan suggested focusing on Columbus' experiences in prison. (Interestingly enough, this is the only point of information omitted by most teachers, despite its significance in the understanding of the conflicts underlying Columbus' mission. It seems that the intention is to present a stereotyped, sugarcoated portrait and to avoid struggle and controversy.)

The responses to the third question ("What does Columbus Day mean to you?") suggest an explanation for the two types of reactions to it. The teachers who were factual in their speech and lesson planning tended to answer that Columbus Day had no meaning to them as adults.

It is only for children. For teachers—a day of vacation.

We learned one thing about him in public school and then it proved to be wrong when we studied history in college. We feel skeptical.

There was laughter in the group when the third question was read. The laughter expressed the skepticism of the participants. However, the teachers who searched for the personal struggle in Columbus' life tended to answer the third question by saying:

He stands for one of the great misunderstood people. Whether he was really great or not does not bother me. The important thing is the symbol.

We are a unique country composed of immigrants from almost all over the world. Our history is one long story of the struggle and courage of the immigrants. Columbus' importance is that he was the first immigrant (in America).

These comments suggest (1) a positive correlation between the teacher's own responding to subject matter and a C-

oriented way of teaching and (2) a positive correlation between lack of the teacher's responding to subject matter and
an *A*-oriented way of teaching.

That the nature of knowledge communicated to children
is related to the personal meaning the teacher experiences
came out in some of the interviews. The following is a hard-
working novice teacher speaking about a lesson she had given:

I taught my third grade about transportation. They are pretty
bright and eager to learn. We spoke about ways different people go
to work, and then we put it on a chart. [Opens the rolled chart]. It
reads

> People go to work by car.
> People go to work by bus.
> People go to work by train.

They enjoyed the lesson, but I don't think that they learned much.
They learned to read and write. They enjoyed participating. But con-
tent-wise, it was not much . . . Planning the lesson on transportation,
I thought about an interesting central theme—*the world is small*,
but my mother (a teacher) said it would be too difficult for the
children to grasp. They are not *ready* . . .

What a person prizes, he does. What the teacher values,
she teaches. The problem of the young teacher is to understand the diversions which undermine her ability to experience rich value in subject matter. In the case under discussion,
the teacher stopped listening to her own sound judgment of
what is central and valuable, and when she had guilt feelings
about a certain depth that was not achieved and meaning that
was not tapped, she quieted her conscience. "The children are
not ready." With this rationalization, too many novice teachers
commit the elementary school child to six years of "readiness."

In this case the young teacher does not develop her own
interpretation of the subject matter because she trusts the
judgment of another more experienced teacher rather than
her own. The insecurities of a beginner make her dependent
rather than independent. This dependency, which interferes
with the teacher's ability to look at subject matter creatively,

is seen in many interviews. Typical comments are:

The expectation is that we will follow the course syllabus. There is no place and time for the new teacher to develop her own ideas.

How can you be like teacher C? I spoke about it with my cooperating teacher. She says that the Board of Education is dogmatic. Democracy in education is only for the children. Little free thinking is allowed to teachers.

Teacher C is an independent thinker. She follows her own ideas, not only those of others. But look at the way most of us plan our work. We are dependent on the teacher's manual. (Opens a teacher's guide to a primer and shows it to the instructor.) The author tells you the exact words to be used. Now, they have guides with an arrangement where you can take the instruction page out. You can read it while you teach. I am often tempted to read the instructions aloud rather than use my own words. It is exactly the opposite of teacher C.

This interview data illustrate the novice's feeling that not only internal insecurities, but also external pressures, interfere with her freedom to develop her own ideas. The objective observer of the school life may claim that the teacher is freer than she thinks herself to be. However, the perception of the beginning teacher is that she is supposed to follow the "notes" developed by others. She feels that she is expected to be dependent.

A common difficulty of many of the teachers under discussion was the development of their own "notes," their own meaning of what is important in the knowledge to be taught. They depended to a great extent on the notes of others—the authority figures and the textbook. The teacher is the most important factor determining the quality of the classroom experience. The teacher who applies notes mechanically will tend to emphasize repetitive teaching. The teacher who learns to develop and experience his own meaning will move in the direction of interaction between the learner and the subject matter—in the direction of creativity.

The pupils experience the various types (somewhat stereotypes) of teachers portrayed here, identify with them, and learn the essence of their being. From teacher A they learn the rigid search for specificity; and from teacher B, the importance of basic understanding. It is only in experiencing the involvement of teacher C that they learn the importance of the active search for subjective interpretation, that is, putting one's own personal meaning into the subject matter. Recognizing this challenge of the creative model, interviewees say:

I would like to be a child in teacher C's class because I would have to approach the story in terms of my own experience . . . I would understand my environment better and have more knowledge about my own reactions and personality. It is this kind of teaching which helps people like me develop new ideas in terms of their potentialities.

Teachers A and B stand for two different schools of thought. However, for both of them the center is the subject matter rather than the child. It is only teacher C whose emphasis is on the interaction between the child and the content of the lesson. Out of this interaction, a new meaning is created. It is most rewarding to the class and the teacher.

Suzuki, the Japanese philosopher,[S19] emphasizes that unless it grows out of oneself, no knowledge is really of value to the individual. A borrowed plumage never grows . . .

In conference, the college instructor often hears students complain about their lack of ability to identify a research problem or develop a project.

My problem is that I don't have the right study skills.

I would like the librarian to show us how to locate information, perhaps this would help.

If I knew the expected format, perhaps I could get started.

These future teachers see the solution of their learning problem in an additional dose of study skills and correct format. As classroom teachers they will tend to communicate the same emphasis to children. These may be the students who later, as teachers, will come to emphasize syntax in the study of poetry, who will react to a child's composition describing the death of his cat with the one-word comment, "skip!"

(meaning, write double space), who will equate research in the classroom with skill in using the encyclopedia.

What many of these future teachers did not learn both as pupils and college students is that their major difficulty in starting a project is not the relative lack of "study skills," but rather their lack of emotional and intellectual involvement in subject matter. Despite many years of formal education, they did not find themselves as people. They never reached the stage of knowing in what they are *interested*. They were so busy with the external knowledge of mastering facts, skills, words, and correct forms that they failed to concentrate on the creative aspect—their own interest.

The personal meaning of problem identification to some teachers is described in my article "The Personal Significance of an Action Research Problem to Teachers."[S8] Following is an excerpt from an interview.[S6:72-73]

College Instructor: I am interested in knowing how you got the idea to work on the project, "Humor in My Classroom."
Teacher: I guess it is much deeper than I thought. You see, all my life I was a bookworm. I was a very good student. Everyone liked me, but no one was excited about me. I was always in the right, but I was never "right"—I mean having something original. I went into teaching. I guess this is the only thing I was prepared to do. But perhaps there was another reason involved: working with children puts you at ease—you let yourself go.

The teacher who has the room next to mine often yells at her children, a thing that I seldom do. Actually I have the better reputation as a good teacher. But from time to time you hear roars of laughter coming from her room, a thing that seldom happens in mine. Now you understand why I am working on humor.

The greatest challenge for educators is to make knowledge a part of the lives of students and to make subject matter personally meaningful. In essence, this is the starting point for creative learning. The repetitively skewed school curriculum, overemphasizing study skills, word learning, and literary comprehension, undermines the ability of the novice to realize himself as a person and as a teacher.

A teacher who skillfully attempts to develop creative interpretations in others and fails himself to experience his

own sense of meaning, tends to move through the motions
of asking the right questions, without these questions having
real meaning to him. This is the kind of teacher who asks
children to think about why they like or dislike a certain
character described in a story, without himself exploring the
question; he may ask for imagery as a response to a mood
poem, while he himself fails to form any imaginative answer.

Children tend to sense a lack of involvement in this teacher; they know that he moves through the correct motions but
somewhere misses the spirit of the activity. To put it in somewhat extreme terms, there are situations where the educator
has to learn to withdraw as a teacher and come forth as a
person. If the teacher plays only the role of a skilled technician, he tends to withdraw as a person and come forth only
as a teacher. In an atmosphere of this nature, creativity becomes an expression of virtuosity rather than an immersion
in an intellectual and emotional experience.

from the known to the unknown

While the subjective meaning of the subject matter to
the teacher is one condition of creative teaching, another
characteristic denoting the *C* orientation is the movement
from the known to the unknown. Teachers who perceive this
element in the behavior of teacher *C* say:

Teacher *C* illustrates in her teaching a simple attempt to help children to create new ideas based on the known subject matter of the
story. The teacher encourages discussion and role-playing of possible
feelings and behavior of the characters. The analyses and scenes
developed by the children are not reported in the story. The pictures
are discussed in terms of what happened before and what will
happen later.

The difference between teachers *B* and *C* is clear. Teacher *B* wants
children to think and understand the subject matter. Teacher *C*
wants children to think and interpret the subject matter. In teacher
B's class, all the good thinkers will come out with the same answer.

In teacher C's class, all the good thinkers will come out with different answers, as if each child rewrites the story in his own way.

Creative thinking involves the production of new ideas—movement from the known to the unknown. Progress depends upon new solutions; that is, upon the creative thinking that children are able to do.

In an article dealing with some aspects of creativity,[L1] it is suggested that college students who are successful in mathematics tend to be characterized by turbulence, both in feelings and thoughts. They tolerate and even prefer disorder. They find thought, fantasy, and creativity ways of making order out of disorder. In contrast, the article suggests that the *best* elementary school teacher personality is a person who has a great deal of self-control and has things well organized and running smoothly.

Reading these findings, one gets the impression that the successful mathematician is a *creator* of new knowledge and is able to move toward the unknown, while the successful elementary school teacher is a transmitter of predigested knowledge and is able only to impart the known.

These findings have validity if the criteria of "teacher success" are of smooth and orderly discipline, repetition of specifics (level A), and some emphasis on the development of basic ideas inherent in the subject matter (level B). As measured by these criteria, the "successful teacher" is a technician rather than a creator—a transmitter of predigested knowledge.

However, the discussion of teacher C by the novice teachers reveals that, at least in terms of their professional ego ideal, they want to move ahead from a sole preoccuption with transmission of subject matter to the developing of knowledge. They are not satisfied with being technicians only, but they wish to experience the rewards of creating and developing this ability in children. They do not perceive their role as merely emphasizing the ready-made and neat package presented by the book, but want to expand their professional role in the direction of ordering a new knowledge and fostering in their pupils the readiness to move from the known to the unknown.

toward the unknown: difficulties

If a young teacher develops her own subjective interpretation of a certain subject matter, and if, in terms of the teacher's professional orientation, she wants to encourage in children the creative ability to move from the known to the unknown, what are the factors which interfere with the teacher's progress in this direction? Interviewees say:

Teacher A is oriented toward security. It is so much easier to present a lesson and get all your facts across. You know what you want to do, you plan on it, and you do it. Unless you have undergone the experience many times, it is difficult to structure your work along C lines.

Remember the experiment on rubber? I wanted to ask them (refers to a fifth-grade class) to find some of the qualities of this material, without giving them any further instructions. But I changed my mind. You will get stuck and fail to come out with what you had in mind. If things don't work out as you structured them, then you are horrified . . . While the children are working, you look at them and think: "What are they doing? Where are they going? What will they ask?" A sense of timing is important in teaching. You see how time flies, and you don't know exactly where your class is.

Teacher C's movement from the known to the unknown is characterized by a phase of disorder. The learner starts with the known, such as a problem, a story, or a picture, and then experiences a phase of disorder where he moves in divergent directions. He reacts to the stimulus (the known) in his own individualistic way. Not being clear about the direction, he tries different ideas. He may pass an incubation period. Finally, the learner reaches his own insight and orders a new knowledge.

Barron attempted to determine how creative people respond to order and disorder. He says that the way in which the common human need for order is related to the constructive possibilities and fruitful challenges which may be found in apparent disorder provided the focus for an early series of his experimental studies.[B2:151-155]

There is little doubt that most people dislike being confronted with disorder. In individuals who turn out original work in science or in art, however a reversal of the usual attitude may be observed . . . Behind the inclination to like and to construct what is not too simply ordered, there appears to be a very strong need to achieve the most difficult and far-reaching ordering.

In other words, the creative response to disorder is to find a new order more satisfying than any that could be evoked by a simpler configuration.

Barron's subjects are highly creative individuals. They are tolerant of disorder and ambiguity. Their response is a search for a new and more satisfying order. The teachers under discussion here were not selected in terms of the creativity variable, and as the above interview points out, their reaction to this phase of disorder is a feeling of threat and loss of power.

In some respects, the task of the teachers in coping with disorder is more difficult than the task which confronted Barron's subjects—the scientists. The latter reacted to the "disorder test situation" working individually. The former have to cope with the phase of disorder while they are teaching a group of youngsters; that is, while they are in a leadership role. To quote from an interview:

I was working on remedial reading exercises. The group read several paragraphs about a class reporter and then answered comprehension questions of the A type, such as the name of the reporter and where he went. I had a very small group, so I decided to try some of the C approach. I decided to ask a general question based on the story, but one which did not have only one correct answer. I asked: "What would you do if you were a reporter?" The first two responses were: Who wants this junk?", and, "I'll make money."

You see, this approach is threatening to the teacher, because you don't know what you are going to get. If I had a full class I would feel lost. The class would laugh and they would start fooling around.

To repeat, the normal human difficulty of coping with the phase of disorder is accentuated by the teacher's role of leadership and control. In the perception of many teachers, guidance of the class in movement from the known to the unknown, and good discipline are too often incompatible roles.

These young educational practitioners operate in terms of their role expectation of what a teacher is. The idealism, the giving of one's self, and the sense of fulfillment that the teacher's image calls for enhance the novice's desire to try to guide children toward the *C* orientation of ordering new knowledge. However, other dimensions of the teacher's image deter this type of experimentation.

My problem is that I look too young. Perhaps I should wear my hair differently—then the children will accept me as an authority.

Today I saw my girlfriend (another novice teacher) teaching. I never saw her in this light. She was so serious and full of authority.

The role expectation of the teacher is that he should be an all-knowing authority, definite and creative. In daily life, adults sometimes say: "Don't be a teacher." They mean: "Don't tell me what to do." These dimensions of the teacher's image undermine the teacher's ability to tackle the phase of disorder, denoting the movement from the known to the unknown.

The role expectation of teachers is that they will be able to make quick decisions. Tolerance for ambiguity and disorder, inherent in the creative process, calls for some postponement of decision-making. It warns against premature structuring. The traditional role expectation of the teacher and the tolerance for some disorder are in conflict. As stressed by Heil,[H7] intolerance of uncertainty and the need for a smooth-functioning operation is a major characteristic of many teachers.

The problem becomes even more difficult when the teacher, examining his teaching behavior, must distinguish between tolerance for ambiguity and irresolution, between the ability to delay a choice of direction and indecisiveness.[G3] The basic difference between these two seemingly similar manifestations of teaching behavior is not the external manifestation itself, but rather the sense of strength which the teacher experiences. If one waits patiently for the ripe moment of creating structure, he has tolerance for uncertainty. It is only when one waits because he feels lost and hopes that "the situation will take care of itself," that he is indecisive.

The movement from the known to the unknown is central in the process of creativity. The young teacher who settles solely for the *A* and *B* orientation because of the threats of the unknown and the security of the known is deterring both his professional and personal growth.

suggested observations

The reader is urged to observe curricular practices with the following interrelated questions in mind:

Are the students encouraged to tackle a difficult but manageable task, or is their assignment cut into small pieces?

Is the teacher's plan flexible and open to accommodate the students' suggestions and ideas, or is it rigid, moving smoothly through predetermined lines?

Does the lesson have a phase of "disorder" in which students struggle to move from the known to the unknown, or is the movement constricted and overstructured?

To better understand these points the discussion will examine teaching behavior in the area of science.

curricular illustrations

Teacher: What do I have in my hand?
Child: A magnet.
Teacher: What does it do?
Child: It picks up nails.
Teacher: What else?
Child: Paper clips and metals.
Teacher: [Puts two boxes on the table; one is marked "yes" and the other "no."] Let's see what are the things that the magnets pick up.

At this point it could have been possible to confront the class with this major question and ask them to suggest ways and materials for proceeding to find the answer. Following this approach means that the learner plays a role in developing the experiment. It calls on the teacher to have a flexible plan which permits the accommodation of the ideas suggested by children. However, as the continuation of the above science lesson illustrates, the novice tends to be teacher-centered in his behavior. He *demonstrates*, rather than encouraging children to experiment.

Teacher: Will the magnet lift the ruler?
Child: [Comes to the demonstration table; tries to lift the ruler with a magnet.] No. [He puts the ruler in the "no" box.]
Teacher: Who will come try the thumbtack?
Child: [Comes to the desk; tries the object and puts it in the "yes" box.]

The overstructured approach to guiding experiments cuts the learning task into small chewable pieces. Observing the process of this Pablum approach to learning, one notices the lack of *confrontation* with a difficult task. Learning becomes smooth movement rather than a struggle for a solution.

For example, in a lesson on sound the concept was developed that when objects made of the same matter are struck, the smaller the object, the higher is the tone; and the larger the object, the lower is the tone. The teacher utilized a variety of materials, among which were eight bells whose tones represent the scale. However, rather than letting the children have all eight "melody bells" at once and letting the pupil discover that the bells represent the notes of the scale, the teacher followed a "less difficult" approach. First, the two bells which produce the lowest tones on the scale were presented and compared; then, the second pair, and so on, until the eight bells were arranged in the scale order. The activity was enjoyable. The relation between size and tone was stressed. However, the challenge of a difficulty and, therefore, the level of discovery, was limited.

In a conference, this criticism was brought before the young teacher. She decided to try the lesson again with another group. The following is part of her report:

After some discussion and experimentation on the relationship between size and tone, I took out the eight "melody bells" and gave them to a small group of children. I asked them to find the order. They started to ring the bells and put them in order. They made many mistakes and several times had to change the sequence. When finally the group had the eight bells in order, they rang the bells in turn and the class cheered.

I asked them to try it again and find a way of arranging the bells in sequence without use of the tone (melody). They found out that the bells are equal in size, but the inner moving piece of metal is different in size. They measured the length of the metal piece and arranged the bells in order. They rang the bell in turn and saw that they were playing the scale. Again the class cheered.

A major approach to develop the ability of children to identify problems is to balance the overstructured methodology in science with provisions for a more open-ended situation. Brenda Lansdown describes this approach in the article "Orbiting a Science Program."[L2:180] Materials are distributed to the group and their manipulation encouraged. Such manipulation leads the pupils to make discoveries of scientific relations. For instance, to help children discover the principles of buoyancy, the following materials are suggested:

A dish of water for each group of four children. Things which float, like wood.... Things which sink like marbles, a penny... Things which sink and float like plastic sponges.

Small groups are instructed to see what they can find out and to record the questions which they want to raise for general class discussion. After a period of free experimentation the teacher calls on the children to join in a discussion of their questions and findings.

The raising of questions by children confronts the teacher with the task of accommodating the pupil's sense of direction. The preplanned route must be modified, or even drastically changed. The teacher is confronted with the task of structuring the questions, deciding on the order of the discussion, and making choices of which question should be followed by the

class as a whole and which should be left for a small group
or even individual assignment. In brief, the creative orientation calls on the teacher to experience a stage of *disorder*
before *structuring* a *new order*.

divergent thinking

Many of the interviewees pointed out that in contrast to
models *A* and *B*, teacher *C* did not respond to or judge his
students in terms of right or wrong. For example,

I was impressed with teacher *C*'s way of evaluating children's answers. In answering the questions of teachers *A* and *B*, the children
know that they are right or wrong. In answering the questions of
teacher *C*, the students know that it is accepted as the individual's
interpretation, by the teacher and by the class.

An important function of the teacher is to be a transmitter
of organized knowledge, called here levels *A* and *B*. Inherent
in this concept is the teacher's role of reacting to the pupil in
terms of reinforcing correct responses and discouraging false
answers.

The pupil is usually aware that his teacher, his parents,
his friends, or he himself, can find out whether he knows or
does not know a computation skill, a generalization in science,
the spelling of a word, the rules of a game, a norm of behavior.
The realization of right or wrong is essential in developing
consciousness of checking reality, and setting goals for the
learner's aspiration. It structures learning by giving the child
a way of evaluating whether he objectively knows.

The process of social learning achieved by judging in
terms of right or wrong is well recognized and does not need
further elaboration at this point. There is a need, however,
to discuss the dangers inherent in *overemphasis* on this process
of learning. A teacher says:

It is not difficult to see that in teacher *C*'s class children are freer and
therefore more creative (than in the *A* and *B* classes). An important
factor is the way teacher *C* responds to them. In the *A* and *B* classes,

what counts is the ideas of the teacher and the book. There is not much room for the child's own ideas. In teacher C's class, the child is free to react in his own way. He is more independent. The end result is the creation of variety of additions to the story.

In the group's perception, the C approach to evaluation encourages divergent rather than convergent responses and, therefore, places a high premium on the *subjective and independent* thinking of the learner. In doing so it promotes creativity. The relationship between divergency and creativity needs elaboration. Two kinds of productive thinking operations generate new knowledge from known and remembered information: convergent and divergent thinking.

In convergent thinking, the information leads to one correct answer or to a recognized best answer. This type of thinking is inherent in the B orientation. The B teacher channels or controls the thinking of the learners in the direction of the correct answer or conclusion.

In divergent thinking operations, denoting the C orientation, the learner thinks in different directions, sometimes searching (the phase of disorder), sometimes seeking variety. In Guilford's language:[G8:9]

It is less goal-bound. There is freedom to go off in different directions . . . Rejecting the old solutions and striking out in some new direction is necessary, and the resourceful organism will probably succeed.

The B orientation encourages a convergent thinker who focuses on the stimulus (the story, picture, etc.), since he seeks objectivity which others will recognize as correct. He conforms to the standards and expectations of others, mainly the elders.

The C orientation encourages a divergent thinker who personalizes the stimulus and reacts to it in terms of his own subjective perception. He is tuned to himself and not only to the crowd and its norms. The stimulus is still very important and has to be understood, but the response draws primarily on the resourcefulness of the individual.

A study comparing the highly creative and the highly intelligent adolescent concludes that[G2:17]

The high I.Q.'s tended to converge upon stereotyped meaning, to perceive personal success by conventional standards, to move toward the model provided by teachers, to seek out careers that conform to what is expected of them.

The high-creatives tended to diverge from stereotyped meanings, to move away from the model provided by teachers, to seek out careers that do not conform to what is expected of them.

The emphasis on judging in terms of right or wrong is an attempt to teach the child to be rational and face reality. However, it is also a way of fostering the dependence on, and subservience to, reality, rationality, and external norms.

From birth, the child is put into a constricting maze of rearing practices which accentuate his adaptation to the realities of the external world. He learns that his source of strength, his way of fulfillment, and his means of being accepted can be reached by looking at the external, objective, and uniform norms of right and wrong.

The parent-surrogate (the teacher), the school culture, and the peer group only accentuate the dependence on the external objective of truism. Through a continuous, comprehensive, and deliberate system of formal education, the child conforms to the realities of knowledge, taste, and behavior required by the rational society. He is right or wrong, good or bad, A or F, 100% or zero, popular or rejected, depending on whether he is rational and conforming.

In this process of learning the *overconsciousness* of the external world of right and wrong, a rich potential is lost. The development of the individual's ability to reach knowledge through listening to his inward and maybe even irrational self, is pushed to the background.

The creative individual is the one who reaches for knowledge not only by developing his conscious faculty, but also by turning to the dimly realized life of his inward self. Reaching the latter means having contact with the life of the unconscious, with fantasy, reverie, and the world of imagination. This knowledge gained by inner orientation cannot be classified into the rigidity of true and false.

The learner who is channeled toward thinking solely in terms of external norms of right and wrong may become intelligent, informed, and productive. However, he would not become creative. His opportunity to be enriched by the primitiveness and originality of his inward life may be lost. By encouraging different interpretations and by emphasizing that not all knowledge can be classified as right or wrong, model *C* illustrates a search for balance between objectivity and subjectivity.

divergency: difficulties

As suggested earlier, the novice teachers realized that the acceptance and encouragement of a variety of interpretations was conducive to a learning climate of divergency and creativity. In the interviews, the question was raised whether they followed this approach in their own teaching, and if not— why not?

The answers reveal that one of the major areas where divergency rather than convergency is encouraged is creative writing.

I start a story and ask them to write an end. I show them a picture and ask them to tell a story. I stress not to stick to the facts, but rather to be imaginative. Then we read their writings and enjoy it.

It is interesting to note that in *creative* writing, where the goal of creativity is explicitly stated, the emphasis is on divergency rather than judgment in terms of right or wrong. However, this educational objective is not perceived as central in the *major* subject areas.

When I think about creativity, I think about music, writing, dance, and art. I play music to my class and let them express their feelings in movements they develop. I don't show them what to do . . . But when it comes to our main work—reading, arithmetic, and science, there we have to teach the subject matter and see that the children comprehend.

In the perception of many teachers, the school curriculum consists of the *major* subjects, which are the province of the *A* and *B* orientations, and the *minor* subjects, where the *C* approach is dominant. Creativity is "extra." Divergency can be encouraged only if "time permits," that is, only if "the important subject matter is covered." A student teacher says:

I was impressed with teacher *C* and decided to adopt his approach. I had to teach my fifth grade the story of Dr. Doolittle. It deals with a doctor who gave up his flourishing medical practice, filled his house with animals, and took care of them.

I encouraged the children to read between the lines and discuss Dr. Doolittle's personality, his sense of values and his fight against public pressure. I encouraged them to disagree in their evaluation of the man. Some saw him as queer and others as a man of principles. My cooperating teacher was very complimentary, saying it was original, and then added, "But with these children we don't have time to do it. It will be impossible to cover the subject matter. They need to learn the language first" . . . I don't know where I stand now.

The notion expressed above is that the development of divergency and creativity are "extra-curricular," to be worked on only if the essentials of the *A* and *B* levels of knowledge are accomplished.

The beginning teacher, harassed by a tradition of a primarily *A*-oriented school and by his own anxiety over control and direction, starts to confuse the reading of many pages with getting meaning out of reading. Under external and internal pressure to achieve, the novice stops listening to his own sense of values and joins the rush toward false production— covering subject matter.

Gradually the correctness of the specifics of the subject matter itself becomes crucial and even sacred, and the divergent responses of the learner become secondary, or are even omitted. The following extreme illustration demonstrates under a magnifying glass the dynamics involved.

A slow first grade class of Puerto Rican origin was studying a story describing a child who walked through the forest and asked various animals for a gift for his mother. The children dramatized the story.

One boy was a "goat" and was asked: "May I have a gift for my mother?" The "goat" answered: "Glon, glon, I don't have a gift for your mother." The teacher interrupted: "What did the goat say?" The "goat" repeated: "Glon, glon, I don't have a gift for your mother." The teacher interrupted again: "Class, how is it written in the book?" The class answered: "Glan, glan, I don't have a gift for your mother."

In this lesson, no effort was made to encourage *divergent* responses to the experience of walking in the forest and speaking to animals. Despite their limited vocabulary and articulation ability, the children could express their feelings of fear, threat, joy, and discovery in the way they walked in the "forest," or in their voices when they spoke to the "animals."

No attempt was made to develop divergent interpretations. The emphasis was, rather, on reinforcing a correct response to a trivial detail. The above observation illustrates the *sclerosis* of knowledge which too often interferes with the novice's ability to move in the direction of divergence and creativity.

divergent thinking and the achievement test

An important factor contributing to the emphasis on the correct response and discouraging divergent thinking is the achievement test. Its relationship to the teaching practices of the novice is often mentioned in the interviews.

A new teacher is very impatient to see definite results quickly: teach a lesson, give a test. With teacher A it is on the table. You give a lesson, you quiz them and that's it. With teacher C it is drawn out over a longer period, and you don't know whether they absorbed.

This reaction illustrates a need for closure and evaluation. The A teacher can satisfy this need by testing. The A teaching and the testing program are interwoven into one logical and coherent unit. The test has a direct impact on the teaching behavior of teachers. Bothered by the problem of what to teach, they look for a guide in the course syllabi, teacher's manual, and the achievement tests.

Last week the principal said that my class was going to have a reading test. I am responsible for the reading program this week.

I was not sure that I had taught them the right things, so I took out a test from the library. We prepared for the test by practicing similar questions   I don't have to invent these questions, I find them in the workbook.

As early as the elementary school level the program is often test-oriented. Sometimes it is a deliberate plan of a teacher threatened by the exposure of the class achievement and the comparison with other classes. However, even in the class of the secure teacher, the test is an important factor. A similar educational philosophy often permeates the curriculum and the test. Both are primarily level *A*-centered. It is difficult to expect the promotion of divergency under these pressures.

To support the contention that the testing program stresses the *A* and overlooks the *C* orientation, the discussion will examine one typical item, from one of the best-known reading comprehension tests. [L7:8]

When my brother Ted and I were sick, a man from the Health Department came to our house. He put a sign with the words "Mumps—Keep Out" on our door. When the other boys saw that red sign, they knew they could not play with us. We had to stay at home until the man came back and took down the sign.

    I. Who is telling this story?
      (1) Ted's mother.
      (2) Ted's brother.
      (3) One of Ted's playmates.
      (4) A man from the Health Department.

   II. What was the matter with Ted?
      (1) He did not want to play with the other boys.
      (2) He did not like to go to school.
      (3) He was angry with his sister.
      (4) He was sick.

  III. Why was the sign put on the door?
      (1) To scare the people in the neighborhood.
      (2) To let the doctor know someone was sick.
      (3) To help keep other children from catching the mumps.
      (4) To tell the attendance officer why the children were
          not in school.

IV. Who took the sign down?
   (1) The man who put it up.
   (2) Another man from the Health Department.
   (3) Ted's doctor.
   (4) Ted.

V. What does this story show?
   (1) That boys are more likely to catch mumps than girls.
   (2) That children will get sick if they play outdoors.
   (3) That the Health Department tries to protect children from diseases that are catching.
   (4) That sick children get very lonesome.

Do these test items, in terms of their impact on the reading program, encourage specificity, convergent thinking, or divergent thinking? Do they encourage a level *A*, *B*, or *C* curriculum?

Out of the five questions of reading comprehension, three tap level *A* of knowledge (I, II, and IV), two level *B* (III, and V), and *none* level *C*.

One does not have to read and comprehend the whole story, but rather, repeat one phrase in order to know the correct answer to the *A*-oriented questions. For instance, it is sufficient to read four words ("When my brother Ted") to answer question I ("Who is telling the story?"), to read the first line ("When my brother Ted and I were sick") to answer question II ("What was the matter with Ted?"). The answer is given in one phrase or sentence. One does not have to put things together to produce, or to think.

The answers to questions III and V call for productive thinking of the convergent type. For instance, to answer question III ("Why was the sign put on the door?"), it is not sufficient to read: "When the other boys saw that red sign, they knew they could not play with us." The subject must add his own understanding that the children could not play with the sick boys because mumps are contagious. This is not stated explicitly in the text. Then the subject produces the conclusion: "To help keep other children from catching the mumps."

To repeat, out of five questions, three are level *A*; two are level *B*; and none are level *C*-centered. However, when one examines *teacher*-made tests, the ratio is even less balanced. An examination of tests developed by the novice teachers under discussion shows that around 80 per cent of the items are *A*-, 20 per cent are *B*-, and none are *C*-oriented. The emphasis is on recall of specifics, a "touch" of convergent thinking, and no attention to divergence.

The test is one of the most formulated expressions of the teacher's philosophy and objectives. It expresses an attempt to spell out in detail the nature of knowledge that, in the teacher's understanding, has to be learned. School testing permeates the practitioner's methodology. It is often a philosophy which leaves little room for creativity, divergence, or intuitive thinking.

Speak with professional people—a scientist, a medical doctor, or a teacher. What most of them prize in their colleagues is intuition and the ability to come out with fresh ideas. The testing philosophy, with its preoccupation—almost obsession—with recall and the correctness of the end result, discourages the development of intuitiveness, divergence, and originality. It discourages the learner from making an intelligent guess, or from developing an intuitive feeling into a confusing problem.

Within the last several years the whole movement that is called "objective testing" has come under severe criticism. For instance, Bruner, in his book *The Process of Education*, says:[B12:66]

The assignment of grades in school typically emphasizes the acquisition of factual knowledge, primarily because that is what is most easily evaluated; moreover, it tends to emphasize the correct answer, since it is the correct answer on the straightforward exam that can be graded as correct.

The present testing philosophy teaches the learner to rely primarily on his memory and to be overconscious of specific facts. The child quickly learns that he is penalized for being interested in the *process*, for questioning the surface truth, or for searching for a divergent response. The present testing philosophy teaches the novice teacher not only to stress level *A* of knowledge out of all proportion, but also to overemphasize the end result and pay little attention to the process. In an interview, a teacher said in a definite and authoritative voice: "I give them a test and I want to know whether they know or don't know. That's all."

"Does he know, or doesn't he know?" becomes the central question, rather than the way the child arrives at knowledge. The process of learning, that is, the way the learner thinks, his attitude toward discovery and inquiry, are pushed to the background by a so-called objective test which measures only true or false *final* answers.

The test is surrounded by such an aura of scientific infallibility that the novice teacher fails to recognize its limitations in terms of validity (what it measures) and objectivity. However, some writers on this topic are very critical. For instance, in an article entitled "The Tyranny of Multiple-Choice Tests,"[H12] Hoffman calls for a re-examination of the major assumptions underlying the construction and use of tests. The test constructor should look for ways of evaluating not only the acquisition of information, but also divergency and creativity. In terms of the science of testing, it may mean movement from the present overemphasis on multiple choice in the direction of projective materials, rating techniques, and interviews.

The search for balance in the testing program is an integral part of a search for balance in the meaning of knowledge. A more balanced philosophy of education and curriculum organization are interrelated with a more balanced testing program.

It is interesting to note that one of the most important tests in the literature, the Stanford-Binet Test of Intelligence, in one phase of its work (Responses to Pictures, 3½ Years Old) attempted to develop a scoring system based on differentiation of three levels of difficulty comparable to levels *A*, *B*, and *C*, under discussion here.

In the author's words:[T3:204]

The test was originally intended to differentiate the three difficulty levels represented by *enumeration, description* and *interpretation*. However, levels II and III did not prove to be entirely satisfatory and only difficulty I has been retained in the present form.

The significance of this illustration is in the fact that the test-builders recognized that description (*B*) is a higher level than enumeration (*A*), and interpretation (*C*) is higher than description. They recognized, also, the need for a scoring system to tap these levels of difficulty.

Pioneering work in developing tests which measure creativity in children is reported by Getzels and Jackson in their book, *Creativity and Intelligence*, [G3] and by Torrance in his book, *Guiding Creative Talent*. [T5] The realization is growing among educators that intelligence and creativity, convergent and divergent thinking, are not identical, or even highly related abilities. Torrance reports[T4:7] that in one study:

The highly creative group ranked in the upper twenty percent of their classes on creativity but not on intelligence. The highly intelligent group ranked in the upper twenty percent on intelligence but not on creativity . . . About seventy percent of the top twenty percent on creativity would have been excluded from gifted groups selected on the basis of I.Q. alone.

Getzels and Jackson identify two major intellective modes. The first mode focuses on the understanding of the known by learning the predetermined. The second mode moves toward the revision of the known, the exploration of the undetermined, and the new creation.

A person for whom the first mode or process is primary tends toward the *usual* and *expected*. A person for whom the second mode is primary tends toward the *novel* and *speculative*. The one favors certainty, the other risk . . .

Psychologists use different terms in discussing these two modes. Guilford speaks about "convergent and divergent thinking"; Maslow, about "defense" and "growth"; Rogers, about "defensiveness" and "openness"; Schachtel, about "embeddedness" and "independence." Whatever formulation is used, the position is that one mode stands for "intellectual acquisitiveness and conformity, the other intellectual inventiveness and innovation."[G3:14]

Whereas both modes are *equally* important, it is primarily

the first one which is stressed by the present intelligence test. There is an urgent need for enlarging our limited concept of intelligence and intelligence testing to encompass the creative and innovating orientation.

democratic teaching

The written reactions and the interview data show that the role-playing demonstration of teacher *C* intensified and solidified the rejection of *A* as a constricting teacher, aroused doubts as to whether the democratic leadership of *B* was sufficiently deep and comprehensive, and focused the group's attention primarily on the role of the learner in the process of learning. The teachers were impressed with the attempt of teacher *C* to bring pupils into the *planning* of some aspects of the lesson. They felt that they were sensitized to a deeper understanding of *democratic teaching*.

My understanding of democratic teaching changed. I called teacher *A* democratic because he was friendly. I equated democratic behavior with being nice. I called teacher *B* democratic because he gave children a view of the total project. He set a goal so that they would know where they were going. I respect his emphasis on thinking.

Now comes teacher *C* who believes in the individuality of the learner and who encourages children to participate in planning. In the *B* class, children work toward goals set by the teacher. They learn subject matter decided only by the teacher. The outcome is known. In the *C* class, children participate in developing the goal and the content.

The democratic process in learning, with its emphasis on pupil-teacher interaction, is one of the most valued ideals of modern education. It is also one of the most elusive concepts. The depth and meaning of the cooperative process of teacher-student participation is often misunderstood by both theorist and practitioner of education. No wonder it is confused by the novice teachers.

Many teachers called teacher *A* democratic, emphasizing

primarily his being "nice," his use of praise, and the amount
of participation in his class. At the beginning, they failed to
recognize his manipulative and constricting approach.

The majority of the group perceived B as democratic primarily because he raised long-range objectives and because of
his respect for the children's ability to think. They started to
question the A orientation and recognized its authoritarian
and controlling qualities.

Under the impact of the C demonstration, the teachers
came to realize that even the B approach lacked democratic
emphasis to some extent. The children have to work toward
goals set only by the teacher. The subject matter, outcomes,
and process of learning are predetermined. They identified
with the C orientation and its richer provisions for the expressions of the individuality of the learner. They perceived it as
a step ahead on the road toward democratic teaching.

teacher- or child-centeredness

Despite the potential promise inherent in the B approach
of unifying subject matter and creating basic Gestalt, this
approach still suffers from a major limitation. As Syngg
points out,[S14:Part 2] the attempt is to change the behavior of the
learner by manipulating the environment *outside* the perceived self. The B orientation attempts to change the course
of study, to manipulate the organization of content and materials with the hope that it will affect the learner. Unless
educators are prepared to go beyond the external steps of
subject-matter integration and stress the interaction between
the learner and the subject matter, the goal of curriculum improvement may not be fully attained.

The C orientation is an attempt to move in this direction
by emphasizing not only the integration of subject matter and
its uniting structure, but rather by developing a curriculum
pattern based on continuous interaction between the learner
and learning. The emphasis is on a somewhat emerging curriculum, a curriculum which is neither child- nor teacher-
centered. A child-centered curriculum tends to be laissez-faire.
A teacher-centered curriculum tends to be authoritarian in

nature. Both of these approaches have their strengths and limitations.

The child-centered curriculum stems from an idealistic belief in the resourcefulness of children. The belief is that there is richness and uniqueness in every individual, but that these qualities are sometimes latent, or covered by a shell. The function of education is primarily to help children realize what *they* want, what potential *they* have, and where *they* want to go, and then to help them get there.

The teacher-centered curriculum is a belief that the child is molded by the values and the norms of the culture surrounding him. It is the function of organized education to see that learning the modes of the culture will not be a trial-and-error process. The teacher, being an authority, has to select the knowledge and values that have to be learned. The teacher has a responsibility to direct the immature child and lead him toward maturity.

The child-centered approach suffers from a naive conception of the meaning of growth. Growth is not only a process of "unfolding the child's potentialities." Growth is a result of the experiences which impinge on the child. It is the function of the teacher to select the right experiences to help the child grow in a healthy direction.

The teacher-centered approach underestimates the power of children and the importance of self-direction. In some cases, at least, it develops a teacher authority who is preoccupied with his own conception of the knowledge to be taught and is not *open* to the needs and perceptions of children.

The C orientation is an attempt to look for a balance between the child- and the teacher-centered positions and to build on the strength in both of them. The C teacher in the role-playing demonstration initiates the activity in an authority-centered way. He develops his own interpretation of the subject matter. He directs and structures. However, as the activity proceeds, he permits children, individually and in groups, to come into the planning and develop the lesson in their own divergent ways. He encourages children to move from the known to the unknown, unknown even to the teacher. The teacher is not laissez-faire; he does not follow a "do-anything-you-want-to-do" approach. The C teacher creates a setup and structure for systematic and serious study, which encourages children to learn by identifying with an adult authority and also by developing their own sense of self-direction.

The teacher who is A-oriented reveals to his pupils a short-range objective; the one who is B-oriented reveals to his followers a long-range objective. Whereas the difference between these two approaches is fundamental, the similarity is fundamental, too. In both ways of teaching, it is the teacher who presents an objective which the pupils had almost no part in planning.

Observing the teachers under discussion here, one finds that in performing lessons they often conceal the next topic from their pupils, and hide the new posters, records, and other materials. This behavior is significant and revealing in terms of the democratic quality or criterion of the teacher-pupil relations. The teacher wants to arouse class interest by surprising and fascinating the pupils with the richness of the materials which she prepared and preplanned. In the A and B classes, children are going to be surprised by the goal and by the presentation. The pupils' function is primarily to absorb and accept rather than initiate and plan.

In following the A and B orientations, the teacher tends to stress primarily the technique of explanation. Facing the class is a dynamic, sometimes even overpowering, young teacher who "monopolizes the stage." He attempts to be interesting by asking questions (sometimes bombarding them with questions), demonstrating, planning, and acting. The children's role expectation is to be "motivated" to move where the leader wants them to go, and be interested in doing what the leader wants them to do.

It is not difficult to recognize in this description the attributes of leadership which is skewed in the authoritarian direction. It is the teacher alone who determines the goal and plans the program of the group. To use Lewin's terminology, it is the leader's "field of power" which keeps the pupils going. Children's initiative, self-direction, and involvement in learning are often insufficiently promoted under such conditions of teacher-pupil cooperation. As one interviewee puts it:

Teacher C makes provisions for children to work on a common interest. In the role-playing they plan for a few minutes before presenting their idea. In C as a way of teaching, it may mean getting involved in a long-range project. They (the children) will develop independence and responsibility in working on their own ideas, without the teacher stopping them every few minutes and telling them to work on another task.

task involvement or reinforcement?

A basic attribute of democratic teaching is the encouragement of *task* involvement. The pupil learns subject matter because the knowledge is intrinsically meaningful to him. A basic attribute of teacher-centered teaching is the use of extrinsic motivation, even coercion or manipulation. An interviewee says:

I always thought it is good to compliment children and praise them. I believed that reward is better than punishment. Now I see that the use of reward may be a manipulative technique, to make children do what the teacher wants them to do.

The excessive use of praise is, at least in some cases, the major tool of a benevolent autocracy.

Teacher A is a master of praise and reward. She asks many questions, gives many assignments, and gets immediate results. Each "result" is rewarded. It gave us a feeling of artificial behavior, but we decided she is a friendly and warm person. I guess we took it for granted this is the way one should behave at school.

The artificiality of A's rewarding behavior was recognized; however, it was compatible with the group's image of a "nice" school teacher. Teacher B's rewarding behavior is less extreme and, therefore, is not manipulative in nature. An interviewee says:

Teacher *B* raises few thought questions which tap the children's understanding of the main ideas. The children work hard to reach the correct answer. My feeling is that when they were praised, they deserved it. It was a praise well-earned.

The difference between the "rewarding behavior" of *A* and *B* is fundamental. However, one should recognize that both of them use praise for the same goal—approving behavior which agrees with the specific objectives and values of the leader. The rewarded children are those who please the leader.

Rewards are not limited to marks, promotions, or stars; nor is punishment limited to non-promotion or expulsion from the group. A nod of approval, a reassuring smile, a frown, and criticism are subtle ways in which the teacher rewards or promotes a particular act of behavior.

Through a system of punishment and rewards the child often learns to work not for his own goals, but for the adult's (teacher's) objectives. The positive impact of this process is fully recognized. It is a major channel of socialization. Generally, children learn to accept the rewarded goal and it becomes their own. However, the overuse of reward has, in many cases, negative effects.

The intrinsic relationship between the learner and the subject matter is sometimes supplemented by the relationship between the learner and the reward. In the language of learning theorists[H10] the learner aims for the reward, an indication that a task has been completed, rather than for the *success* inherent in the mastering of the task itself. A common illustration is the pupil who is encouraged to learn to read in order to get a high grade (reward) rather than to satisfy his own quest for knowledge (success).

The direct personal relations between the learner and the subject matter often disappear. One learns for the culminating symbol of graduation. Of course, graduation satisfies a personal need too. In satisfying it, however, the subject matter learned becomes secondary.

In contrast to the *A* and *B*, the *C* orientation illustrates a teaching behavior which is not based primarily on the law of effect, or the reinforcement theory. Teacher *C* limits his use of reward or punishment. He centers his educational approach on Lewin's belief in the power of the intrinsic motivation of task involvement.

In a discussion of "Field Theory and Learning,"[L3] Lewin points out some of the difficulties in applying the law of effect drawn from "maze experiments" to *classroom* situations. Psychologists have tended to perform their experiments in confining runways or with subjects strapped to the apparatus. They overlooked the importance of the factor of the maze barrier on the results of their experiments. The animal is compelled to learn an intrinsically disliked task not only because of the fear of punishment, but also because the maze barrier does not permit it to run away and "leave the field." In terms of classroom practices, it means that the teacher who wants to resort to punitive motivation in the learning process must not only employ punishment but also erect authoritarian and "police" barriers around the learner; or, using Lewin's example, put him in a maze.

Teachers *A* and *B* can be rewarding or punitive in nature. When they are rewarding, the reward is *externally* related to the task of learning. In an attempt to obtain such rewards, children tend to develop a variety of shortcuts. For example, copying on an examination is an attempt to get reward without working on the learning task.

One of the greatest challenges for the educator is to make knowledge a part of the lives of students and to make subject matter personally meaningful. The *C* demonstration illustrates a beginning of movement in this direction. Each child is encouraged to try to be successful in working on a task he sets for himself; to experience progress toward his own level of aspiration. The pupil works not because of the approval or disapproval of his elders (teachers), but because he is ego-involved in the task. Underlying the ideal of democracy in education is task involvement in learning.

individual worth

Observing at work the overwhelming majority of teachers who follow the *A* and *B* patterns of rewarding behavior, one finds that the signs of approval and disapproval are not distributed equally among all pupils. Already in the first grade the class is sorted into two groups: the approved and the disapproved. The approved pupils are those who obey the teacher's request for attention; they follow the directions, do neat, clean work, keep obviously busy, and finish their work on time. The disapproved pupils are those who, for various reasons, cannot keep up with the others and cannot measure up to the same standards, or those who want to assert their independence and do it their own way.

Those who belong to the disapproved group introject the teacher's evaluation of them. They tend to lose their security and initiative and stop investing effort in mastering the subject matter. They tend to develop a defeatist approach toward the school and the teacher, which in turn brings about more disapproval from the teacher and, consequently, further passivity toward the educating agent. A look at a typical class discussion illustrates this point.

In order to arouse interest and keep the discussion going, the teacher tends to raise many questions. It is not a discussion where everyone contributes from his experiences, hopes, and uncertainties. It is an aggressive search for the correct answer which often only a few pupils can provide immediately.

The teacher, being interested in a "good discussion," tends to prefer those who can produce the right answer and sometimes tends to ignore the other pupils. A discussion pattern is established where the class is divided into an active group, which has something to contribute, and a passive group which, in some cases at least, is considered by the teacher and by itself as lacking in ability to contribute; it is considered, to put it somewhat extremely, as worthless.

Democracy in education means the belief in the worth of an individual. If this last sentence should become an item on a scale testing the educational beliefs of teachers, the response of all of them would be "strongly agree." However, the above observations of teachers in action suggest that a wide gap exists between one's professed ideals and his teaching behavior.

Teacher C illustrates an attempt to implement the democratic belief in the work of every individual.

Teacher C looks at the child's answer or work from the point of view of the child. He tries to understand what the child wanted to say and where he wanted to go. He respects children.

To conclude, democratic teaching does not mean only nice and friendly human relations, nor the sole emphasis on unity of subject matter and productive thinking. Democratic teaching means primarily cooperative planning, task involvement, and respect for the worth of the individual student. These three are interrelated.

Movement from repetitive toward creative teaching cannot be realized without an understanding of the deeper dynamics of democratic teaching.

democratic teaching: difficulties

Democratic teaching was perceived by the novice teachers as a major characteristic denoting the C orientation. Some of the difficulties experienced by teachers in translating the ideal of democracy into the language of teaching behavior will be discussed in this section.

A major problem is the difficulty in understanding the nature of freedom inherent in democratic teaching and its confusion with an atmosphere of laissez-faire. This difficulty can be observed both on the *conceptual* and *behavioral* levels. The following experiment illustrates cognitive confusions involved.

In a college class, three staff meetings were demonstrated through role-playing before a group of teachers. In the first "staff meeting" the "principal" played a *laissez-faire* role. One could not distinguish his role from those of the other group members. The nature of his participation in terms of its quality and quantity resembled the participation of the other members. There was no attempt on his part to move the discussion ahead, reach conclusions, etc. After the first demonstration was over, the group was instructed to indicate whether the principal played a laissez-faire, democratic, or authoritarian role. The majority answered, "democratic"; the minority, "laissez-faire"; and none, "authoritarian."

A second "staff meeting" was demonstrated where the "principal" played a *democratic* role. He identified the problems and developed an agenda cooperatively with the staff. He was attentive to human relations, attempted to clarify and synthesize positions, and moved the discussion ahead.

The group of teachers was again instructed to decide whether the principal played a laissez-faire, democratic, or authoritarian role. The responses were almost equally divided between "democratic" and "authoritarian."

In the third "staff meeting" the "principal" played an *authoritarian* role. He dictated a preplanned agenda, made decisions, and assigned tasks without encouraging the group to present their ideas. Without exception, the teachers decided that the last "principal" portrayed an authoritarian leader.

On the perceptual level, the teachers were in some agreement with regard to the operation of authoritarian leadership but in disagreement with regard to the nature of laissez-faire and democratic behavior. Their misconceptions show a very definite trend which has significant educational implications: it is the laissez-faire teacher who is perceived as democratic and not vice-versa; it is the democratic teacher who is often perceived as authoritarian and not vice-versa.

To put it in other words, it is the laissez-faire teacher, the one who does not *assert* leadership, direction, and power, who is perceived as meeting the *ideal* of democratic behavior. It is the democratic individual, the one who asserts some degree of leadership, who is often perceived negatively as authoritarian. On the professed verbal level, democratic leadership is equated with lack of assertion of direct power.

Traditionally, the role of the teacher is seen in an assertive light. The dictionary defines the term "teach" as, "to make to know how; show how; hence, to train or accustom to some action." In many languages the teacher is called "instructor," that is, the one who gives instructions or orders. The professed belief that democratic leadership means lack of assertion is a reversal of the traditional image of the teacher. How does this reversal affect the teacher's behavior?

One conception of democratic leadership translated into the language of teaching behavior is withdrawal, non-direction, and delegation of complete responsibility to children; a teaching behavior which is more laissez-faire than democratic. This pattern is especially prevalent when the subject matter is *art*, the area that traditionally is considered the province of creativity. In many instances, observing coloring activities, "cut-and glue" projects, the novice teacher would come to me and say:

I let them have free time to express their own ideas. I don't want to impose mine and stifle their creativity. Don't you think it is a workshop atmosphere?

Free time for children to do what they want, and non-direction on the part of the leader, is equated in this typical illustration with democratic teaching and with the process of promoting creativity.

It is relatively easy to surrender the traditional role of the teacher—the one who structures and directs—in the general area of art. This area is conventionally seen as one where norms of production are not established, definite achievement is not expected; an area with relatively no pressure of standards. It is also relatively easy to resign the role of directiveness in the arts because the tendency is to perceive them as secondary in status in the hierarchy of school subjects. To put it somewhat radically, the arts are not really seen as serious business, but rather as extracurricular, or even as frills. Let the children express their creativity by doing what they want, by drawing pictures, or by putting on a skit. This will be lots of fun.

The role of directiveness is diminished primarily when the activity is denoted by lack of norms of achievement and an atmosphere of fun rather than systematic and hard work. This is a sad commentary on one frequent approach to democratic teaching and creativity.

A second area known to be the domain of democratic teaching is *social studies*. The teacher is aware that the teaching of social studies calls for the application of the principles of the democratic process. Should the teacher, whose professed value of democratic leadership is characterized by withdrawal, apply non-directiveness to the teaching of social studies?

The answer to this question is negative. Social studies is perceived as a fundamental area of the curriculum. It has subject matter to be covered and achievement to be reached. It is a serious business. The teacher cannot afford to abdicate the responsibility of leadership and invest complete authority in the children. On the contrary, the obstacle to democratic teaching in the area of social studies is a high degree of teacher-centered teaching, or "pseudo-democracy." The last term refers to the known practice of moving through the external motions of democratic teaching, but, in reality, manipulating children to do what the teacher wants them to do. An example might be "guiding" the child to decide on a topic or on committees that the teacher "had in mind." In cases of this nature, the teacher realizes that his teaching behavior is pseudo-democratic; that he only pays lip service to the ideal.

To conclude, both on the conceptual and behavioral levels, many teachers have difficulty with the principles of democratic teaching. The major issue is the definition of the nature of freedom for children, as opposed to direction on the part of teachers.

the role of freedom and structure

Some proponents of an extreme atmosphere of freedom in the elementary school claim that the end result will be a higher level of creativity. The function of the teacher, according to this freedom-centered position, is to provide a permissive atmosphere and to supply tools and materials for the development of self-expression. Any attempt in direction or setting standards is seen as a danger stifling the innate talents of children. Direction is seen as imposing the teacher's own set of values and channeling children into the prevalent pattern of production. The Rogerian psychology of non-directive therapy was adopted by some educational theorists and practitioners[A5] and contributed toward the building of the image of the "ideal teacher": permissive, non-directive, and objective.

The impact of these educational and psychological theories on the beginning teacher was a mixed blessing. On the one hand, the novice was sensitized to the importance of identifying children's interests and following the child. Teachers realized, at least on the verbal level, that autocratic and overstructured teaching is a deterrent to the growth of children's creativity. On the other hand, the emphasis on the relationship between freedom, child-centeredness, and creativity sometimes led many young teachers to the equation of democratic leadership and the creative process with laissez-faire oriented behavior, or to "pseudo-democratic" behavior.

The C orientation is based on the belief that creativity means neither child- nor teacher-centeredness. Teacher C starts the lesson with a definite structure and sense of direction. He does not abdicate the teacher's responsibility, but rather, leads. However, in the middle of the lesson children are encouraged to come into the preplanned structure and develop their own orientation. They are expected to work seriously and systematically, and present their accomplishment—that is, the structure they reached. They are expected to work hard on achieving the task.

Democratic teaching, as an element of the creative process, means the initiation by the teacher of a flexible structure and direction that accommodates the direction and structure suggested by children. It is an attempt to reach a synthesis between the child- and teacher-centered schools of thought.

conclusion

The formulation of the repetitive-creative continuum is based on the modern findings concerning modes of thinking. Whereas the leading researchers in this area stress primarily the measurement of creative abilities, the contribution of the present study is the conceptualization of the thinking modes of memorization, convergent and divergent thinking as total and distinct teaching behaviors and climates. The central difference underlying these teaching climates is their perception of the role of the learner.

The A climate perceives the child as relatively powerless.

He can only repeat the given known; he can only enumerate facts without using them. He needs continuous support and continuous "triggering" by the teacher.

The *B* climate perceives the learner as more powerful. He is not bound to the concrete but can exercise his own power. He can dare act, generalize, abstract, use data. He can dare fly, but he is restricted by the need for objectivity and the predetermined channeling of the teacher.

The *C* climate encourages the learner to rely on and utilize his potential, not to be bound to the concrete model, but rather to dare grope ideationally toward the creation of new and not predetermined knowledge. It is a climate which nurtures power to learn and create beyond the boundaries of the safe familiarity of the present and the predictable, and sparks in the individual the desire to outreach himself.

selected bibliography

GETZELS, JACOB and JACKSON, PHILIP, *Creativity and Intelligence.* New York: John Wiley & Sons, Inc., 1962. A pioneering study into the nature of giftedness. Of special interest are Chapters 1 and 2 and the last section of Chapter 3.

HOLT, JOHN, *How Children Fail.* New York: Dell Publishing Company, Inc., 1965. An insightful discussion of the process of learning.

RATHS, LOUIS E., HARRIMAN, MERRIL, and SIMON, B. SIDNEY, *Values and Teaching.* Columbus, Ohio: Charles E. Merrill Books, 1966. An analysis of the problems involved in working with values in the classroom.

SHUMSKY, ABRAHAM, *Creative Teaching in the Elementary School.* New York: Appleton-Century-Crofts, 1965. Part II analyzes and illustrates the repetitive and the creative aspects of the methodology of the various subject areas.

TORRANCE, E. PAUL, *Guiding Creative Talent.* Englewood Cliffs, N.J.: Prentice-Hall, Inc., 1962. A comprehensive and original discussion of creativity.

two

*in search of teaching style:
the teaching experience*

4

the student-teaching experience

While participating in college courses, observing the cooperating teacher, and reading educational literature, the student teacher asks a fundamental question: "What does all this mean in terms of my teaching?" Along with the teacher education process, the novice is actively searching for his identity as a teacher, for his own style of teaching. Is he going to be permissive or demanding, critical or supporting? Is he going to emphasize factual information, convergent, or divergent thinking? Is he going to emphasis individual and committee work or the "frontal approach" of teaching the class as a whole?

The impact of the praticum on this search for style is very significant. In expressing their own evaluation, student teachers consider the practicum as the most important single experience in their preparation for teaching. To the incomplete sentence, "The student-teaching experience . . .," typical reactions were:

. . . is the most meaningful learning I have ever had.

. . . is the first time I understood the problem of education.

. . . is my opportunity to try my wings.

. . . is the entrance to the world of the teacher.

While there is no research to compare the relative impact of the cooperating teacher on the novice's search for a style of teaching, it is a common observation that it is significant. Because of her advantage in working with trainees in an action-type program, her influence is perhaps greater than that of the college teacher.

Discussions with cooperating teachers show that they themselves believe in their strong educational influence. They credit the theory of learning through doing for their success in molding, or at least affecting, the novice's way of teaching. They believe that their direct contact with children, their deep understanding of the practical aspects of implementing educational theory, makes their teaching realistic and, therefore, most meaningful.

It is the purpose of this chapter to examine the student-teaching experience (with emphasis on the relationship with the cooperating teacher) in terms of its impact on the quality of the novice's teaching behavior.

relating to the cooperating teacher

the promise

Educational literature calls the cooperating teachers key figures in teacher-education programs.[S17] Most student teachers, in first meeting the cooperating teacher in action, feel that they have finally met the reality of teaching. They have a feeling of coming closer to a better grasp of teaching.

In comparing the college instructor with the cooperating teacher, the student teachers tend to identify with the latter. The cooperating teacher represents the reference group to which the trainee aspires: "Looking at her I see myself in the same situation. When I take over, I play her role." This cannot be said about the college instructor.

The cooperating teacher illustrates in her behavior, in a comprehensive and concrete way, the total professional role that has to be learned in its most real and natural setting. While the college instructor illustrates verbally, the cooperating teacher instructs in action. Attempts to demonstrate the effectiveness of a curricular innovation in a college course are perceived by some prospective teachers as unrealistic laboratory experimentation.

Was it designed for an ideal situation? Most of us here don't have the accommodations or the necessary materials.

It is almost like the unrealistic education film they (the college instructors) show of a teacher working with a committee of six pupils. You wonder what the other thirty are doing.

Generally words cannot communicate with the clarity of a picture. But perhaps more important, the learner may feel skeptical in listening to words. He is more receptive when observing a curricular innovation which "works" in a field situation.

Such comments on the part of student teachers may be interpreted as a reflection of a concrete and practical approach to knowledge. Frequently this interpretation is correct. However, just as frequently these attitudes reflect the gaps felt by students between principles of education and the knowledge of how to handle children. These practical attitudes can be interpreted as a healthy search for meaningful knowledge.

In the college class the student is a member of a large group. His relations to the instructor are affected by the size of the group and the formal regulations of the course. The problem to be discussed is generally decided by the instructor, or cooperatively, by various class members. The student has a relatively passive position in the teaching-learning relations.

The relationship between the student teacher and the cooperating teacher is potentially more personal and reciprocal. It is a relationship between two people with the common bond of having to work with the same group of children. The common task brings them closer as people and, to some extent, reduces the status barrier.

Having a student teacher may require a great investment in terms of time and energy on the part of the cooperating teacher. However, the cooperating teacher not only gives; she also receives. The student teacher is not only an observer or one who asks time-consuming questions; he also cooperates by helping with the various teaching responsibilities.

For instance, while the cooperating teacher works with one group in reading, the student teacher may work with another. In a modern teaching situation where a balance among teaching the whole class, group, and individual work is constantly sought, an assistant ready to take over one of the groups or to work with a slow child is most advantageous. As reported by student teachers, their first involvement in the class work is generally in helping a slow learner.

The most common criterion of evaluation used by cooperating teachers is whether the student teacher is "helpful and cooperative." The cooperating teacher is appreciative of the trainee who contributes to the class welfare, helps in record keeping, in checking papers and tests. This appreciation is seen in statements like the following:

I remember Mary Brown whom I had two years ago. She was most cooperative and helpful. I still have the relief map she did with my group.

The student teacher not only helps in teaching but also exchanges roles—takes over the class. This experience is a source of closeness between the cooperating teacher and the novice. The latter is influenced by the experienced teacher's way of teaching and often even imitates her. The cooperating teacher herself often has a strong sense of identification with the student teacher. She may experience nostalgic feelings about her own student-teaching experience. ("I remember the first lesson I ever taught.") She enjoys the sense of achievement in attributing the student teacher's accomplishments to her own teaching.

Working with a student teacher is not only a source of emotional satisfaction, but also a source of intellectual stimulation. In spite of his lack of experience the novice, as some cooperating teachers put it, is their link with college—the source of new ideas. The student teacher is fresh with discussions of the latest trends in education innovations. Being less threatening than any other status leader (principals, consultants, or college professors) the novice can introduce new ideas that may intellectually challenge the cooperating teacher.

The need to stop and explain her practices to the inquisitive novice is an opportunity for the senior teacher to look for their deeper meaning and examine the rationale of her practices. As some cooperating teachers see it, they don't relate any more only to the relatively immature minds of children, but are also challenged by the adult mind of a student teacher.

The fact that the practicum can be a satisfying and educational experience for both novice and senior teacher does not mean that there are no problems involved in these relations.

bringing in a stranger

One study on the problem of cooperating teaching[A3] suggests that the training of student teachers is somewhat less than the sheer joy pictured by public relations personnel at the college. The fact is that, in addition to the normal class load, the cooperating teacher has to guide the student teacher in practice teaching, to be acquainted with rules and regulations, to assist in securing and organizing materials, to schedule conferences, and so on. All this, suggests the above study, lays a demanding and time-consuming burden on the teacher. As difficult as this burden may be it would seem that the most taxing aspect of this role stems not so much from the tangible elements of time, energy, and effort, but primarily from the intangible undercurrents of bringing a stranger into the intricacies of teacher-class relations. Putting it somewhat extremely, bringing in a student teacher may sometimes mean opening one's home to a stranger.

A student teacher who enters a classroom may normally go in with the expectation of observing techniques of teaching and learning the skills. He may view the cooperating teacher primarily as a source of ideas and methodology.

Cooperating teachers, however, are more than mere audiovisual machines which demonstrate techniques. They are people. The most significant thing they invest in teaching is their personality. Teaching is primarily an expression of intimate relations between an adult and a group of children.

Teaching a group of children is more than a livelihood, imparting subject matter, or developing attitudes. Teaching is often a way by which one attempts to find himself as a person; a way one lives in a home and builds his home—in the psychological sense of the word *home*. Into these intricate relations between a person and the meaning of his "home" a newcomer is admitted, not for a lecture or a short course, but rather to become a continuous observer and somewhat a partner.

Bringing in a student teacher is difficult because teaching is more than a skill; it is a personal process. Teaching consists to a great extent of intuitive, subjective, and spontaneous reactions. Many of the techniques used by teachers may never be verbally explained to others because they result from subtle and unrealized communication between the teacher and her students. It is as if an inner sense of timing, an inner sensitivity, exists within the teacher which helps her move and respond to the needs and behavior of children.

The teacher uses her self as a tool in the teaching process. Teaching is an art which develops out of using one's own self; out of learning more about others by way of understanding one's own reactions to others.

It seems that in some cases the fact that teaching is primarily a personal relationship serves to establish a strong bond between the experienced and the novice teacher. Perhaps these are the cooperating teachers which the student teachers describe by expressions such as the following:

Help us beyond the call of duty.

Take us under their wings.

Want us to be almost their daughters.

Enjoy tremendously when we are successful.

On the other hand, in at least some cases, the newcomer is a damper to the cooperating teacher's spontaneity and sense of personal fulfillment. Perhaps these are the cooperating teachers of whom some perceptive student teachers report their indirect rejecting remarks or rejective actions:

You were absent today and we had a wonderful lesson. Why do we have some of our best work when you are not here?

Any time I (the student teacher) develop relations with some children she runs over and takes them from me. Is she jealous?

This discussion is no attempt to justify comments of this nature. It only attempts to explain and understand them.

lack of role definition

Another difficulty underlying the relationship between the novice and the cooperating teacher is the lack of a sufficient delineation of their mutual roles. Both parties are not entirely sure of their rights and responsibilities and do not know what to expect from each other.

Compare the relationship of the student teacher and the cooperating teacher with that of the student teacher and the college instructor. The latter is pretty well defined. It is expected that the instructor will set the course requirement, such as assigning readings, papers, or administering tests. It is expected that the instructor will examine the students' oral and written work, criticize and grade it. It is expected that the student teacher will participate in college discussions, introduce ideas, question, and sometimes even disagree with the instructor's position.

When it comes to the relationship with the cooperating teacher, the roles of each party are not clear. There is definitely disagreements in answering questions such as the following: Should the cooperating teacher assign homework or leave it up to the student teacher? Should the cooperating teacher criticize or only answer the questions raised by the trainee? Should the student teacher suggest curricular innovations or disagree with the practices of the senior teacher? Or should his role be limited to accepting things with no questioning?

This confusion about role definition and expectation can be seen in the following excerpts from an interview:

At first our relationship was one of mutual confusion. She (the cooperating teacher) didn't know what to expect of me and I didn't know what to expect of her. I spent most of my time in the back of the room watching her teach. This ridiculous siuation persisted until I asked my teacher if she thought I was ready to teach a lesson.

After this our relations improved. The teacher was willing to give her opinions and criticisms of my lessons. She no longer felt guilty about asking me to teach and I was no longer afraid to ask if I could give a lesson.

An examination of the logs of student teachers shows that the lack of clarity in role expectations is a source of stress and, most important, a major deterrent to learning. The data also suggest that those student teachers who, on their own initiative or in collaboration with the cooperating teacher and college instructor, were able to reach mutual understanding in the role expectation, utilized the practicum experience more productively.

the status problem

In a college course a group of student teachers was asked to report one incident which occurred in their classrooms. Examination of the responses showed that the most frequent category was the relations of the cooperating teacher to children. The second most frequent category was the impact of the cooperating teacher's attitude on the *status* of the student teacher. It is evident that the latter is sensitive—and even, perhaps, oversensitive—to the status problem.

Being preoccupied with the fear of lack of control over pupils, being driven by the need to be respected, one of the novice's first questions is: "Am I going to be introduced to the children as a student or a teacher?" Being introduced as a student is perceived as a threat to their status. The introduction as a teacher is an invitation for an attitude of equality.

The lack of clarity about their status is illustrated by the following two extreme incidents: One student teacher lined up with the children on the first morning and walked in the line into the classroom. This is an extreme expression of the feeling that one is a student rather than a teacher.

The second extreme is the incident of a student teacher who, in presenting herself to the cooperating teacher, reprimanded the class: "I would like you to be quiet and respectful when I am introduced to you for the first time." This is an extreme manifestation of anxiety over the respected status of a teacher.

The majority of the logs discuss the first introduction to the class in terms of the status threat. However, the status problem is not limited to the first initiation. The trainees want the cooperating teachers to treat them with equal respect, especially in front of children; to support in disciplinary situations so that their word will be the rule; to avoid criticizing or correcting them in front of children.

They see interruptions as lowering of status.

I told the class a story and then asked them to develop their own ending. Several children did not want to write and I insisted that they should do it. As we were arguing, the cooperating teacher returned and without consulting me said, "O.K. boys and girls, stop what you are doing and let's do some arithmetic." The children looked at me with laughter in their eyes.

They praise the cooperating teacher who helps them learn to assert themselves.

One day when teacher Z was administering a citywide test to other classes and I was on my own, I had great difficulty in getting the class to the room quietly. I scolded, I asked for a straight line, etc., but all to no avail. I finally gave up and led the mob (for it was a mob) to the room. At the door teacher Z greeted me and told me that if I did not positively assert myself now I would never be able to gain control of this class. She tactfully whispered instructions to me and left me to myself at the front.

They complain about the cooperating teacher who builds her own status by means of competition rather than mutual respect and support.

It is particularly in the upper grades of the elementary school that children will realize that the student teacher is only second in command and is in the process of learning a profession. It is thus somewhat naive to attempt to hide the fact that the newcomer is a student teacher.

It is more realistic for the children to learn that every organization has a power hierarchy. In the school structure it is usually the principal, the assistant principal, the teacher the student teacher. Each one of these people has a right to assert his leadership within the limits of the setup. It may also be helpful for children to see a young person in an apprenticeship position, as many of them live in a culture which is detached from the experience of work.

The student teacher may give homework to children, provided it has been previously approved by the cooperating teacher. Of course he may finish a lesson, assuming the time limit was agreed on in advance. Much of the misunderstanding derives from lack of communication and lack of cooperative planning of the various tasks to be accomplished in a specific day.

The vision of the student teacher is sometimes limited only to the specific activity he has to conduct, such as an art lesson. He may take too much time developing this activity, not being aware of the other pressures, such as preparation for a citywide test. An interruption of the art activity may be perceived by the novice as a threat to his status, while objectively it may be necessary in order that time be provided to clean the room before departing for the day.

I would like to suggest that many student teachers are too sensitive to status problems. They may forget that the main objective of the practicum is learning to teach rather than building status. Unwittingly they often seem ready to sacrifice their education for the sake of security.

In the college situation the prospective teacher is a student—a well-delineated role. In the field he is a student teacher —a student to the cooperating teacher and a teacher to the children at the same time. The involvement in both roles is a source of difficulty to the student teacher. In his preoccupation with playing the teacher's role, the novice may overlook his function as the one whose main objective is to learn and thereby make mistakes, get help, and try again.

Another difficulty underlying the status problem is lack of sufficient communication between the two parties involved. Student teachers report that to the extent that they are able to establish communication with the cooperating teacher, their feeling about their status in the classroom improves tremendously.

Here are a few points which a teacher and a student teacher may want to discuss in order to improve their communication.

Should the student teacher participate while the cooperating teacher is teaching the class as a whole, and vice-versa?

How, where, and when should comments about ways of improving be made?

To what extent can the student teacher participate, or act independently, in disciplining children or giving homework?

How long should a specific activity last?

How closely should the student follow the teacher's routines and to what extent is the novice permitted to introduce new routines?

How closely should the trainee follow the mentor's way of teaching and to what extent should he experiment with his own ideas?

observation: a passive or active process?

The first function of the student teacher in his field practicum is to observe the class operation. In terms of the amount of time spent in the classroom, observation is the most time-consuming activity. Even when the novice starts to move toward other aspects of his training, such as assisting teaching and independent teaching, he still spends many of his practicum hours in observation. Observation remains a continuous process through all stages of student teaching, although it may change in terms of time emphasis.

the function

The main purpose of the activity termed here *observation*, is to help the student integrate the theory of education and its practice. As the discussion will show, when this purpose is fully understood and is kept in focus, observation becomes an enriching experience. When the above main purpose is overlooked, observation may become a drudgery.

Student teachers generally look forward to the experience of observation as they recognize the difference between knowledge derived from attendance at lectures and that derived from observations of live illustrations. And indeed, one of the most valuable aspects of the observation experience is that the novice makes progress in learning to think in the analytic language of a situation, rather than solely in the synthetic language of a generalization. The ideas of unit planning, motivation, committee work, or creative writing become more meaningful by being spelled out. He makes progress in visualizing many specific situations of various aspects of teaching, which results in increased clarity, confidence, and a growing readiness to teach.

An educational idea observed in operation in a classroom, such as individualized reading, is convincing. The observer watches the matrix of all the factors (including interruptions by the public address system) as they impinge on each other, and begins to believe that "it can be done." The convincing aspect of the observation experience is illustrated by the fact that the novice tends to use it as "evidence" that a certain curricular innovation is operational. In brief, observation can be a most potentially meaningful experience in the education of the prospective teacher.

a passive or an active process?

As reported by student teachers, the seemingly simple practice of observation varies tremendously in different field situations. For instance, on one extreme is the trainee who sits and watches for weeks, and on the other end is the one who in the first hour is plunged into taking the class over while the cooperating teacher leaves the class. The majority of student teachers fall between these extremes. They spend some time in observation and are gradually initiated into teaching.

Complaining about a prolonged stage of observation, a student teacher says:

Long periods of observation are a waste of time. You see the
same thing again and again. You feel as useful as a fifth wheel.
You don't feel that you are an integral part of the group.

Other trainees speak about feeling "like a piece of furniture" or complain that they "do only one thing—sit." They
wish that the teacher would permit them to take a more active
role in classroom affairs.

Complaints about prolonged periods of observation are
sometimes valid and will be discussed in another section. The
point discussed here is that for too many student teachers,
observation implies a passive process. The *active* aspect of
observation is not sufficiently understood.

An examination of the logs written by student teachers
shows that there is hardly a person who does not report his
observation of the field situation. Some reports are comprehensive and rich; others are sketchy or even poor. They describe, agree and disagree, compare with previous experience
and with a theory of education. Some students, on the other
hand, go through the motions of observing in a relatively passive way. They see things and accept them for what they are.

The basic difference between the active and the passive
observers (if one can divide the group into these two distinct
categories) is the *motivation*—that is, what they want to get
out of the experience. Excerpts from the log of two trainees,
located in the same school and dealing with the same observation, illustrate this point.

Today was the turn of my teacher to supervise the children as
they walk into the classrooms. I went with her to see how it works.
She told me that generally the children line up in the yard, but
on that particular day they gathered in the auditorium because
of bad weather. When we reached the place it was bedlam. The
teacher used her whistle and the miracle happened. The children
lined up and were quietly led by monitors to their rooms.

While this observation is primarily descriptive, it brings
out a very definite frame of reference: "It is my function to
know how it is done, so tomorrow I'll be able to do it in the

same way." The above observer expresses her admiration to an approach which "works," and the ability to change noisy disorder into quiet order.

The anecdote reflects the type of approach which concentrates on *imitating* the tested practices of elders. There was no attempt to examine the observed practices in terms of basic principles of education.

The importance of knowing the school practices cannot be overemphasized. It is important to know how children get into their respective classrooms in the morning, the procedures for leaving for lunch, fire drill, etc. An efficient organization on the school and classroom level facilitates learning. Without the ability to establish order, and without knowledge of the school policies, it will hardly be possible for the novice to make progress.

However, critical questions can be raised with regard to such observed practices as the one described above, which may lead the novice beyond the level of merely knowing the school practices without searching for their theoretical rationale.

An excerpt from a log, describing the same situation, will illustrate this point.

When the weather is cold, they wait in the auditorium and line up there. I went to see it today and I felt lost. I wonder how the children feel in this big, noisy crowd. Are these policies consistent with the professed objective of being attentive to individual children? Why cannot a child in coming to school walk directly into the classroom on his own, and be greeted as an individual by the teacher?"

The ability of this student teacher to observe is not limited by the sole need to know practices which work, or to the administration of a senior teacher who is able to control a poor situation. Her thinking is diagnostic. She looks for the *why* and not only the *what*. She is interested in what happens to children, not only in saving her own skin.

This ability to examine the observed classroom analytically and critically in terms of educational principles we will term an *active experience*. While observation for the sake of imitation is relatively passive, the "active observer" can go on and on for days and weeks observing the same classroom operation without feeling bored. What keeps him going is not only what he observes, but also his personal interpretations and thoughts which interact with the observation. In contrast, the "passive observer" learns the practices quickly. Then he develops the feeling that he sees more and more of the same known thing. He does not *react*, he only absorbs.

Whether the novice will develop a constructive educational orientation which is personally meaningful and whether he will develop experimental attitudes in his practice teaching will depend to a great extent on his ability to experience *actively* the observed field situation.

the function of the cooperating teacher

One factor determining the quality of the observation is of course the perceptiveness of the student teacher, his ability to see theory in action and his ability to look for the meaning of action in theory. Another factor determining the quality of this experience is the nature of the communication with the cooperating teacher.

Student teachers report various practices in this area, ranging from passivity and lack of involvement to active guidance. The passive cooperating teacher is sometimes one who has never accepted the student teacher imposed on her by the administration. In most cases, however, she is the one who is not sure of her role definition and does not want to impose herself on her guest, but rather waits for the student teacher to raise questions. To the student she may appear aloof and cold.

There are many more complaints on the passivity of the cooperating teacher at the beginning of the observation stage than at the end. As the ice between the two adults gradually thaws and a relationship is established, both parties start to play a more active role: the cooperating teacher in guiding the observation, and the student teacher in raising questions or making comments.

It should be emphasized that the majority of cooperating teachers enjoy their role of guiding the student teacher. They feel it is a source of intellectual stimulation and emotional satisfaction. The novice, on the other hand, finds the briefing about the purpose of the lesson and its relation to the total unit most helpful. He is appreciative of the cooperating teacher who stops in the middle of the lesson to make comments about the ongoing activity, a change of plans, or difficulties encountered by specific children. He feels at home with the cooperating teacher who encourages him to raise questions and share observations.

The student teachers who do not get guidance of this nature report that sometimes they have the feeling of sitting in the dark, moving (or more correctly, being moved) step-by-step together with the pupils. Their field of perception and vision becomes very limited. They may find it difficult to relate the specific questions which the teacher raises to the broader goals of education. In some cases, the end result of this limited vision is the feeling of uselessness.

To repeat again, the stage of observation is an enriching experience to the extent that there is give-and-take between the mentor and the student teacher, and to the extent that the latter is able to generalize the meaning of the observation.

assisting teaching

Somewhat artificially, and only for the purpose of organizing the discussion, the analysis of the student-teaching practicum is divided here into two main stages: observation and actual teaching. These two are not entirely sequential experiences, but rather overlapping. With the movement toward actual practice teaching, the activity of observation is reduced only in terms of the relative amount of time devoted to it, but it continues to be an important aspect of the practicum to its last day.

Many student teachers feel that the movement from observation to actual teaching is too slow. This feeling stems partly from an underestimation of the importance of observation as a preparation for teaching, and partly from an eagerness to rush and try the real taste of teaching.

It is evident that the active student teacher, the one who

shows interest, the one who makes suggestions, has a better chance of getting the green light from the cooperating teacher than the trainee who "only sits." His first step in this direction is generally cooperating in or assisting teaching.

The terms *cooperating in teaching* or *assisting teaching*, refer to teaching situations in which the *cooperating and the student teacher share responsibility* in working with the class. For instance, the cooperating teacher illustrates arithmetic problems on the blackboard, and the student teacher helps check whether the children worked them out correctly in their notebooks; or, each of the two teachers may work with a separate group during reading.

Especially in the modern elementary school, which stresses the need for individualized instruction, there are many opportunities for an assistant teacher to perform a useful function, as a major deterrent to individualized instruction is the burden of class size. Many dedicated teachers ask: "How can I devote time to one individual? What will the other thirty do? Waste time in busy work?" It should be recognized that from the point of view of the individualization of instruction, the availability of a student teacher to assist is a major contribution.

As reported by student teachers, they move from observation to teaching by assisting. Generally they start by helping an individual, who is usually academically slow, and gradually move toward working with a small group of slow learners. This initiation has many advantages. An interviewee says:

I find it easier to relate to a small group than to the class as a whole. I am not handicapped by the fear of being on the stage before the class as a whole. The children themselves find it easier to relate and contribute. It is easier for me to know whether the children learned, or to find out about the nature of their mistakes. I am encouraged by being accepted by the group. I feel it prepares me for the more strenuous task of teaching the whole class.

assisting teaching: difficulties

The advantages of the phase of assisting teaching are obvious and do not call for elaboration. They are primarily related to the personal face-to-face relations which the novice develops with the learners.

There are some difficulties characteristic of the assisting phase. An interviewee says:

I enjoy this type of work. I know that I benefit from it. But it is only being a helper. I am not on my own, responsible for the preparation of the total program for the whole class.

The assisting work is generally denoted by some degree of dependency of the student teacher and by limited *planning* on his part of the work that has to be done. He is too much like a worker who "fills in" because he happens to be there, rather than the one who plans ahead and organizes a systematic program of working with a slow learner.

As reported by student teachers, their own *preparation* for assisting is small in comparison to their preparation when they have to take over the class as a whole. It often results from the notion that the novice's role is only to fall in line and join, rather than participate in, the preparation and planning of the work.

To vitalize the assistance phase of the novice's experience, it is helpful to raise questions like the following:

Is the student teacher aware of the total program, and does he see his own contribution as part of this totality?

Does the novice plan and prepare for his activity? Does he know in advance what the nature of the activity may be, how much time is allotted for it, etc.?

Is there a systematic program and continuity in the novice's assistance work, or is it only sporadic?

Is there guidance of the novice's work, such as cooperative planning of the activity and an evaluation of his learning gains?

It is this last point, the evaluation of what has been learned, which should be central in the assisting teaching of the novice. While student teachers generally find that the assisting phase is helpful in terms of their own training, a few wonder at times whether the purpose underlying the assisting work is the education of the novice to become a teacher, or the service to the cooperating teacher and the school. In some extreme cases they ask: "Are we cheap labor?"

The type of work required of the student teacher at this phase may seem somewhat remotely related to teaching a class, but carries as much significance in his training as other functions of the student-teaching experience. There are menial jobs constituting just plain good housekeeping that have to be done in school. Adjusting shades, taking care of the light and heat in the room, straightening chairs, checking supplies, all are part of the duties of a teacher. The trainee has to be aware of all these chores that have to be done, and must carry his share of the responsibility. There are many records to be kept and special forms that one has to be acquainted with. Standardized and teacher-made tests have to be administered and scored. Bulletin boards have to be planned, materials prepared, and worksheets mimeographed. All these are part of the teaching assignment and the student teacher has to practice them.

When is a student teacher *misused* so that instead of being a learner he becomes a teacher's aid? Milner answers this question when he warns cooperating teachers:[M12:19]

But watch out! Don't turn all the work over to him and then forget about it. It is easy to slip into the habit of thinking: a student teacher? Good. I'll give him some of the jobs to do that I dislike so much . . . He's got to find out that teaching isn't all fun.

When the assistance phase of the practicum is skewed day after day in the direction of clerical responsibilities and record-keeping, then the student teacher becomes a *convenient service man rather than a learner.* The cooperating teacher may find it helpful to differentiate in her own mind between situations helpful to the student teacher and situations which seem to exploit him, by using one major criterion: What does the prospective teacher learn from the activity? To test this criterion consider the following illustration.

In two different schools the practicing student teachers were asked to administer a reading-readiness test to the first graders and then to score the results. In one school their function was limited to testing and scoring alone. In the second school they had, in addition, an orientation by the assistant principal on the nature of the tests and a discussion with each cooperating teacher on the meaning of the results and their application to the classroom work. The student teachers practicing in the first school found their experience "an imposition," while those in the second school found their test work "a rewarding teaching experience."

To conclude, in his rush toward independent teaching (teaching the whole class) the novice tends to attach little significance to assisting teaching. He looks at it primarily as a "temporary stage" leading to the final goal, failing to comprehend the full learning potential within the experience itself.

Assisting teaching offers the student teacher an opportunity to learn to teach within the optimal conditions of a small setup and to gain intimate contact with individual children as learners. Teaching is not limited to the function of giving a lesson to the whole class. It has many functions and assignments. Mistakenly they are sometimes seen as secondary or even insignificant. Assisting is an opportunity to practice, one by one, the variety of the role components of the teaching position and understand their function.

suggested activities

It may be useful for the student teacher to discuss with the cooperating teacher the diversity of her role responsibilities and then ask himself: "Did I try each one of these elements?" In many cases, the novice will find that some aspects were overlooked.

Some teacher's responsibilities which have to be checked are:

Examine textbooks for readability.
Arrange the closet.
Keep health records.
Arrange the bulletin board.
Give a diagnostic test to a child.
Prepare work sheets.
Supervise playground.
Supervise lunchtime.

Prepare a test.
Prepare art materials.
Evaluate and check written work.
Arrange rollbook.
Work with children's cumulative records.
Plan a science corner.
Give remedial help to a child.
Organize the class library.

It is the responsibility of both the student teacher and the cooperating teacher to try to make the assisting phase a learning experience. The prevalent practice of "exploiting student teachers" should definitely be denounced.

independent teaching

As perceived by student teachers, the summit of the practicum experience is that of teaching independently, without assistance from the cooperating teacher; the novice teaches a lesson or more, and the cooperating teacher observes. To the incomplete sentence, "I wish my cooperating teacher . . .," prevalent answers are "would give me more opportunities to teach on my own;" "would permit me to take over more often."

evidence of readiness

There are more complaints about cooperating teachers who are slow in letting the student teacher take over than about cooperating teachers who rush the trainee in this direction. It seems that the movement from assisting to independent teaching is relatively more difficult than the movement from observation to assisting teaching. The latter movement is often natural and does not call for a "formal agreement" between the two adults. For instance, in noticing a child who has problems in arithmetic, or the classroom teacher checking written work, the novice may step over and assist. In contrast, the student teacher cannot step over and *teach* the class. His teaching must follow a formal decision with the cooperating teacher.

The novice who is eager to try his wings and be in charge, therefore, often fails to examine some of the factors which interfere with the attainment of his objective. In order to tap the perceptions of the difficulties involved in the movement from assisting to independent teaching, a group of student teachers was asked to role-play an informal chat among cooperating teachers discussing their feelings about the trainees. The following are illustrations of the comments made.

The student teacher interferes with the class routines. It took a long time to have them well trained and I would not like to have to start again.

It must be confusing to children and I must be sure first that the student teacher follows my methods.

No one can do the job as well. I am under time pressure. The course of study must be covered and with these children it is not an easy job. I know I'll have to go over and teach the same subject matter again.

The general tone of the above comments is a critical attitude toward the cooperating teacher. Many student teachers seem to feel that the senior teacher is reluctant to let them assume more responsibility with the class. But what they seem to overlook is the fact that the cooperating teacher has responsibilities both to her class and to the trainee. She has to protect the rights and further the education of both parties. In terms of her first responsibility, she cannot let her class become guinea pigs for the floundering of a student teacher. She feels that education is a serious business and time should not be wasted. Furthermore, the zeal for learning should not be dulled by the floundering of a novice.

In terms of her second responsibility, the education of a prospective teacher, she cannot follow the hands-off policy or sink-or-swim. She must be sure that the novice will swim. Mistakes and difficulties are to be expected, as they are a normal part of learning. But there is a basic difference between mistakes and a complete failure stemming from lack of readiness.

As the logs show, the student teacher himself is critical of the cooperating teacher who "plunges" him too early into "taking over" and then "takes a walk." It is this cooperating teacher (fortunately rare) who is perceived as one who misuses the trainee as "cheap labor" rather than someone who is there to guide the learner.

The main criterion to be followed in moving from assisting to independent teaching is the *readiness* of the student teacher. Providing evidence of being ready is mainly the responsibility of the student teacher, which shows up in his behavior and attitude toward the student-teaching practicum.

In my visits to schools I find that the cooperating teacher is highly complimentary of the student teacher who has initiative.

Come and see the science corner Miss Martin prepared with the group.

She has so many ideas. The children immediately take to her.

They value most cooperation and initiative to help. They question the ability, or at least the readiness, of the one who is passive.

I cannot tell you much about this student. She just sits. I'll have to wait.

She did not come out yet. Perhaps she needs to take her time.

The fact is that the same cooperating teacher will permit one trainee to start independent teaching early and another trainee to start only late in the semester. The decision depends on her perception of the readiness shown by the specific student teacher. It will be useful for the novice to examine his own participation in the practicum, in terms of the criterion of readiness. The following are illustrations of points to be checked.

Systematic work with an individual or a group.

Initiative in organizing a special project.

Discussions with the cooperating teacher of learning problems of specific children.

Knowledge of the course of study, textbooks, and other materials used in the classroom.

Participation in planning of the unit under study.

Familiarity with the class routines and management.

the problem of planning

Student teachers generally know in advance when they are going to teach the class and, therefore, have time to prepare and plan. However, some student teachers report that they are called on to teach without having an opportunity to prepare in advance. ("The teacher was called out and I had to take over.")

Following are some of the practices, student teachers report, which are followed when there is a lack of advance planning.

I continue with her work.

She leaves an assignment on the blackboard.

She tells them to practice their spelling and I supervise it.

She gives me instructions of the pages to be covered.

Not being prepared, the student teacher tends to cling to the textbook or the assignment on the blackboard. He tends to become a supervisor of busy work rather than the one who develops creative ideas.

Portrayed by these responses is an apprentice whose whole entity is following and copying the cooperating teacher. His sense of teaching does not come from reliance on his own resources. He fails to experience the excitement of discovering his own power and becoming independent. He rather imitates. Children may be quick to sense that little new can be expected from this novice.

The importance of comprehensive planning of the independent teaching activities cannot be overemphasized. It is an opportunity for the novice to think through his own interpretation of the subject matter to be taught—a main characteristic of creative teaching.

Student teachers vary in the nature and amount of their planning for independent teaching. They range from those who write lesson plans to those who preplan only by reading materials (teacher guides, books, etc.) with the expectation that the structure of the lesson will develop spontaneously once the teacher is confronted with the group.

The lack of systematic planning is defended by some student teachers on such bases as:

Emphasis on spontaneity.

I don't want to be rigid. I must develop the lesson in terms of their responses.

Only when I am faced with children can I create.

In reality, lack of systematic planning as a means of promoting spontaneity is often used as an excuse for the novice who finds it difficult to foresee the expected lesson. Planning a lesson means developing a "play" which predicts the development of the theme through the interacting between the teacher and the children. Writing this "play," or thinking it through, enhances the novice's ability of "being" in the lesson and "feeling" the expected interaction.

The novice who is versed in his plan tends to feel secure during the lesson. He knows what he wants to say and where he wants to go. He feels that he is able to be in control. It is often the person who plans well who is also more able to be open to the ideas, questions, and suggestions of children, and encourage them to come into his plans.

The novice who does not plan sufficiently tends to be

occupied with the anxiety of what will happen next. His ability to listen to children is undermined. To avoid floundering and relieve anxiety he tends to rely on one method and adapt it to many situations. Rather than being spontaneous, his teaching tends to become trite.

My observation has indicated that there is a positive correlation between comprehensive planning and successful teaching; between superficial planning and trite teaching.

It should be realized, however, that comprehensive planning alone is no assurance of successful teaching. For instance, some student teachers, in their first steps of independent teaching, tend to consult their lesson plan and read from their notes. In reading notes they stop listening to themselves, to the interaction between themselves and children, and rely solely on the external crutch of the preplanned program. It seems that to some extent at least their planning remains in the notes and does not become an integral part of their ideas; it is as if their teaching is borrowed from the notes rather than created. This practice often expresses the alienation of the student teacher from his teaching, a behavior which violates the creative emphasis on personal meaning.

Some student teachers feel that they must follow the lesson plan to the dot and, consequently, fail to bring in and utilize what evolves in the classroom. Discussions with these student teachers reveal that there are many factors which explain this behavior.

One factor is a misconception of the role of the lesson plan, which is often seen as something they must implement smoothly and meticulously rather than as a tentative structure which has to accommodate the unpredictable in the classroom. In their operational values they are teacher-centered, believing that their sense of order and sequence is the best one and, therefore, should not be modified.

Another factor is the security in the known plan and the fear of the unknown changes. Following the lesson plan generates the satisfaction of knowing where one goes. The difficulty in shifting is that it calls for readjustments and new decisions with regard to the direction. The insecure beginner may be threatened by these unknowns. Student teachers reiterate, in interviews, that while being observed by an authority they tend to be more reluctant to modify plans than when they are on their own. The main issue is to develop a plan which helps the teacher live the lesson and free him at the same time to be open to the ideas and plans of children. At the beginning it is desirable to develop this plan in detailed writing, gradually moving to a general outline with increased teaching experience.

practicing the teacher's total role

In the course of student teaching the number of lessons taken over by the student teacher gradually increases and becomes a daily arrangement. At the beginning he teaches only individual and discrete lessons, but later he becomes responsible for an area of instruction, such as arithmetic or science, or for a unit of instruction, such as weather, clothing, or transportation. Toward the end of the practicum the novice may take on the responsibility for a full day or even several successive days of teaching. While in the beginning student teaching consists primarily of observation and occasional teaching, toward the end the balance changes toward more emphasis on assisting and independent teaching. In the last month or weeks of student teaching, observation should play a minor role.

The importance of being responsible for a large area of instruction, in terms of subject matter and duration, cannot be overemphasized. As the vision of the novice tends to be narrow, he looks at one lesson, one practice or problem, as separate entities. He tends to be present-oriented without taking into account what has happened to the group in the past or what their plans may be for the future.

A lesson does not exist in a vacuum. Teaching is much more than the preparation and the implementation of discrete lessons. To the extent that the novice can be responsible for large blocks of time and large areas of study, he may come closer to experiencing the total role of the teacher and thus come to broaden his vision of the meaning of teaching. It is perhaps impossible under student-teaching conditions (as many student teachers point out) to realize the full role of a teacher. Even if the senior teacher is not in the classroom, the student teacher operates in terms of the former's power. Despite this reality, the objective should be to come as close as possible to the goal of the total role.

One factor which explains the importance of practicing the total teacher's role rather than discrete lessons is the emphasis of modern education on the value of the *unity* of subject matter. This trend toward unity stems from a criticism of traditional education as being too fragmentary and compartmentalized. Experimentation with curriculum patterns within the last era, the movement from the subject matter to the correlated curriculum, the innovation of the broad field and the core curriculum can probably be seen as an expression of the trend to search for unity in subject matter.

When a student teacher plans or teaches a single lesson and fails to see its relation to the total unit, he ignores this emphasis on unity. This type of student teacher may teach, for instance, about the nest in a single lesson and fail to put it in the broader context of the life of the birds, or the problems of adjustment to the environment. He will tend to fail to see the need for integration into broad units or major ideas and concepts and thus have limited success in developing a high level of thinking.

The emphasis of modern education on unity of subject matter goes hand in hand with the emphasis on the increased role of the learner. A preoccupation with discrete lessons leads, sometimes unwittingly, to a de-emphasis on the above function.

Teaching, when approached as a series of discrete lessons, may not only ignore the significance of emphasizing continuity in learning, but also may present the danger of overlooking the role of *balance* in the curriculum. A student teacher may tend to be interested in the success or the quality of one lesson, not realizing that the quality of his lesson is at least partly dependent on its relation to other aspects of teaching and its balance with other activities of the day.

Taking over the class for the whole day is an opportunity to examine practical, though sometimes overlooked, questions, such as the following:

Is there a balance between sedentary activities and moving? Our schools no longer have a recess period at the end of each period as was practiced in the traditional school. When does the child then have an opportunity to move around? Is he expected to sit for three successive hours?

Is there a balance between teaching the class as a whole, working with groups or with individuals? Whereas this balance may be better achieved in the present school than in the traditional setup, is there, nevertheless, in a specific classroom, an overemphasis on one of the above organizational patterns?

Is there a balance between intellectual discussion and other activities, in moving from a discussion of current events to a discussion of literature? Would it be better to balance the over-emphasis on class discussion by introducing reading in literature?

Is there a balance between difficult learning activities and easier ones, and attention to their proper sequence? It may not be the best practice to start the day, as too many teachers do, with "red tape" activities or with spelling. Both do not call for the investment of a high degree of intellectual energy. It is better to start with a class discussion of a subject area.

These are only illustrations of the problem of the day balance. The student teacher who looks at teaching as a lesson plan may fail to become sensitive to this problem. Teaching a unit, and especially teaching the class for several days, may be even more demanding and educative in terms of the balance criterion. Here are illustrations of questions to be examined in this circumstance:

Is there a balance between committee presentations and teacher-directed discussion or between individual interests and common learning for the whole class in unit teaching? For some teachers a unit utilizes individual interests and committee presentations; for others the term *unit* is only a "respectful title"; under its disguise they can continue with traditional instruction.

Is there a balance of emphasis on various subject areas? In the self-contained classroom, where planning is mainly in the hand of the teacher, there is a common tendency to emphasize an

area in which the teacher feels strong and to underemphasize or
even neglect subjects in which one is not very competent (As reported by student teachers, the amount of time spent on science
is too often limited.)

Is there a balance among the *A*, *B*, and *C* orientations in teaching?
As suggested in this study, there is room for more emphasis on
the development of convergent thinking and creativity.

In brief, a practicum limited to the planning and teaching of
discrete lessons tends to be denoted by a narrow vision of the
broader dimensions of teaching.
    As reported by student teachers, the topic of the unit to
be taught is generally determined by the cooperating teacher.
For instance, she advises the trainee whether the class is going
to study the water supply of New York City, housing, or the
westward migration. The choice of the subject of instruction
is generally up to the student teacher and is often made in
terms of the special competency of the student teacher. The
choice of subject area is often made by the student teacher in
terms of his observation of the limitation of the senior teacher
in a certain area.

impact on teaching style

    Prior to the actual experience of student teaching, the
prospective teacher reads, writes, and thinks about the role of
the teacher. Now for the first time he is taking the role himself as an observer of classroom practices, as an assistant,
and as an independent teacher. What is the impact of role-
taking on the student teacher? Examination of the group's
reactions reveal both positive trends and unresolved difficulties.
    A prevalent reaction to the practicum is a deeper aware-
ness of the dimensions of the teaching problem. An interviewee says:

Only when you teach do you really understand what it is all about.
You are faced with the problem. You must think and act . . . In
observing the classroom teacher I tend to take it for granted that
what she is doing is the right thing. I don't have to make choices.

I follow her actions and get the false impression that the problem is simple.

Another student teacher brought the following example to illustrate the point that in teaching one finds out that the problem is more complex than expected.

I was working on developing an experience chart with the children. The title was: "The Circus Comes To Town." I am critical of the teacher who asks children to contribute and then uses her own ideas, or selects only what she had in mind. So I decided to put down the children's statements as they were given and add only the name of the contributor. The kids got a kick out of it, but I found out that not being selective, the story lacked continuity. So we had to do what I didn't plan on—rewrite the story.

As seen in this example, role-taking means that the behavioral role is generally more complex than its *predicted* intellectual formulation. Therefore role-taking, such as delegating responsibilities to children, evaluating compositions, or starting committee work, leads to better insight into the broader dimensions of the problem.

Role-taking is perceived by the student teacher as a most important educational experience and by many subjects as *the* most important one. The confrontation with the need for "action" is a dynamic force which promotes further learning. The conventional emphasis on "first learn then act," is changed into a new pattern of continuous interaction between learning and action: learning $\longrightarrow$ action $\longrightarrow$ learning $\longrightarrow$ action, and so on. The surge of interest in learning is identified by the student teachers themselves, and also can be seen by the increased amount of non-assigned educational literature they read on their own. The search for knowledge deepens when a new dimension is added, namely, the search for knowledge on how to behave as a teacher.

Another positive impact of role-taking is a gradual increase in the feeling of competency. Teaching is partly a skill (in the broad sense of the word) and therefore has to be practiced. There is much skill to be mastered and many practices to become acquainted with. The novice speaks about an improved sense of timing, better ability in leading a discussion, growing sensitivity to the individual differences, with a corresponding ability to adapt the content to these differences, growth in realistic planning, and a richer development of a repertoire in terms of content and techniques. As some student teachers put it: "I start to feel like a ham."

In terms of relating to children, the positive impact is seen through a better awareness of their needs, and a more realistic expectation of the leadership problem. They learn that relating to children is more than being permissive or authoritarian. Teaching is a complex role which calls for different patterns of behavior in different situations.

imitative or creative?

Role-taking, along with its positive impact, raises a question in the mind of the student teacher about *the expression of his individuality as a teacher.* The difficult and unresolved problem is whether the novice's teaching behavior is going to be only an imitation of the senior teacher or is also going to be an expression of the student teacher's own exploration and experimentation.

Excerpts from interviews illustrate the problems involved in searching for self-expression.

Naturally you respect the classroom teacher for achieving what you have yet to attempt to achieve. Along with this respect goes a feeling that her way is the right way since it is getting results.

In theory, and even in your mind, you believe there are many different ways of approaching a problem. However, in reality, when faced with a difficult situation you are more likely to resort to the tried and tested than to attempt a new approach to a situation. It is here that I believe a cooperating teacher has the greatest influence on her student teacher.

The student teacher is appreciative of the functional model of teaching demonstrated by the cooperating teacher, but he also questions whether he is free to find himself. Despite the feeling of progress, there is nevertheless an expression of the apprehension that something is lost in the process, or perhaps unrealized in the student-teacher experience—namely, the expression of individuality as a teacher.

Her relations with the children, her personality, her manner all have an effect on your teaching. Almost unconsciously you pick up her way of teaching which you have been observing for six weeks . . . It becomes difficult to fully express your personality in some-one else's classroom.

This student teacher feels that in some respects he is being molded rather than growing, that he becomes primarily an imitator rather than a creator. What is the basis for these not uncommon feelings? Is there something inherent in the climate of the student-teaching practicum or in the consulta-tive behavior of the senior teacher which contributes toward a feeling of limited freedom? Or does the problem lie less within the objective reality and more in the subjective and selective perception of the novice?

The data collected in this study does not suggest a con-clusive answer to this question. It only permits some specula-tion. Look at the following responses to the incomplete sen-tence "Introducing new ideas while being a student teacher in a class . . ."

. . . is a challenge.

. . . is a fascinating and rewarding experience.

. . . is rewarding, but also frightening.

. . . may lead to trouble. The teacher may resent you.

. . . may be resented by the class.

Introducing new ideas is seen both as a challenge and a threat. The main source of the threat is perceived primarily in the attitude of the cooperating teacher and in the reactions of the children.

Similar results can be seen in the responses to the in-complete sentence "Changing classroom routines. . . ." Positive reactions approve the idea as contributing toward flexibility and innovations. Negative reactions warn that introducing change in routines . . .

. . . is very difficult as children do not believe there is any way other than their teacher's.

. . . is a source of confusion.

. . . may upset the children and the teacher.

In discussing changing classroom routines, a common expression used by the student teacher is "breaking the classroom routines." In the metaphoric language of the novice, routines are perceived as so solid and rigid that if bent only a little they will tend to *break*. No wonder that, with these perceptions of the classroom climate, the student teacher feels the lack of freedom, often freedom needed for his own exploration and experimentation.

The question should be raised again whether in the objective reality the classroom climate is denoted by more freedom to experiment than the student teacher is willing to recognize and make use of? Whether in reality the cooperating teacher is much more permissive than the student teacher cares to admit?

A group of student teachers was asked at the end of the practicum to discuss as a panel the following topic: "My advice to the young generation of teachers." The *first* point on the agenda was routines, and a major part of the presentation dealt with the need to *routinize* the class. A typical expression used was the advice to "clamp down" on the class in the first weeks of the year. One extreme expression used was, "the first job you have to do is to tame them down." (The dictionary defines *tame* as "to reduce from a wild to a domestic state.") The point was made that

These children are confused in so many other areas of life, that the school should become the secure force in their life. It is the good training of a routinized classroom atmosphere which makes the school a source of security.

This study does not question the point that the development of routines should be an integral part of the teacher's job. It does question, however, the exaggerated proportion given to the role of routines in the thinking of the novice. It is almost as if success in teaching is magically related to success in structuring classroom routines.

The perception of the classroom as a routine-oriented institution which does not tolerate modifications interferes with the novice's ability to develop his individuality. This, however, does not necessarily mean that his perception is always correct in terms of objective reality, as the needs of the student teachers affect their perception. Those who are less open and imaginative as people, those who crave protection and security, those who need the exactness of the model, those who are satisfied with the status quo, tend to perceive routines as the center of their work. Those who are tolerant of ambiguity, those who are actively trying to realize themselves as educators, tend to perceive routine in its proper perspective.

The former group in their student teaching tends to be preoccupied with the imitation of the model. The second group attempts to develop a teaching behavior based both on imitation and on their own exploration. Some student teachers have power to try their own way even under rigid classroom conditions, while other trainees may remain fixated in the imitation stage, even under optimal conditions and a free climate. Freedom to try is primarily a subjective phenomenon!

the consultative role

Another factor which affects the novice's sense of freedom to experiment is his consultative relations with the cooperating teacher. The impact of the latter is expressed mainly in two ways: (1) demonstration and (2) consultation.

To the extent that the objective reality of the "demonstration" is characterized by behavior which permits freedom to children, the student teacher is more likely to encourage freedom in his teaching. If the climate is generally experimental, then the novice may be encouraged to develop ideas and try them in action. To the extent that the model demonstrated is characterized by overemphasis on controlled behavior, it will interfere with the student teacher's desire to explore.

Demonstration is a recognized function of the cooperating teacher. This is her unique contribution to the guidance of student teachers. It somewhat overshadows her second guidance function—consultation. As reported by student teachers, when consultation is stressed in their relations with the senior teacher they feel encouraged to try ideas. When emphasis on consultation is limited, the tendency is to feel that there is no room for trying. As one novice put it:

I get best results when I do what she does. But deep in my heart I am confused on whether all that she does is right and on what I really have to do.

It seems that consultation is conducive to encouraging experimentation in the student teacher in two main ways: (1) It brings the senior and the novice close together as people, and therefore generates a sense of security and freedom in the latter. (2) Consultation is an attempt to look at the dynamics of teaching. The specific pattern of teaching is not accepted as "this is the way to do it," but is rather generalized in terms of its underlying principles. In other words, thinking through educational practices is conducive to experimentation.

As perceived by student teachers, the main strength of the cooperating teacher is in the first function of demonstration, rather than in her second role of consultation. To the incomplete sentence "I wish my cooperating teacher . . . ," a typical response is "would criticize my work more often." To the incomplete sentence the "cooperating teacher criticizes mainly . . . ," the overwhelming majority responds:

She does not.

She never criticizes but simply says thank you.

It seems that many cooperating teachers themselves perceive their main contribution as demonstration and tend to de-emphasize consultation. In a conference a cooperating teacher said to me:

I work very intensively with my student teacher. While she is teaching, I take *your role* and jot down detailed notes to be discussed later in a conference.

In the perception of this dedicated cooperating teacher, the intensive examination of the teaching behavior of the novice is not within the exact boundaries of her role, but rather is more characteristic of the consultation role of the college instructor.

When the novice is faced with the experience of a forceful model of teaching behavior (the senior teacher) without sufficient systematic and deliberate attempt to help him analyze the dynamics and explore other possible directions, he is faced with the two alternatives: (1) to copy the pervasive and concrete teaching behavior, the "sure-proof," "the one which works," or (2) to mobilize his resources and in addition to learning from the model adapt it with his own personal interpretation.

Under the insecure condition of being a beginner and a guest in a classroom, with the not uncommon and often mistaken perception that the strength of the classroom climate is primarily the routines, the tendency of too many beginners is to emphasize the imitator-repeater role of the learner and to "postpone" the role of pursuing the expression of their individuality in teaching.

expression of individuality

The emphasis given to the importance of the expression of individuality in student teaching can be challenged. The question can be raised: Isn't the primary function of the student teacher to learn the existing practices? Is exploration a proper objective for the novice who still has to do the ground work before he is ready to spread his wings? It can be argued that individuality should not be a major objective of student teaching, but is rather an aspect of independent and full-time teaching. To use Mackinnon's terminology,[M1] the student teacher should learn both by "sense perception" and "intuitive perception." The first is stress on things as they are, on ties to the model. The second is an alertness to the as yet not realized and to be explored practices, on ideational movement from an original stimulus.

The emphasis on sense and intuitive perception are not sequential tasks of learning, but are rather simultaneous processes. One is not a prerequisite to the other, but rather feeds and enriches the other. In terms of school practices, it is not fully correct to assume that the teaching of reading skills is a prerequisite to the teaching of literature and poetry. They should be taught simultaneously. In terms of student teaching, learning through both sense and intuitive perception—that is, imitation of the model and exploration—are the task of the novice.

When these two processes are seen as sequential tasks, the second task may never be realized. The end result may be the type of teacher of whom it is said: "She teaches for twenty years, but has only one year of experience."

To experience a sense of freedom to try, to actively search for improved ways of working, is a challenging, but a threatening, task. The challenge and threat involved can be understood in terms of the broader theory of motivation underlying this study. As Maslow suggests in his article on "Defense and Growth":[M2:3738]

Every human being has both sets of forces within him. One set clings to safety . . . hanging on to the past . . . afraid to take chances, afraid to jeopardize what he already has, afraid of independence, freedom, separation. The other set of forces impels him forward toward . . . uniqueness of self, toward full functioning of all his capacities . . . safety has both anxieties and delights; growth has both anxieties and delights.

It seems that it is not at all difficult to relieve, at times, the anxiety over lack of growth. The mechanism used frequently is that of externalizing the source of the trouble and blaming it on factors outside oneself. In another investigation, exploring the attitudes of *experienced* teachers toward experimentation, I got reactions like the following:[S6:203]

Attempting to do anything new brings down the wrath of the system on your head.

Our fear is a direct product of a dogmatic board of education. Democracy in education is for the children. Little free thinking is allowed to teachers.

The prevalent reaction of the experienced teachers was perception of the external threat of the *authority figures*—principal, board of education, etc.—concerning experimentation. It was the rare response which dealt with the experience of the *internal* threat.

It is my observation that both experienced and novice teachers tend to have more freedom to experiment than they are willing to make use of. Student teachers often admit that when they make a suggestion for a new approach to the cooperating teacher, she generally reacts: "It is interesting; why don't you go ahead and try it?"

It is of utmost significance to start on the level of student teaching to avoid overemphasis on repetitive teaching; to see the practice of exploration and the search for the expression of individuality as an integral part of the definition of the teacher's role.

selected bibliography

AMIDON, EDMUND and HUNTER, ELIZABETH, *Improving Teaching.* New York: Holt, Rinehart and Winston, Inc., 1966. A down-to-earth analysis of the verbal interaction in the classroom.

BELLACK, ARNO (Editor), *Theory and Research in Teaching.* New York: Bureau of Publications, Teachers College, Columbia University, 1963. A report of several studies focusing on the analysis of teachers' classroom behavior.

BROWN, THOMAS and BANICH, SERAFINA, *Student Teaching in the Elementary School.* New York: Harper & Row, Publishers, 1962. A systematic and comprehensive discussion.

5

the activation of the learner

A central theme permeating this study is that modern educational theory rejects passive learning. It is, rather, dedicated to the activation of the learner. It wants to diminish the role of the learner as a listener and accentuate his role as a speaker. (On several occasions I have seen listeners fall asleep; I have never yet seen a speaker fall asleep.)

In light of the goal of developing "active learners," the discussion is going to examine and compare two of the most common patterns of teaching: lessons and units.

the lesson

the goal

The goal is the main theme under which the subject matter and the activities of the lesson are organized. For instance, as part of teaching about life in other countries, the novice may want to teach the well-known story, "The River" by Pearl Buck. He examines the subject matter (the story) first and only then develops the objective: compare the values and way of life of the Chinese girl portrayed, with the life of the children in the class.

The social climate in the classroom, and the needs and

interests of children, can play a main role in identification
of lesson goals. In a school participating in the open enrollment setup in New York City (a provision whereby parents
may register their children in schools outside of their neighborhood), a teacher noticed social distance between the children
who were bussed in and those who lived in the school district.
She decided to teach about similarities and differences between people.

The lesson's goal can be a development of a question
raised by children in a previous session or a task children
wanted to accomplish. This is especially common in classes
where cooperative planning is encouraged. For instance, as
part of a study of the turtle, a point was made that it was
cold-blooded. Some children raised questions with regard to
the function of this characteristic in the life of animals. It
was decided to take up this topic in a special lesson.

As seen in these illustrations, the goal for a lesson serves
two important functions. It is a way of looking at the specific
lesson in the light of the broader context of the classroom
curriculum, and it is a guide for determining the specific
subject matter to be taught in a lesson.

Examining the work of the novice, one finds that in some
cases the above functions are not understood and, consequently, the goal for a lesson is either not formulated at all or is
stated in vague terms. Interviews with student teachers suggest two main explanations of this lack of emphasis on goal
formulation. Some student teachers feel that the goal is an
"expectation" dictated by the professed values and norms of
the educational culture and, primarily, by the college instructor. They feel that goal formulation is part of "theory," and
that it does not have a direct and practical impact on the
lesson.

Another factor which explains this lack of emphasis on
the lesson's goal is the difficulty in identifying the main theme
of the lesson. The lesson is perceived primarily as an aggregation of facts and details—the A orientation without the
ability to see the uniting idea—that is, the B or the C orientation. It is this kind of practitioner who tends to pay lip service
to goal formulation and who formulates his lesson goals in

vague terms: "to understand the story," "to understand the problems facing Washington," or "to study about Holland." No attempt is made by him to clarify for the teacher the meaning of the story, the problems facing Washington, or the concepts which may be developed through learning about Dutch life.

A lesson goal does not necessarily aim only at the development of the understanding of specific subject matter. Another type of lesson goal deals with the development of desirable attitudes or ways of behavior, such as scientific thinking, imagination, cooperative work, self-directiveness, or curiosity.

These attitudinal goals determine the approach or the methodology of the lesson. Referring back to teachers A, B, and C, they all approach the same subject matter in such different ways primarily because A believes in specificity and recall, B believes in convergent thinking, and C believes in creativity. The science teacher who believes in scientific thinking will emphasize experimentation and observation. The one who is not oriented in this direction will limit presentation to reading and discussion.

As may be seen from these illustrations, the development of lesson goals, in terms of subject matter and attitudes, is not a simple objective process. Looking at the same subject matter and relating to the same children, teachers may come out with somewhat different objectives. What may seem the same topic, such as transportation, is taught by one teacher with a goal emphasizing means of transportation, by another emphasizing that the world is small, and by another as a search for development of a better system. Whether he is conscious of it or not, the objective of the lesson is the product of the teacher's educational philosophy.

the content

The same topic in science (electricity), or in social studies (the American Revolution), can be taught on the elementary school or on the university level. The teacher should decide on the depth and comprehensiveness of the subject matter to be taught in order that it will be adapted to the mentality and interests of a specific group of children.

As the discussion suggests, in developing the subject matter the novice should keep in mind two main considerations. The first is the extent to which there is a direct relationship between the teacher's goal and the specific subject matter. Will the lesson on the American Revolution attain the goal of understanding the main factors which caused the historical event? Or will it be used in the context of helping children develop a better understanding of the African Revolution?

An examination of lesson plans and observations of lessons taught in the classroom show that the relation between the goal and the subject matter is an important point which calls for a great improvement. There are far too many lessons in which the forest cannot be seen because of the many trees— too many lessons in which the subject matter taught does not lead to the crystallization of the main idea—the objective. In some cases the feeling is that the novice jotted down an objective only because he is expected to, and did not think through its structuring impact on the lesson.

A second consideration to be kept in mind is the suitability of the subject matter to children. There are teachers who want to teach *social studies* to children, and there are others who want to teach *children* social studies. It is the latter who generally do a more meaningful job of subject matter development. It is not enough to be involved with the structure of the subject matter and to simplify it for children, but it is as important to have insight into the process of concept formation in children.

starting the lesson

The actual presentation of a lesson has to start in a way that suggests to the learner that meaningful problems are here to be mastered, and must evoke in him a desire to master them. Teachers generally call this starting point "motivation." (This is a somewhat oversimplified term because, in the long run, everything that is done in a lesson, and not only the starting point, has a motivational value.)

There is a variety of ways of creating motivation in a lesson. In my observation, student teachers are ingenious in this area. They usually relate the lesson to an experience the children have had. For instance, they discuss the visit of the fireman and then raise the question, "But really, how does he extinguish fire? Can we try to extinguish fire here in the classroom?" Or they relate the lesson to the unit under discussion; they may summarize the class study of communication up to the development of the radio and then raise the question of the limitation of radio in terms of the visual images. From here they move to the discussion of television, which answers this problem.

A strong "motivation" technique is to emphasize a contradiction or to identify points of confusion due to insufficient knowledge. An illustration of emphasis on *contradiction* is examining, through magazines, the present friendly Anglo-American relations and then raising the question, "So why were they at war during Washington's time?" An illustration of motivation through emphasis on the recognition of *insufficient knowledge* is working on arithmetic problems where division is seen only as partitioning, and then discovering, through introducing a new problem, that division also has another function—measurement division.

The above illustrations show that the success of the beginning of the lesson as a motivating factor for learning stems from the fact that it identifies a problem for the learners and therefore sets the children's objective for the lesson. To the extent that the children are aware of an existing *difficulty* (How does the fireman extinguish fire? What is the difference between the two paintings?), they are motivated to work on the lesson's objective.

The assumption underlying the above discussion is that children are curious and that they have a healthy appetite for learning. The cooperative search for the identification of a *difficulty* will arouse this appetite and create motivation for learning. Lack of understanding of the value of identification of a difficulty as a motivation for learning may result in the use of "pseudo-motivation." Here is an illustration:

Children, what did you have for breakfast today?
Eggs.
I mean, what did you drink?
Milk.
What else?
Juice.
Yes.
Water.

In this illustration, by no means atypical, the relation between the objective—study about water—and the "motivation" is based only on *associative thinking*. The fact that a
specific child was drinking water for breakfast does not suggest an identification of a difficulty that has to be resolved.
The strength of a "motivation-discussion" of this nature is
limited, as it will arouse only those who are anxious to please
the teacher.

the children's perception of
the objective

The beginning of the lesson, called *motivation*, is culminated by a statement which combines the teacher's goal and
the objective as perceived by the pupils. Many teachers like to
accentuate the children's objective of the lesson by putting it
on the blackboard or asking children to explain, in their own
words, "What do we want to do today?" The reason for this
emphasis is the realization that being aware of and accepting
the objective will enable children to develop the subject matter
in a more meaningful way and see its unity. The children's
objective is *their perception* of the question which the lesson
has to answer; their perception of the direction toward which
they have to move in order to develop a new concept.

For instance, as part of the discussion of Manhattan, children relate experiences about its congestion. The motivation
leads to a formulation of an objective for the lesson. "Let us
suppose that Manhattan does not have any transportation.
What kind of transportation system can we devise for this

borough?" In the light of this objective, the children examine
a sketch of the area (bridges and roads not identified) and
start to develop a plan. Whether they work on the connection
of Manhattan with New Jersey or the fact that the city is
no longer than wide, they always do it in terms of their
awareness of the objective—a transportation system.

In contrast, when children are not aware of the lesson's
objective, they will be slow, or even fail, to see the unity of
the subject matter. They will discuss the bridges and wait until
the teacher moves them to the discussion of the subways. In
terms of the process of thinking and self-direction, these pupils
will not be searching actively for a solution to the total problem. The quality of the children's thinking is dependent on
the teacher's ability to formulate and elicit a meaningful
objective.

Examination of lesson plans written by student teachers,
and observation of their teaching, show a conspicuous lack
of emphasis on the children's objective. This de-emphasis may
be partly due to the great involvement on the part of the
novice in the lesson and its goal, taking for granted that the
goal is as obvious to children as it is to him. Or, it may be
partly due to an unconscious expression of the teacher's need
to control. It is as if he feels that it is sufficient that the leader
know the goal and, therefore, expects his followers to do
what they are told—namely, move step by step as instructed
and wait at the end of one step for the leader's instructions
concerning movement to the next.

Going back to the previous illustration about transportation in Manhattan, the controlling teacher who spoon-feeds
the children discusses the topic in the following terms:

This is good, today we'll study about water.
Now, let's look at the Lincoln tunnel. Where is it?
In Manhattan.
What does it connect?
New York and New Jersey.
How is it similar to the Washington bridge?
Both connect New York and New Jersey.
How is it different?
One is a bridge, the second is a tunnel.

Very good, children, now let's see, is there anything else south of
the Lincoln tunnel which connects with New Jersey?
The Holland Tunnel.
Very good. Where is the Holland Tunnel?

This orderliness, specificity, and the step-by-step advance-
ment are subtle ways of controlling the class. There is no movement unless the teacher moves because there is no total goal
in terms of which children can initiate their own steps.

Imagine that a cooperative statement of an objective for
the above lesson was formulated, such as "to devise a transportation system which connects Manhattan with other places."
The end result would tend to be an element of *freedom* for
children to suggest various means of transportation, to move
on their own from one subtopic to another.

It is evident that guiding the students to formulate the
lesson's objective tends to emphasize the common task facing
the group, raises a meaningful goal to be achieved, and encourages freedom and initiative to think and participate. The
cooperative identification of the lesson's objective is an attempt to alleviate a major difficulty inherent in lesson planning
—the *involvement* of children in learning.

Underlying the lesson approach is a problem of leadership. It is the leader, the teacher, who invests time, thought,
and energy in the preparation of the lesson. He reads books,
develops materials, devises a plan. It is the leader who is involved and is interested in the plan. The problem is how to
make children involve themselves in the same questions with
which the teacher is involved; how to make pupils realize
that the idea selected for its importance in the teacher's perception can also become important to them.

The answer to the problem of leadership may lie in a
lesson plan which makes use of a cooperative search for the
identification of the difficulty and the cooperative formulation
of an objective. It is the function of the motivation discussion
and the sharing on the part of children in the development
of an objective to help the learner get involved in the goal
of the specific area of learning. Without these elements of lesson planning learning may tend to become a passive process of
imposition.

Once the children's objective is formulated, the class has to move to work on the common task. Two important and interrelated considerations are the methods and the materials to be used in presenting the subject matter.

methods and materials

Elementary education has moved a long way from the traditional practices emphasizing lecturing and the assign-study-recite-test method. The lecture approach, rarely used in the elementary school, does not emphasize the active role of the learner, since it puts him primarily in the position of an absorber. The second method, more commonly used in the elementary school, makes use of the teacher's assignment of reading or exercises, followed by testing of the reproduced assignment. Here, too, the frame of reference is the predetermined subject matter in the text, rather than the involvement of the learner in the delineation of a problem and the cooperative formulation of an objective for learning.

The novice is generally aware of the need for a methodology which attempts to bring out the pupil and encourage him to *participate*; participation is a value very close to the heart of student teachers. Consequently, the most common method used by them in presenting subject matter is the *teacher-led discussion*.

In comparison with the lecture or the assign-study-recite-test method, the emphasis on discussion with its goal of participation is very valid. However, as suggested previously in this study, the novice's conception of leading a discussion is often limited. The pattern is too often on teacher-child-teacher-child conversation with lack of sufficient emphasis on the pattern of teacher-child-child-child-teacher discussion where children interact among themselves.

The novice's teacher-centeredness in leading a discussion is a product of the *A* emphasis in his operation values and his great need for control and security. It is usually true that those student teachers who are able to operate on the *B* and *C* level are more successful in making the method of discussion an experience of interaction among children.

Similar observations can be made concerning the use of the method of *experimentation* commonly employed by the student teacher. Its strength lies in the emphasis on scientific and productive thinking, whereas its limitation is that when used by the novice primarily as demonstration and directed observation, it becomes a learning situation which de-emphasizes experimentation by children or use of the learner's free observation for science learning. Again it is evident that the novice tends to be teacher-centered in his approach to the method of experimentation and observation.

There is a variety of methods that can be utilized in lesson planning: discussion, experimentation, reading, construction, committee work. The novice is confronted with making a choice of the most appropriate method for his specific lesson. Is he going to begin with experimentation and later move to discussion, or vice-versa? Is he going to teach the class as a whole or suggest individual and group work? Does he want to begin by teaching the class as a whole and later move to group work, or do it the other way around?

Similar questions can be raised with regard to the problem of materials. There is a variety of materials used in the school, such as books, audiovisual equipment, or science instruments. Which is to be used in the specific lesson and how is it going to be employed?

Generally it can be said that one important difference between successful teachers and poor teachers is the variety of methods and materials they employ. The novice, being industrious and dedicated, is very aware of the importance of utilizing a variety of methods and materials. Much credit for this should go to the cooperating teachers who, generally, do not tend to limit their work to the traditional reading-recitation or to the use of a single textbook for all children. In many classrooms the basal readers have been replaced, or at least supplemented, by a class library. Variety in methods, as well as variety in materials, can be seen in many classrooms today. Such experience is positive in its impact on the novice's ability to plan. He stresses the use of concrete and representative material and makes use of a variety of teaching materials and techniques.

Both in his lesson plan and in the implementation of that plan the student teacher shows one recurring difficulty—namely, the lack of a good sense of timing and of the ability to shift from one method or material to another. In some cases the novice tends to be slow in moving from one approach to another and sometimes fails to sense that even a group eager to learn will gradually lose interest if a discussion, for instance, is too lengthy. A shift in the method of presentation from class discussion to experiments conducted in small groups, or a shift to writing, may generate new life and interest in learning.

In other cases, the novice tends to shift from one type of activity to another too rapidly. In his too early shifting or the over-reliance on the rich variety of methods and materials, he may overlook the fact that the material has to be *used* in order to be effective. An illustration of overrushed planning and teaching is the student teacher who reads a story to his class about the circus and, without pausing for any discussion or reaction to the story, moves to present the main characters arranged as cut-outs on a flannel board. The novice may be impressed by the variety of the materials—story, cut-outs, flannel board—but a closer examination shows that they were not utilized to bring out learning.

Another illustration of misuse of materials is a lesson in individualized reading where children "sell books." The emphasis is on the visual materials (wheels and covers) made by children rather than on the characters of the story and what they stand for. In other words, the danger is that the concrete materials will become the focus rather than the generalizations and the ideas that they have to help develop.

Throughout the presentation of new subject matter by the use of various methods and materials, one fundamental criterion has to be kept in mind—the goal of the lesson. As suggested earlier, the subject-matter goal determines the specific knowledge to be presented, and the attitude or skill goals determine the *method* of presentation.

With regard to the latter, if the goal is scientific thinking, then the method of presentation should not be the *A* orientation of repetition and recall. If the goal is skills in cooperative work, then the method should not be teacher-centered but rather based on the practice of, and the sensitivity to, the experience of group work.

Only too often do intangible objectives, such as creativity, critical thinking, or cooperative work, express superficial vales to which one pays only lip service. It is with the implementation of such values through the method and materials aspect of the lesson that the spirit of the objective is translated into the language of behavior.

summary

The culmination of the presentation is to develop a summary or to draw conclusions for the lesson. The function of the summary is to synthesize the learning reached in the light of the stated objective. A common practice in summarizing the lesson is asking children to restate the objective ("What were we looking for?") and then state the answer ("What did we find out?")

The summary is generally well-stated in the lesson plans of student teachers in the form of generalizations or evaluation of the learned subject matter. However, when it comes to practice, under the time pressure of other obligations, the summary is often pushed aside. Children in many cases move from one lesson (social studies) to another (arithmetic) not because they have reached some closure in their intellectual endeavor, but rather because of external circumstances.

Summarizing is an important aspect of the lesson and should not be rushed. The children themselves should reiterate the objective of the lesson and in *their own words* should draw the generalizations. The poor practice of telling children "what we have learned today" and then asking them to repeat it (recite it) or copy it in their own notes is not unknown. Summarizing should be approached as an expression of productive thinking, of putting things together, of applying and creating, rather than as a process of repetition and specificity.

Summarizing is not necessarily an oral process. It is possible to summarize through other media, such as writing or dramatization. For instance, when the science experiment is over the pupils may describe the problem, procedure, and findings in writing.

Summarizing does not necessarily mean drawing generalizations; it can also be a process which emphasizes application or divergent thinking. For instance, as a culmination of a lesson discussing punctuation, the children apply their learning by punctuating a composition. Or, as a culmination of reading and discussing a story, the pupils move from the known to the unknown by adding a part or a scene to show their personal interpretation of the dynamics involved.

It is an effective practice to have a brief discussion of the work which still *has to be done* on the specific topic as part of the summary aspect. The student teacher is often interested only in a single lesson. For the regular teacher, and especially for the pupils, a lesson does not exist in isolation but is rather a part of a larger unit. The emphasis on the unfinished business, that is, on things that have to be done next time as a result and a continuation of the learning gained today, is conducive to the development of a unit in subject matter. The child is helped to see the total picture.

There is also a psychological aspect of motivation and involvement in suggesting the direction for the next lesson. The field vision of the learner is not limited to one lesson alone. He does not have to wait in the dark until the teacher next day unwraps an unknown package to reveal a new objective. In other words, one function of the discussion of "what we will do next time" is to activate the learner.

the assignment

So that you may better understand the concept of activation, the following discussion will center on what is generally the last part of the lesson plan—the assignment.

One known and important function of the assignment is for the learner to review the material presented in the lesson. This can be done at home or at a special work time at school. The former is generally referred to as *homework* and the latter as *seat work*. Typical examples of assignments may be drill on arithmetic exercises or review of readings in social studies and then answering questions on the topic. The commercial publications are very prolific in this area and have produced the workbook whose main function is review.

However, looking at the function of the assignment primarily in terms of review is very limiting. Too often the emphasis is only on the repetitive A orientation. Whether one calls the assignment *drill*, or a nicer word, *practice*, or a still nicer word, *review*, one cannot avoid the feeling that too much of it is what teachers call "busy work."

Limiting the assignment only to one function—review— is an underestimation of the importance of encouraging the learner to go ahead on his own with the subject matter. It stems from a philosophy which perceives the child as a helpless creature who can only absorb rather than create; a philosophy which believes that the only important knowledge is communicated by the teacher, underestimating that discovered by the learner. It is a position which perceives the responsibility to move ahead, to initiate further learning as the prerogative of the leader only. The child has to follow the leader and review.

A second function of the assignment is to give the pupils an opportunity to go beyond the review, to react to the subject matter learned in the lesson, apply it, and create something new on their own. For instance, in a science lesson a class studies the topic "air takes space." They see that a napkin put in the end of a glass turned over in water does not become wet. The water does not fill the whole glass as the napkin is protected by a barrier of air. As an assignment the children have to develop other experiments or suggest other observations which show that air takes space.

The review function of the assignment means that the pupil is past-oriented; what will happen next is not his concern. The creation and application function of the assignment means that the learner is future-oriented, that he is aware of (the former tends not to be even aware), and involved in, the coming lesson. The development of the next lesson is at least partly dependent on the quality of his preparation and contribution.

There are not many more important principles in education than activating the learner in sharing in the responsibility for the progress of his learning. There are few principles which are so often violated by teachers. Perceiving the role of the assignment not only as review but also as creation of new learning which extends the field vision of the learner and encourages him to share in the responsibility for the next lesson, is a step toward the education of the active learner.

conclusions

As suggested earlier, a lesson plan is a culmination of the teaching philosophy of the teacher. The discussion here was limited to the main steps a teacher may move through in organizing his ideas into a lesson.

In the reality of actual teaching, the lesson steps presented here in a sequential fashion may not proceed in this order at all. The researcher following the steps of research design often finds out that he has to reformulate the problem or add a hypothesis at the advanced step of data analysis. Similarly, the teacher following the steps of lesson planning may often find that he begins the lesson with the children's objective or that he has to change his own goal in midstream.

The structure of a lesson presented here is an attempt to help the novice plan. Followed rigidly, it becomes a routinized procedure which stops the teacher from being open to the children's suggestions and sense of direction. As stated in the discussion of model *C* (the creative teacher), a major problem of planning is to develop a flexible structure which is a foundation for the learner's own structure.

Despite the usefulness of the lesson plan described here, one should be aware of its major limitation—planning is limited to one lesson; the horizons of the learner and his involvement with a specific objective are limited to a short-range goal. Productive and creative thinking call for *long-range* planning in the light of a *long-range* goal. Therefore, to the extent that it is possible the pupils should be sensitized to the broader context of the lesson, that is—the unit.

the unit

A group of novice teachers was asked to explain the unit approach to planning. Without exception, they stressed the principle of integration of subject matter; some spoke about committee work, and with few exceptions they failed to discuss the *activation of the learner*.

unity of subject matter

In essence the unit approach is a product of the progressive education movement, which called for a unifying concept of subject matter. It held that the "subject-matter approach" meant compartmentalized and fragmentary learning, lacked in depth of meaning, and was limited in its potential for creating unity of ideas. It criticized the subject organization which emphasized the exposition of its own logical sequence and failed to pay due attention to the interests and activities of children. It warned that confinement to the subject organization tends to be historical and predetermined in nature and is therefore too often presented in a social vacuum. It took issue with the overemphasis on the past and the relative inattention to emerging present issues and controversies. It questioned the educational value of an approach which focused on the center of a discipline rather than on moral and value problems of people.

A comphehensive and scholarly critique of the subject-matter curriculum, and an analysis of its development, are presented in the book *Fundamentals of Curriculum Development*.[S12] In terms of the discussion presented there, it is sufficient to describe the three curricular modifications in the subject-matter organization which affected the trend toward unification in social studies.

The first modification toward unity of subject matter was

the *correlated curriculum*. In this pattern, two or more subjects are articulated and the relationship between or among them is made a part of instruction. Subject boundaries remain intact. For example, history and geography may be taught so as to reinforce each other. The geography of Egypt taught in a geography lesson may be correlated with the study of the early history of the Egyptians taught in a separate history lesson. The stress on the relationship between the subjects is believed to help reduce compartmentalization.

The second modification in the direction of unity of subject matter was the *broad field curriculum*. Whereas the correlated curriculum follows the separate subject-matter organization, the broad field curriculum is, in essence, the first attempt to break away from highly delineated disciplinary structures and organize learning in terms of broader divisions. Typical illustrations are social studies, language arts, or the science-hygiene integrations, where broader blocks of time are assigned to each division. The teacher is free to develop a topic, such as a study of a specific country, in terms of the subject-matter areas involved in the division.

The third modification, the *core curriculum*, is the most advanced pattern in terms of the process of movement toward integration of subject matter. It is based on a complete breakdown of subject lines. The center of the curriculum is not a broad field, typical of the previous pattern, but rather a central problem. In order to work on a given problem, the learner is guided to draw on whatever needed subject areas pertain to his problems. It is the function of reaching a meaningful understanding of the problem which determines the subject matter, rather than the artificial boundaries of the traditional subject organization.

Examination of the work of the novice suggests that the core pattern of unity of subject-matter organization has a strong impact on the work of the teacher. In essence, the core pattern, or as it is called on the elementary school level, the *unit* organization of subject matter, is the most prevalent approach in social studies. It is common for teachers to equate the social studies methodology with unit teaching. In this discipline the unit is an attempt by the teacher to organize learning experiences around a social problem and draw on subject matter from any area which may contribute to a better understanding of the topic. Typical illustrations are the problems of transportation, shelter, adaptability to various climates, or life in a foreign country.

The unit pattern of planning has a definite positive impact on the novice teacher. He is encouraged not to limit himself to the piecemeal planning of a discrete lesson, but rather to plan in terms of a long-range objective. The lesson becomes an integral part of a broader scheme.

The unity criterion underlying the unit pattern rejects the traditional aggregation of lessons and attempts to move toward the productive thinking inherent in the integration approach to subject matter. To the extent that the teacher is more aware of his long-range goal, to the extent that he sees the relationship between the small part (the lesson or the activity) and the whole (the unit), and to the extent that he views subject matter as an integral part of a broader generalization, the probability is that, that insight will be communicated to children.

unity: difficulties

The unit is a promising approach. However, it is only an organizational pattern. It is evident that in some cases the unit is used as a cliché without depth of meaning; as a new word one is expected to use, while traditional practices continue.

In terms of the criterion of unity of subject matter, observation of novice teachers suggests two not uncommon mistakes:

The first mistake is that of giving the unit a "nice title" such as, "Living in Our Community," or "How Does Man Live in Cold Countries?" without thinking through the main concepts to be developed. Under this "pseudo-unit" arrangement, teaching is only an aggregation of lessons with little unity of relations among them.

A second typical mistake is the temptation, or even the sense of obligation which some novice teachers have, to in-

clude every subject area in each unit they teach. Rather than
thinking in terms of how to study a problem and make it
meaningful, they think about how to correlate various disciplines with the topic.

The vantage point should be the needs of the problem
under study rather than the discipline. The teacher guided
by this criterion may often find that some important skills
or important knowledge cannot be fed into the topic. The
implication is that the unit is not all-inclusive. While one unit
is in process, some areas of the curriculum, such as arithmetic
or certain skills, may need a separate and independent treatment.

Whether or not the unit approach achieves its goal of
enhancing the integration of subject matter depends on the
teacher's perception of this practice. Only if the depth of the
rationale for unity of the main idea is pursued does the unit
become conducive to curricular organization and productive
thinking.

the activation of the learner

The discussion in the previous section dealing with the
criterion of integration of subject matter was "teacher-centered" in nature. It was the *teacher* who was encouraged to
think through the main objectives and look for the interrelationship between the main idea—the unit— and the subparts—
the lessons. The following question, however, must be raised:
What is the role of the learner?

Traditionally the ideal teaching situation is one in which
the teacher is able to command the confidence and respect of
his followers and to induce them to accept the presented subject matter. The teacher is the central authority, and the children are the followers. They move because he "motivates"
them to move. The power to decide on the direction, route, and
pace is invested in the teacher.

Progressive education raised a new ideal for teaching:
to facilitate the process of learning and to help the child define
and achieve his goals. The word "education" derives from the
Latin *educere*, which means drawing out of a person something

potential or latent. The principle of "activating the learner" is based on the belief in the power of education to bring people out and to generate self-direction.

Therefore, the attributes of the modern teacher, as perceived by the progressive education school of thought, are in sensitizing the pupil to realize what *he* wants, what potential *he* has, where *he* wants to go, and to help him to go there. The theorist of progressive education does not speak about "teaching," but rather about "helping the child learn." This is not a play on words. It is an expression of a basic philosophy. The main function of the teacher is to activate the learner.

Dewey says that no other aspect in education is more important in progressive education than the participation of the learner in the setting of the goal and the development of the plans for his learning.[D8] As a result of active participation, the pupil tends to assume a greater responsibility for the progress of his own learning than he would under conditions of merely following directions.

It is interesting to note that a similar position about learning is presented by Suzuki in *Zen Buddhism*.[S19:93] Suzuki describes a monk who asks his friend to teach him the mystery of life so that he can become a master. His friend answers:

I am willing to help you in any way, but there are . . . things in which I cannot be of any help to you. These you must look after yourself. . . . When you are hungry or thirsty, my eating of food or drinking does not fill your stomach. You must drink and eat yourself. . . . And then it will be nobody but yourself that will carry this corpse of yours along this highway.

One must take the responsibility for his own learning. It cannot be done for him by others. The emphasis should be on the learner learning, rather than on the teacher teaching. The ultimate in education is the independence of the learner from his teachers. In Zen the expression of this independence is described as the burning of notes or the monk twisting the nose of his master.[S19] Fortunately for us teachers, progressive education does not suggest such symbolic acts. It limits its appeal to stress on intrinsic learning and a higher degree of self-direction.

The impact of progressive education on unit planning is expressed not only in the trend toward integration of subject matter but also a more responsible role for the learner. The pupil plays the self-directive role of an initiator of activities. He is not merely motivated to move from one lesson to another.

The unit is different from the lesson, not only because it consists of *many* lessons (the duration of a typical unit is four or six weeks), but also because of the role played in it by the learner. The latter criterion of the unit concept is sometimes overlooked. For instance, some reading-readiness books are organized in terms of units: the family, the farm, the school, etc. In other words, *with the exception of social studies*, the typical unit taught at school tends to be based on the first criterion of a long-range theme with some attempt to integrate subjects. It is generally not an attempt to *activate the learner*.

activation: lessons versus units

To create a better understanding of the process of activating the learner, the discussion will compare the way in which novice teachers teach lessons with the way they tend to implement units.

In teaching a lesson the novice teacher attempts to arouse the class interest by surprising the pupils with the richness of the materials that she has prepared. In some cases the teacher even conceals the next topic or hides the new materials from the pupils. It must be a surprise.

This not uncommon behavior suggests that teachers expect children to wait passively for the new direction to be presented by the teacher in each new lesson. In unit teaching, the teacher attempts to balance the above teacher-centeredness with provisions for cooperative planning and self-direction.

How does the novice move toward a more democratic behavior in unit teaching? A position often advocated in educational literature maintains that the topic of the unit shall be decided cooperatively by the teacher and the class.[H1] As reported by novice teachers, they seldom follow this recommendation. In most cases the topic is predetermined by the teacher in accordance with the curriculum guide, the textbook, a significant current event, or an interest which the teacher happens to have.

The first step toward the involvement of children in co-operative planning is children's participation in the identification of the major issues in the topic. After some study of the topic (reading, discussion, viewing a film), the children, guided by the teacher, attempt to formulate the major questions to be studied. Following is an illustration taken from a unit about Japan.

1. How did the geography of Japan affect the life of the people?
2. What is the Japanese industry, and why?
3. What kinds of homes do they build?
4. What is the history of Japan?
5. What are the Japanese arts and sport?

The conventional school practice is denoted by pupils' search for an *answer*; it rarely has pupils searching for a *question*. Count the number of questions raised by the teacher versus the number raised by children in a typical lesson. The ratio is often 100:1. This unhealthy ratio illustrates the extreme overemphasis on teacher-centeredness in the teaching behavior.

The unit in social studies is one of the few instances, and sometimes the only instance, where raising questions by children is *institutionalized* into the classroom work pattern. Observing the teaching behavior of the young teachers under discussion, it can be said that the social studies unit is partly developed in terms of the main questions raised by children. The same *cannot* be said about the way these novice teachers develop a science or a language arts unit. The latter tends to be more teacher-centered.

The value of cooperative formulation of the major problems inherent in the specific unit is not only the expression of interest or the indication of insight. Cooperative formulation is valuable because it is a cooperative attempt to identify long-range objectives.

According to the lesson practice, the pupil achieves the objective at the end of the lesson. Unless he has homework related to the lesson he may be waiting passively for the next lesson when the teacher is going to "unveil" the new objective.

The long-range objective in the unit is a goal toward which the learner may move independently, under the guidance of the teacher. In one of the educational films portraying unit work, the first scene follows a class discussion; a few minutes later the door opens and the teacher enters. This class was to a great extent self-directive. It worked in terms of its established and accepted long-range goals. Consider the following questions:

1. What would happen to a typical class if a teacher were late?
2. What could be done to improve self-directiveness in the learning process?

The activation of the learner in working on a unit is expressed not only by his participation in the setting of the long-range goals, but also in provisions for relative *freedom to move toward* the goal. In contrast to the lesson pattern where the learner is moved by a series of questions and assignments and is almost constantly led by the teacher's pace, here the learner has a higher degree of freedom. He can set his own pace in moving ahead. He takes an active part in choosing materials best suited for the study of his problem, such as collecting information from various books.

The progress toward the goal involves much of what teachers call "doing research." Whereas research may be too big a word to describe the child's activity, it is an indication of the respect which the educator shows for the learner's independent search for knowledge.

In contrast to the traditional practice of limiting the study to one textbook, the learner is encouraged to consult a variety of textbooks, trade books, encyclopedias, and other resource materials. He can be imaginative with regard to the type of resources he wants to utilize: books, people, records, objects for demonstration. He has a say in the way his completed work will be presented: as a written essay, through the use of pictures and graphs, as an oral report.

activation: units versus
programmed instruction

The learning process underlying the conception of the unit can be better understood if compared with the learning theory underlying programmed instruction. Both practices reject passive learning and are dedicated to the activation of the learner. However, their conceptions of activation are very different, and in some respects, are even contradictory in nature.

Figuratively speaking, programming visualizes the learner as standing in the corner of a room and moving in the shortest direct line toward the other side, not knowing in advance where exactly he is moving. His vision is limited to one step (frame). If he makes a mistake, he is taught the correct step. If he is "right" he is requested to move ahead another step. His route is predetermined. The pace is up to the learner.

The unit approach visualizes the learner as standing in the corner of the room and deciding on a goal—reaching the other side. Every move he makes is in the light of the final goal he wants to reach. He is free to decide on the nature of his "transportation" (different activities and not only a programmed text). He may get stuck on the way and have to retreat not merely one step, but even back to the starting point. . . .

Whereas both programming and the unit approach are valuable learning practices, the latter would seem to have a richer potential for *creative thinking*. In comparing the logical order of presentation and the psychological order of creation, Dewey[D8:26] says that the difference between them is like:

. . . the difference between the notes which an explorer makes in a new country, blazing a trail and finding his way along as best he may, and the finished map that is constructed after the country has been thoroughly explored.

The unit approach resembles "the notes which the explorer

makes in a new country," while programming resembles "the finished map."

committee work

As seen by the proponents of progressive education, the ultimate criterion of knowledge is its expression in actual behavior. There is a cleavage between academic learning and operational values, which has to be cemented. Therefore, the personal experience of the learner and his daily human relations are an extremely valuable source for learning which is neglected in traditional education.

As an integral part of the stress on the self-image of the learner and on interpersonal relations, a notable change in teaching methodology became evident in the increase of the amount of *group work*. Whereas the unit is not identical with committee work (hypothetically, it is possible for a unit to be developed by the class as a whole and by individual research), in practice some amount of group work is prevalent in the above unit more than in any other area of the curriculum.

In terms of theory, committee work is an expression of two fundamental values underlying the position of progressive education. One was discussed previously—the activation of the learner. The second is the value of group process for the development of the democratic personality.

Citizenship education seeks to develop not only the intellectual understanding of the law and the structure of government but also the ability to join in groups to study and resolve immediate social problems; it can aid the development of these skills through experiences which provide opportunities to practice democratic living in the classroom.

In the past, the conventional practice had been to confine democratic living to school government and other extracurricular activities and to leave the main school function, namely learning, in an authoritarian domain. One of the most significant contributions of progressive education was to penetrate the main castle of authoritarian teaching and introduce an element of group work.

Committee work is an opportunity for each child to experience a leadership and follower role. The need to resolve an issue or achieve a common task is a factor potentially conducive to high morale. The fact that one has a contribution to make to the group welfare, that one is recognized by the group, tends to generate responsibility and a sense of belongingness. Thus the normal need for self-esteem may find its satisfaction in a committee setup.

The trust which many teachers have in the constructive and educational value of group work is illustrated by the fact that committee work is one of the most common topics selected for research projects on the graduate level. Typical examples are:

"The Impact of Group Work on Class Morale"
"Helping the Isolate Through Committee Participation"
"Committee Work and Intergroup Cohesion"

committee work: difficulties

The above discussion stressed the role of the unit in the activation of two interrelated agents—the learner and group work. Although the novice teacher values unit work, complaints about difficulties or even dissatisfaction with this approach are often expressed. Some concerns are a sense that children waste time, inequitable sharing on the part of children, domineering behavior on the part of a few leaders, and perhaps most important, lack of full knowledge of what the class has mastered and lack of surety as to what every child is doing at a given time.

The practice of individualization of instruction, which is a significant aspect of unit work, may result in some lack of unity or cohesiveness of subject matter; a feeling that people are studying in the same room but not working on the same task. In order to overcome this difficulty, both the teacher and the class should continually examine their progress in the light of the generalizations to be developed. The balance between what should be common learning to the class as a whole and what is individual interest is an important criterion to be considered by the teacher. The fact that individual research and committee work are central in unit work does not mean that there is no room for a study of a core of subject matter by the class as a whole. In a unit, the class should be taught on three levels: class, committee, and individual work, the three enriching and interacting with each other.

To guide committee work is a difficult task. Children should be introduced to committee operation gradually. As a beginning, only one committee should be organized. The size of the committee should generally not exceed five children. Committees of young or immature children should be smaller. At the beginning, the progress of the committee should be checked after every meeting, by having the group present an oral or written report to the teacher. An assignment should be decided upon at the end of each session. The teacher should participate as an observer in several of the working sessions and analyze with the committee its way of proceeding both in terms of (1) the process, namely, the relationship among group members and (2) the content.

The visitor to an elementary classroom on the intermediate level often discovers special charts dealing with the proper leadership behavior of "a good chairman" or "a good committee member." Typical illustrations of the role of the leader are these:

> should try to keep his committee on the topic
> should call on different children
> should summarize the discussion

Illustrations of the functions of the group member are these:

> stick to the point
> help the group make progress
> respect the ideas of others
> contribute information

Facilitating productive relations among committee members is a significant aspect of learning. It is important that both teacher and children move ahead from the somewhat moralistic presentation of a chart toward an examination of their own group process in actual behavior. The human-relationship climate in the small group should be frequently evaluated. One of the main questions to be raised is the extent to which there is *give-and-take* among the group members about the *content* of the unit. As reported by novice teachers, too many committees serve mainly in the capacity of an administrative function responsible for allocation of roles. The committee becomes a setup for discrete presentations.

As reported by novice teachers, committees tend too often to rush prematurely into a discussion of the nature of the *culminating activity*. (Will the presentation be in the form of a television skit or a puppet show?) I am not trying to underestimate the importance of these considerations. They are a source of enthusiasm and involvement. They offer an opportunity for an expression of ingenuity. However, they are only secondary to the main issue—the discussion of the content to be learned.

In some classes the culminating activity is evaluated in terms of the quality of the performance. For instance, "Did the children speak in a clear voice? Was the exhibit attractive?" A dull performance may kill the enthusiasm of even a receptive audience. However, the major emphasis of the evaluation should be on the *intellectual* quality of the presentation. The "performance" is only secondary. The function of the school is to educate people to think rather than to be entertaining and too often superficial masters of ceremonies.

A related point is the need to examine the *activity* aspect which is characteristic of group work. The traditional school stressed reading and recitation. The modern school attempts, in addition, to incorporate "activities" into the program. It believes in learning by doing.

Especially today when the education of the socially deprived child has become the central educational problem, the emphasis on a motoric style of learning, on sensory perception, on involving children with doing or role-playing, is very valuable.

Despite the importance of activities, observation of classroom practices suggests that in some cases these activities are too time-consuming or even wasteful. Whereas the enjoyment and aesthetic values of the activity should be considered, the most important criterion is its contribution to the development of significant concepts.

The traditional school was criticized for its narrow methodology and too great a reliance on book knowledge. It is also possible to err in the opposite direction—doing for the sake of doing. Therefore, the teacher should ask himself the practical question—What do the pupils learn from the activity? For instance, role-playing is a very enjoyable activity. But is the end result of the acting-out mainly joy? Does role-playing lead to a better insight into the personality dynamics and the motivation of the characters? Does it lead to a deeper expression of feelings or the ability to think on a higher level of divergency?

Similar criticisms can be made about another prevalent activity of committee work—the scrapbook. Were the pictures collected to impress the teacher with a bulky collection, or were they utilized for formulation of issues and concepts? Generally, children find it easier to speak when they illustrate with materials. Therefore, materials such as scrapbooks should be utilized for the development of language facility and concept formation. The materials in most cases are not ends in themselves.

conclusion

The principle of "activation" is not a formula for success. As reported by some novice teachers, the excitement over being "democratic" and "experimental" leads them to a "hands-off" policy. The impact on children is well-known. It tends to be floundering, domineering by the few aggressive members, and limited production.

The impact on the teacher himself is less recognized or discussed. For instance, believing that committee work is the "children's domain," some novice teachers become detached and fail to get involved with the group and with the subject matter—as though the teacher is there to keep order, supply materials, administer, but not to *think with* the children.

In terms of the study of teachers' behavior, which is so central in this book, one is confronted here with important dynamics which should be recognized. The novice who is teacher-centered in his behavior may be very involved with his ideas and plans. The positive in this involvement is the feeling of mastery and its corollary—the communication of solidity to pupils. In the same sense, however, teacher-centeredness can be a product or a cause of a tendency to underestimate the power of children or not to be open and accommodating to the children's sense of direction.

The novice teacher who searches for improved practices and activation of the learner may err in the opposite direction —lack of sufficient planning of subject matter and some neglect of the teacher's formation of his own ideas and perception of the problem. This kind of teacher is too often dependent on what the children are going to produce. He is sometimes detached and may communicate a sense of weakness to pupils.

The problem is how to encourage children's initiative and at the same time maintain the teacher's initiative; how to be in control without being overcontrolling and constricting; how to plan subject matter and, at the same time, accommodate the child's sense of planning. Perhaps it is best summed up with the following question: How can we encourage children to be strong and, at the same time, remain strong teachers?

selected bibliography

CREMIN, LAWRENCE, *The Transformation of the School*. New York: Alfred A. Knopf, Inc., 1961. A scholarly discussion of the impact of progressive education on the school.

HANNA, LAVONE, POTTER, GLADYS, and HAGAMONS, NEVA, *Unit Teaching in the Elementary School*. New York: Holt, Rinehart and Winston, Inc., 1963. A comprehensive discussion of the unit approach.

6

individual differences in learning styles

Adaia Shumsky

An attempt will be made in the following pages to describe individual differences as they are related to the learning-teaching process in the classroom. Out of the vast number of variations in learning four areas will be selected for discussion:

1. **Knowledge-** How do children vary in the kind of skills and general information they bring with them to school, and how can the teacher's awareness of such variations improve the learning-teaching process?

2. **Academic capabilities-** What sort of capabilities in different areas do children bring with them to the classroom, and how can the awareness of variations in this sphere improve the learning-teaching process?

3. **Approach to learning-** How do children differ in the way they go about mastering a task; what are their attitudes; what are their habitual ways of responding to challenge?

4. **Social relations-** How do children relate to one another, and how can the awareness of such relationships improve the learning-teaching process?

knowledge

Every teacher, new or experienced, recognizes the futility in attempting to teach a given course of study to a total classroom and in expecting that it will respond uniformly. In planning any instructional activity the teacher needs to know what the children know, how ready they are to take in, what type of instruction they need, what can or cannot be assumed about their background, etc. For the purpose of illustration let us take a hypothetical fourth grade and see the type of observations that a teacher can make about what children know. The example deals with the question of what children know in the area of reading.

The group consists of twenty-five fourth graders. On the basis of reading achievement tests, five are rated "above average;" seven, "below average;" and twelve, "average." The typical procedure is to divide the class into three reading groups as a way of adjusting the curriculum to the children's level of achievement. One should realize, however, that this awareness of variations in achievement on three levels is not enough. There are, in addition, *qualitative* variations within each group.

The teacher may focus her attention on the slow group and observe what children in this group know about reading. She may find that out of the seven, two still rely heavily on sight vocabulary. They stumble with helplessness when they come across a new word. The teacher may decide to give these children more intensive instruction in word attack techniques. She may also find in this group two or three children who have good word attack techniques but who read slowly and laboriously. She may decide to give these children easy materials of high-interest value to increase the bulk of their reading and consequently their fluency. She may find in this group one youngster who has trouble with vowels and may decide to give him a chance to concentrate a little more intensely on materials and exercises which will strengthen this area. This slow group may have in it a child who, after a closer look, appears not to be a poor reader. He is perhaps a bit overcautious in his reading, afraid to make a mistake, reluctant to call out the words for fear of being ridiculed. This child may do better by getting away from oral reading for a while. Let him do mainly silent reading and check on it individually until such time that his confidence grows.

Let us now, together with the hypothetical teacher, turn our attention to the "average" group. We will soon find nothing "average" about this group except for a grade-level achievement score. Some children in this group read well in a fourth grade reader but have trouble remembering what they read. They seem so intent about the mechanics of reading that they have little energy left to pay attention to the content. These youngsters will need help both in comprehension and reading fluency.

Other youngsters in this group are good grade-level readers but do little reading on their own. They have not yet discovered the pleasures hidden in the world of reading and only engage in it when the teacher requires it. With these youngsters the teacher may have to relate reading to their personal interests, or may have to try to arouse new areas of interest. In this group, the teacher may find children who need to work on increased accuracy, while others tend to be too concerned with accuracy at the cost of fluency.

In the "above average" group, too, there will be major variations. One child may need to be given advanced reading materials of more complex content because not only his skill but also his interests are more typical of older children. Another child may need to be encouraged to try a larger variety of reading materials, as he tends to read only on one particular topic. Another child may need to learn to use different reading techniques in different areas of reading.

A similar diagnostic approach should be taken in the other subject areas, such as arithmetic, spelling, or social studies. In thinking about individual differences in knowledge in these areas, the teacher should consider not only the aspect of the child's comparative ranking in achievement but also about the qualitative aspect of his knowledge.

Knowledge also applies to the child's general fund of information. A teacher may want to find out in relation to a certain general age expectancy, how much the child does know on matters concerning his immediate environment, about science, current political events, history, music, and art. The teacher may want to have an idea about the way in which the child gathers his information. Does he use independent reading and study as a major source; does he have enriching home experiences such as trips, discussion, etc., which add to his fund of knowledge; does he absorb namely by listening in class; or are the mass media the main source of his contact with what is going on in the world around him?

These questions, too, have implications for teaching, as they may be used in class or give a certain direction and impetus to the work of the teacher as she tries to gain more understanding of the individual learners in her classroom.

academic capabilities

We are used to thinking of academic learning ability mainly in terms of I.Q. and often set our expectations according to such quantitative measurements. The child with a "high I.Q." is expected to do well, and if he does not he is considered an "underachiever." A child with lesser measured capabilities is expected to do less.

As this section will suggest, understanding children's capabilities in learning goes beyond the concept of measured intelligence. Their understanding lies in observing *how* children learn and in becoming aware of the variation of the processes which they utilize in learning. Following are a few examples.

A teacher may want to know how the child thinks. She may want to know whether he is facile in re-arranging ideas into new concepts and relating his knowledge to old learnings. She may want to know whether he is quick at grasping relationships and comprehending meanings or whether he retains primarily separate bits of information without easily arranging them into new concepts. She may want to know whether the child has difficulty in both retaining specific subject matter and in interpreting it.

The teacher may further want to know which children

show evidence of original thinking and creativity, which children are capable of seeing beyond the immediate, which can organize, and which tend to go off on tangents, failing to make a distinction between the essential and the trivial.

Being aware of the child's ways of thinking, perceiving, and organizing learning, the teacher may be able to accomplish several goals. She may set different expectations for different children. For instance, the child who deals better with specific bits of learning and does not form concepts easily may need to have ample opportunities to deal with concrete material and relatively less comprehensive subject matter.

She may decide to improve the child's level of thinking by keeping him slowly moving beyond the concrete into abstraction, or by pointing out similarities and differences to help the child arrive at generalizations. She may want to help the child who has good conceptual capabilities soar even higher by exposing him to more complex and challenging problems. She may help the child who lacks the ability to make differentiations improve his way of thinking by constantly pointing out the difference between the essential and nonessential.

In assessing children's capabilities, the teacher needs to become familiar with the modality of learning of which the child is most capable. Some individuals learn well through a variety of modalities. They may be equally facile with numbers as they are with words, in art as they are in science. Other individuals tend to select one particular modality in which they function best and through which they learn best.

Some children think best when they are dealing with well-defined elements and where there is little room for ambiguity. These children will manifest good comprehension of scientific and mathematical phenomena but may be able to give only little in response to a poem or a play. Other youngsters function better in the aesthetic, less defined modality. They may show their best thinking in response to a story, a discussion on human relationship. They are sensitive to feelings and to human problems. Other youngsters shine when they deal with the manipulative modality. These are usually concerned with how things work, what holds things together, how they move, how they grow, how to take them apart and put them together again.

There are numerous modalities in which people function. By becoming aware of the individual preferred modalities of children's learning, the teacher can make it possible for children to learn in the way which seems best suited to their person. Johnny who seems to become restless or apathetic when the class is expected to write a creative story, may not necessarily be expressing resistance or poor motivation. He may be a sort of youngster who cannot tolerate ambiguous, open-ended ideas. His thinking does not flow when he has to create a story or a fantasy. He comes back to life, however, when the content of a lesson deals with concepts which can be well defined.

Wendy, on the other hand, dislikes highly disciplined forms of thinking. She is not at her best with numbers or grammar, but she really gets off the ground when given an opportunity to write a play, project herself into a certain period in history, or interpret a poem.

And then there is Paul who is inventive when the class puts on a puppet show. He knows how to make the stage work. He always takes things apart and puts them together. He must find out how things tick. While Paul may not show his best thinking in math or creative writing, he can certainly show evidence of excellent thinking in his own particular way.

The child's way of handling language is a fairly reliable mirror of his thinking capabilities. Becoming familiar with the child's language pattern may help a teacher know more about him as a learner. The teacher may want to know whether a child can express himself fluently using complex sentences, qualifying phrases, and paying attention to nuances. Or is the child's fluency evident only when he deals with simple descriptive statements, or comments of daily practical matters? Whereas the two types may be equally fluent, the one which expresses complex quality and abstract language may indicate a more developed way of thinking, perceiving, and learning.

Language is often a function of the type of ideation it expresses. When the language is rich it usually expresses a wealth of ideas and images. When the language is meager it often expresses poverty in ideas. These relationships usually exist but should not be taken for granted. We all know the child who has a great deal to say but is blocked in expression or the child who talks a good deal but says little.

The teacher may find it profitable to become acquainted with a child's language. It may often give the teacher a clue about the child's thinking and organizational capabilities and may often point up the need for assistance in a specific area. For instance, the child who has a lot to say and cannot do so may be helped to bridge the gap between his ideas and his expressive tools. The one who is verbose but thinks poorly may be helped through language to organize his thinking better.

In conclusion, having insight into the qualitative difference of the academic capabilities of children, the teacher can (in addition to emphasis on the common elements of the curriculum) give every child an opportunity to use and develop his strongest avenue for learning.

variations in approach to learning

Children in a given classroom may vary not only in the things they know and in their capabilities for learning, but also in the ways in which they approach and deal with a given task. These variations are usually a function of the way in which they approach most life situations. The timid child will probably approach a new learning task with greater timidity than the bold, assertive kind of child. The highly intense, energetic child will approach a new learning task with more zest than the child who is usually passive and indifferent.

An attempt will be made in the following pages to describe a number of ways in which children show diversity in their handling of learning tasks in the classroom. The examples are by no means inclusive. Rather, they serve the purpose of demonstrating a way by which teachers may observe children to get further insight into the learning process.

tempo in learning

The child's individual rate of learning is often confused with capacity. A child may respond very *slowly* but learn no less than one who reacts and absorbs very quickly. Slow tempo is sometimes associated with cautiousness, sometimes with sluggishness. Rapid reactions may be due to impulsiveness and may be accompanied by either inaccuracies or high quality comprehension. In other words, rate or tempo as such can be highly individualistic or can be associated with a wide range of learning behavior.

In attempting to clarify the role of learning pace in different individuals, the teacher may ask the following questions:

Does the child work slowly, cautiously and accurately? Or does he work slowly and inaccurately?

Does he work quickly with good quality outcome?

Or does he wish to "get it over with"?

Is he the kind of child who works at a variable pace depending on the nature of the task?

The failure to recognize that children differ in the amounts of time they need to function in the learning process poses a major threat to growth. When we expect all children to complete an assignment or master a task in a given length of time, we not only ignore the fact that people move at different rates, we actually force certain children into adopting undesirable ways of learning.

Johnny, who usually takes long to do a job, is a careful and rather profound thinker. He is not satisfied with one solution but may attempt to look at a problem from more than one point of view. He may find, on second thought, that he needs to qualify, correct, or add to something he had previously thought about. By forcing Johnny into a preset time limit, we may encourage him to take shortcuts and cut corners; thus, we may be encouraging a lower level of operation.

David needs a great deal of time because his responses

are deliberate. He will not take a step unless the total plan or concept is conceived. He does not plunge into trial and error. By imposing time pressures on David, we are indeed violating a highly desirable way of thinking. We are encouraging him to be more dependent on guesswork than on reason.

Another child may move slowly because he finds the process of thinking, problem solving, and doing, laborious. This type of child generally stands to gain nothing from speeding-up his tempo. Some children need to be prodded to move faster because their attention to meticulous detail is excessive and because they derive little learning benefit from dwelling on insignificant details. Others need prodding because they tend to lose sight of the goal they set out to achieve. They need to be reminded of the goal and the ways to get closer to it.

Some children move so fast they need to be slowed down. They may be satisfied with superficial achievements or they may tend to react impulsively without preplanning.

To enable each child to learn at the pace which would result in optimal learning, flexibility in scheduling, and allowances for individual tempo, variations need to be made in the classroom. This requires flexibility in class organization, curriculum development, and the guidance of the teaching-learning process.

independence in work

A teacher may want to know who children differ in their capacity to work independently. Who are the children who can work with a minimum of adult direction and prodding? Who are those who need quite a bit of help at the initial stage of a given assignment or task and can later proceed on their own? The teacher needs to know who are the children who need intermittent help (including those who do not ask for it vocally) and who are those who consistently need assistance.

Being aware of variation in children along this dimension can help a teacher make appropriate decisions in the area of grouping. She needs to know which children can make use of self-directed activity while the teacher is busy working with a small group or with an individual. The teacher has to plan in such a way that she will be able to get to those children who may need more help and direction when the group as a whole is working on a given project or assignment.

In assigning homework the teacher may need to know who may or may not be able to complete the work without her presence, how to vary homework assignments so that the children who are more dependent may not have to resort to excessive parental help or complete helplessness. While the teacher is working along with the present levels of development in her class, and adjusting instruction to the needs of the dependent child, she also has to work with this child toward achieving increasing independence.

If independent learning is a major educational goal, then the *ability to plan* becomes one of the major tools to achieve this goal. As children vary in their capacity to plan, it becomes an important educational responsibility to help them in this direction.

Some children have a good sense of inner organization and can therefore plan better. They may need less direct help in planning. They can also be helpful in working in groups with other children, where they can help others acquire a more adequate capacity to plan. Others may need a great deal of teacher assistance and direction in learning how to distribute time, how to decide what they should do first and what they should postpone.

The teacher may thus find it necessary to identify those children who can plan long-range work with appropriate time distribution and those who leave things to the last moment. She needs to know who are the children who know how to assign priority to different tasks and those who become confused when expected to attend to more than one responsibility at a time.

In trying to help the children who have difficulty with planning, the teacher must remember that while they are being helped to acquire a better sense of organization, the change may not come easily. They will need to have support in organization and timing provided from the outside by teachers, other adults, and even peers.

attentiveness

Children vary in their attentive capacities. Some can be fully attentive for long periods of time, others for short periods of time. Some are more distractable than others; some show various levels of attention at different times. In order to be aware of individual variations in the capacity to be attentive, a teacher may keep in mind the following questions:

Who are the children persistent in their capacity to attend, and who are the highly distractable children (either by external factors such as noise, or by inner factors such as daydreams)?

Are there children who have adequate attention in non-academic activities and poor attention in academic work?

Are there children who demonstrate good attention capabilities only in areas of special interest to them?

Information of this nature can help the teacher become aware of the child's contact with her instruction. A teacher may thus know whether she needs to stop at intervals and check whether Johnny is still "with it," see that Pam, who is easily distracted, works in a spot where distraction is kept at a minimum; watch Sandy's tendency to get lost in daydreams and call her back to reality by asking a question and probing her attention to a certain topic.

Awareness of individual variations in attention span can also help the teacher determine the length of assignments she should give to different youngsters in her room. Paul, who has the capacity for a long attention span, may be given a long assignment, while Josh, who tends to be distracted every few minutes, may need an assignment broken down into smaller units.

In conclusion, attentiveness is an important factor in learning, as it affects the child's capacity to attend to what is said in class by either teacher or other students. It also affects his ability to remain attentive to a given task, which he is expected to fulfill independently. The teacher's awareness of variations in attention may help her adjust instruction to the specific attention style of an individual child, and when needed, attempt to help the child gradually change in a more positive direction.

reactions to new situations

An important way in which children differ is in their reactions to new situations. A child's characteristic response to newness may affect his initial adjustment to a class at the beginning of each year, may affect a move from one school to another and even from one classroom activity to another. In order to become more keenly aware of the different ways in which children respond to new situations, a teacher may observe the children in her class in view of the following questions:

Does the child tend to accept new situations and new learning as a challenge?

Is he slow to warm-up only at the very initial stage but usually comes around to handle the task with confidence? Or does he "panic" with the introduction of most new materials and situations?

At the beginning of every new school year Lisa has difficulty in getting to school. She complains about frequent headaches or stomachaches. When Lisa gets to school she enters the classroom shivering and remains very anxious most of the time. She does not seem to make much academic headway because she is too anxious to listen and work. A teacher who does not know that Lisa is having her usual reaction to a new class and a new teacher may label Lisa as "problematic" or "neurotic." The teacher may not know that she can help Lisa by introducing into the new situation as much of the familiar old as she can. She may seat Lisa close to an old friend. She may permit Lisa to begin working on some of the books she had last year. She may find out about a favorite interest Lisa has at home and structure a small group activity around it. She may try to bridge the new experience to the familiar one and thus help Lisa overcome her initial dread of the new classroom.

Burt seems comfortable in new social situations but tends

to "freeze" when a completely new subject matter is introduced. His initial reaction to new learning is pessimism and avoidance. Although Burt is a capable youngster he tends to believe he would not get it right. Knowing that Burt tends to react in this manner, the teacher should give him more support during the initial stages of learning new material. She may work with him individually a few times when first introducing long division. This teacher knows that if Burt is helped to face the new concept with less trepidation, he will sail smoothly in a short time.

Teachers are often impressed by the initial enthusiasm of a few children and assume that other children should be equally enthused. If they are not, the teacher takes it to mean that these children are perhaps intellectually less able or even incapable of dealing with the new task. Sensitivity to children's reactions to new situations may often change the teacher's evaluation of the child, may help prevent unnecessary difficulties, and may facilitate learning.

variations in social relations

The ways in which children relate to one another, the roles they take in a social situation, the ways they relate to leadership, have significant implications to the way they learn within the classroom. By being familiar with patterns of social interrelationships in the classroom, a teacher may prevent difficulties and enhance the learning process.

Each classroom has its leaders and followers. Each class has its small group formations and clusters. The leaders themselves vary. Some tend to be protective and benevolent toward the more passive followers. Other leaders may be competitive and impatient and recognize only a small group of youngsters who have similar interests but who do not present a threat to their domination. Some children may show leadership ability in the athletic field, others in academic activities. There are also degrees of leadership—a strong leader who gives the tone to a prestige-bearing cluster in the class, and a weaker leader whose influence only applies to some of the weaker members of the less accepted group in the class.

A teacher may find it worthwhile to become familiar with the variation in the social structure of her class and its impact on the learning process. For example, a teacher is ready to let the class divide into small committees to work on a different aspect of the social studies problems they are studying. How are the committees to be structured? It is usually helpful to organize a group in such a way that it will not consist mainly of assertive children with leadership capabilities and separate groups of passive-dependent followers. It is usually good practice to have in each group one or two youngsters who inspire it. They may help the group become more involved and help carry the group through lulls of passivity. At the same time, however, it may not be too beneficial to group one very strong and domineering child with an extremely passive and retiring committee, since he may tend to take over and prevent the others from exercising their capabilities. By the same token, it may not be desirable to group a highly impatient and critical type of leader with other children who are reticent and sensitive, as this leader may be a detriment to their confidence and their readiness to experiment.

In brief, awareness of the social interrelationship in the classroom helps the teacher group her children in a balanced way, a way which will facilitate the process of productive learning.

conclusion

The discussion in this book has focused on the role of the teacher in activating the learner and in developing a climate of productive thinking. The last chapter stresses that the teacher does not teach an "average" or a "uniform" child, but rather different individuals who vary in terms of their academic potential, personality, and learning styles.

Perhaps the most significant contribution of American education to the world is the commitment to the ideal of helping every child develop his individual characteristics and potential to the highest possible level. We guard the notion that the uniqueness of the individual should not be subservient to and curtailed by governmental or other group power, that conformity has to be rejected and the development of plurality of expression encouraged.

Our concern over preserving the uniqueness of the individual human being is the basis for a variety of forms of educational practices ranging from local control of the school to individualization of instruction within the classroom. It is this value that underlies the teacher's continuous effort to tap the level of ability of individual children, to group children, to attempt to adjust expectations to ability, and to use a large variety of teaching techniques in order to reach the maximum number of individuals in the classroom.

The common practice of ranking or grouping children according to scores on intelligence and achievement tests provides only a partial picture of individual differences. As this chapter illustrates, children vary qualitatively in the way they approach learning, that is, in their learning styles. It is by being aware of such detailed patterns of individual learners that teachers can best build on individual differences.

The discussion of individual differences in learning styles confronts the teacher with some difficult problems and decisions:

What is the *core* of the culture (and in school it will be the core of the curriculum) in terms of subject matter, values, or processes of thinking, which have to be taught to every individual, and what is the domain of individual differences?

What are the individual differences in learning styles which have to be enhanced, and what are the variations which the teacher must accept?

And on the other hand, what are the individual differences in learning styles which hamper the learner and have to be modified and altered?

The questions posed here are at the core of teaching and cannot be easily resolved. They are always present and will always be part of teaching. It is in the constant movement between the polarities of individual versus culture, and the desirable versus the workable, that the art of teaching is created. How much individuality can be permitted to develop before it begins to undermine basic cultural goals cannot be measured or described. It must be felt almost intuitively. The balance between individual versus group, or adjustment versus aspirations for higher goals is never achieved in teaching. It is in the constant movement around the wish to obtain such a balance that a teacher-artist grows.

selected bibliography

CHESS, STELLA, *Your Child is a Person.* New York: The Viking Press Inc., 1965. A discussion of normal variations in child behavior. An interesting chapter on learning styles.

D'EVELYN, KATHERINE E., *Meeting Children's Emotional Needs.* Englewood Cliffs, N.J.: Prentice-Hall, Inc., 1959. An interesting and constructive guide for teachers.

JENNING, HELEN HALL, *Sociometry in Group Relations.* Washington, D.C.: American Council on Education, 1959. Emphasis on social relations in the classroom.

three

*in search of teaching style:
the disadvantaged learner*

7

the teacher and the disadvantaged child

society versus school

Education all over the world is becoming a talisman of hope and the symbol of striving toward success. The school is the most promising means of giving the masses of people what they want. Despite the strong belief in the power of education, it is difficult to ignore the schooling failure of a large part of the population—the slum children. Some of the indices of this failure are scholastic retardation which increases from first grade on, alienation, severe discipline problems, and a significant proportion of dropouts in high school. Says Clark:[C2:119]

The basic story of academic achievement in Harlem is one of inefficiency, inferiority and massive deterioration. The further these students progress in school, the larger the proportion who are retarded and the greater is the discrepancy between their achievement and the achievement of other children in the city. This is also true for their intelligence test scores.

What are the factors responsible for the school failure of a large segment of the slum pupils? There are two main answers to this question: (1) society and (2) the school.

the social position

The social position explains the educational retardation of the disadvantaged learner in terms of the conditions of anomie inherent in slum existence amidst the surrounding affluent society. In his book *The Other America*, Harrington[H3] speaks about the existence of two nations in this country: one is the known, visible affluent society and the second is the land of poverty characterized by helplessness, broken families, slum living, lack of schooling. A disproportionately large segment of the Negro group belongs to "the second America."

In a research survey of the Department of Labor entitled *The Negro Family*, Moynihan[M16:6] warns that

. . . the evidence, not final, but powerfully persuasive is that the Negro family in the urban ghettos is crumbling. A middle class group has managed to save itself, but for vast numbers of the unskilled, poorly educated city working class the fabric of conventional social relationships has all but disintegrated.

In an article "The Disadvantaged Child and the Learning Process," Deutsch elaborates the position that the slum child enters the first grade so poorly equipped to meet school expectations that failure is almost inevitable. Deprivation has a negative impact[D5:168]

. . . on both the formal and the contentual aspects of cognition. . . . Formal equipment would include perceptual discrimination skills, the ability to sustain attention and the ability to use adults as sources of information and for satisfying curiosity. . . . Examples of "contentual equipment" would be the language-symbolic system, environmental information . . . and concepts of comparability and relativity appropriate to the child's age level.

In other words, the social interpretation of school failure of the slum child suggests that he tends to operate far below his maturational ceiling because of his experiential poverty. The Head Start programs stem from the above observation and attempt to compensate for early environmental and experiential poverty by establishing a system of free nursery schools, day-care centers, camps, and kindergartens.

the school

A second position looks for the explanation of the educational failure of a large segment of the slum children within the school life itself. The claim is that the school tends to perpetuate the very pathology it is supposed to remedy. The school tends to cultivate the attitude of evasion, alienation, defensiveness, and lack of industriousness of many disadvantaged children. Clark claims that the teacher does not believe in the power of lower-class children to learn. The use of intelligence tests to brand and label children for life, the various procedures of homogeneous groupings and tracks, the rationalization of cultural deprivation lead to one result:[C2:128]

. . . children who are treated as if they are uneducable almost invariably become uneducable. . . . It all adds up to the fact that they are not being taught, and not being taught they fail. They have a sense of personal humiliation and unworthiness. . . . They hate teachers, they hate schools . . . because they are not being respected as human beings . . . because their dignity and potential as human beings are being obscured and ignored in terms of educationally irrelevant factors—their manners, their speech, their dress, or their apparent disinterest.

Those who blame the school for the failure of the slum child stress that a cultural gap exists between the school teacher who is middle class in origin and values and the lower-class child. The middle-class family is child-oriented and encourages its children to renounce immediate gratification in order to achieve future goals. In contrast the lower-class family tends to be adult and present-oriented and teaches children to admire toughness, physical power, and practicality. It is this variance in familial orientations and parental reward systems which makes it difficult for the middle-class teacher to understand how to reward and motivate lower-class children.[D3]

There is some research evidence to support the position that some middle-class teachers tend to favor middle-class children in a mixed-class situation. Hollingshead, in his book *Elmtown's Youth*[H:13] found a positive relationship between social-class ranking and teachers' evaluation. Davidson and Lang in a study of children's perceptions of their teacher's feelings toward them found that the children perceived correctly their teachers' attitudes toward them. The students who felt that they were less favored tended to have lower achievement and lower self-evaluation than those who considered themselves to be respected by their teachers.[D2]

Further support to the claim that the school is responsible to a great extent for the retardation of the slum child is the *horizontal* mobility by a large number of teachers. The horizontal mobility, with very few exceptions, is transfer of teachers from lower- to middle-class schools and not vice-versa.[H8] In other words, teachers tend to be reluctant to work with the disadvantaged and prefer middle-class neighborhoods.

Coleman, the author of *Equality of Educational Opportunity* says:[C3:13]

Two points then are clear: 1) These minority children have a serious educational deficiency at the start of school, which is obviously not a result of school; and 2) they have an even more serious deficiency at the end of school, which is obviously in part a result of school.

change in perception of the lower-class problem

The education of the disadvantaged learner has become the central focus of research work and experimentation for the last several years. Most of the studies deal with the disadvantaged child and attempt to look at the problem from his frame of reference, such as, his attitude toward school. There is a dearth of research attempting to look at deprivation from the point of view of the *novice teacher*, the one who is generally assigned to work in lower-class communities. What does the novice teacher know about lower-class living? What are his expectations of relating to and teaching the disadvantaged learner? What is the impact of the disadvantaged child on the novice teacher, both intellectually and emotionally?

Many novice teachers are currently interested in studying the life conditions of deprived children. In their college assignment they often choose the culturally disadvantaged as a topic of major focus. They often express great empathy with deprived children as is evident from papers written by novice teachers.

James hated school. I asked him why and he said: "It ain't no good. Those f   teachers don't understand me." He told me that they were always "hollering" at him because he didn't do his homework. "I ain't got no time. After school I watch my kid brothers and sisters. The house is too noisy to do my homework. My father is always drinking. My mother is always hollering and the babies are always cryin'."

The children who attend the school come from overcrowded homes. The rooms are falling apart. Many families would have to share a toilet. The water tends to be rusty. And rats and roaches share family quarters.

Walking from the subway to school I noted broken glass, garbage all over the place, not to mention the occasional drunk or two in the doorways. I noticed an inordinate number of males just sitting around and my students pointed out several prostitutes.

They [disadvantaged students] most often say "hey, teach, what is this nonsense for? Teach, why do we have to learn this stuff? Who wants to go to school, it's a drag."

The problem of the deprived learner had been a central topic of interest for the student of education for many years. Within the last decade, not only did the interest increase in volume and in intensity, but the approach to the problem became more *realistic and mature*.

It is possible to identify two stages in the educational thinking of the teacher about the problem of educational deprivation. The first stage, which dominated the educational scene in the forties and fifties, was characterized by cultural relativism. The second stage, which became dominant in the sixties, is denoted by a high level of realism and determination to change. It is important to understand these two stages and their impact on the educational thinking of the teacher.

acceptance of differences
versus change

In the year 1944 Warner and his associates published a book entitled *Who Shall Be Educated?* It was a landmark in the educational study of the social-class structure in the U.S.A. It demonstrated the challenge of unequal opportunities characterizing the educational system. The American school is an expression of the social-class structure in what and whom it teaches, in who does the teaching, and in what the children learn in and out of school.[W2]

Hollingshead,[H13] in the book *Elmtown's Youth*, studied the impact of social classes on adolescents and found that the social behavior of adolescents is related functionally to the position their families occupy in the social structure of the community. Again, teachers were confronted with comprehensive research evidence documenting that the democratic principle of equal educational opportunities is a myth and that class origin is a major factor determining the lot and development of the individual. Teachers became aware and sensitive to the social-class problem and its impact on education. They were troubled by the problem, groped for a sense of direction, but *did not* make much progress in finding new directions.

A most important contribution to the educational analysis of the social-class problem was the work of Allison Davis and his associates. His work had a great impact on the educational thinking of the classroom teacher. In his best-known work, *Social Class Influences Upon Learning*, Davis[D3] develops a comprehensive socio-psychological rationale which explains the differences in socialization between lower- and middle-class chidren. In contrast to Warner,[W2] who discussed primarily the adult population, and in contrast to Hollingshead,[H13] who dealt with class differences of adolescents, Davis sees the inception of differences already starting at birth.

It is the contrasting child-rearing practices of lower- and middle-class parents, that is, the earliest socializations processes, which lead to the variation in the lower-class personality. The child-rearing practices of lower-class families are characterized by permissiveness and a climate of freedom for gratification of organic drives, whereas the child-rearing practices of middle-class parents are denoted by pressure, demandingness, frustration, rigidity and anxiety.

This thesis is supported with research evidence describing and contrasting the child-rearing practices of the two groups:

1. breast feeding is more prevalent among lower class;
2. more lower-class babies are fed at will;
3. weaning in lower-class families occurs when the child is older;
4. bowel and bladder training begins earlier with middle-class children;
5. middle-class children have home responsibilities earlier;
6. lower-class children are permitted to stay up or stay out later and go to the movies more often.

Middle-class children are taught to postpone immediate gratification of their primary organic satisfaction in order to achieve. According to this position the middle-class parents very often sacrifice their children's happiness by instilling the anxiety about achievement early in the child's life. Inner feelings are thus severely controlled and the child acquires some degree of alienation from his inner experience at an early age.

The impact of these theories of socialization on the class-room teacher was substantial. Teachers began to look at the lower class and the middle class from the frame of reference of *cultural relativism*. These two classes are often perceived as separate cultures, each having its strengths and limitations. The middle class is thus seen as driven by the need for achievement and self-improvement, spurred by frustration, compulsive tendencies, and the drive to "suffer and renounce gratifications." According to this orientation, the lower class suffers from poverty, lack of ability for long-range planning and social climbing. At the same time, however, the lower-class person is perceived as more earthy, closer to his emotions, more capable of expressing his urges and desires, more masculine, and freer to enjoy the good things of life. In contrast to the compulsive and repressed middle-class personality, the lower-class person is seen as a man who is closer to nature.

It is interesting to note that similar conceptions of the contrasting class personalities have been observed by the novelist and playwright, for instance, the description of the expressive lower-class mother in *Rose Tattoo* or the masculine portrayal of the worker in *Street Car Named Desire*. The same search of middle-class people for uninhibited joy and earthiness allegedly inherent in the lower-class personality can also be seen in the practice of "let's go slumming" [visiting nightclubs in slum areas.] The underlying belief is that the impoverished have been spared the corruptions of affluence and are an untapped source for the regeneration of the middle-class culture and its personality constriction.

The impact of the cultural-relativism approach on the classroom teacher was primarily dual. One impact was an increased insight into the dynamics of the relationship between social class and personality development, as the approach brought about more knowledge, understanding, ability to observe, and most important—more appreciation. The second impact was, in my judgment, negative in nature. It made the classroom teacher feel that he has to be "objective" about the problem, an objectivity which in essence was often an attitude of detachment. The effect is evident in the very common expression used by teachers: "One is not supposed to impose middle-class values on lower-class children," or "Let's not be ethnocentric and look at the behavior of the lower-class child from a middle-class point of view." Teachers were reluctant to make a value judgment. They referred to the deprived child as the "*so-called* lower-class child" or to dilapidated slums as "*so-called* bad neighborhoods."

I remember discussions at the college on the social-class issue. When the degrading life conditions of the slum were described, or the dynamics of anomie analyzed, or when statistics on juvenile delinquency or teenage pregnancies were mentioned, a student would comment: "The only difference is that in middle-class communities, the police do not report the majority of juvenile delinquency cases." Or, "There is the same promiscuity in middle-class groups, except that the mothers of the girls take them to the doctor." It often appears that the group of young educators is sticking to the rule of fair play: a bad word about lower class must carry with it a corollary bad word about middle class.

the I.Q. controversy

The reluctance of the education community to judge and make value commitments with regard to lower-class children was intensified by another significant contribution to the study of lower-class mentality. The book *Social Class Influences Upon Learning* discusses a study of social-class cultural influence upon the responses of pupils to intelligence tests and suggests that the commonly used intelligence tests are culturally loaded in favor of middle-class children. While the experience of middle-class children is highly correlated with the content of these tests, only part of the content is familiar to most lower-class children.[D3:48]

The cultural bias of the standard tests of intelligence consists in their having fixed upon only those types of mental behaviors in which the higher and middle socio-economic groups are superior. . . . The tests do not measure the comparative overall mental behavior of the lower socio-economic groups, because they do not use problems which are equally familiar and motivating to all such groups.

The questioning of the validity of the intelligence test only solidified the teachers' conviction that it is not fair to judge lower-class children with middle-class standards. Along with the attack on conventional intelligence tests came a growing feeling of empathy, greater acceptance, and decrease in dogmatism in teachers' views of lower-class children. Such feelings increased understanding and strengthened the desire to see the two cultures living harmoniously side by side. These feelings, however, *did not* move educators sufficiently toward constructive action to help the disadvantaged child get out from under the enormous destructive elements in his life.

the realist's position

The education profession in the forties and the fifties invested much effort in studying lower-class children and in

curricular programs which attempted to diminish prejudice
between social classes, ethnic and religious groups.[W3] The
emphasis was on understanding and acceptance, rather than
on change. Only in the sixties did we see a total change in
orientation. The education community began to come to grips
with the calamity of slum existence and is leading a total war
on poverty. The social goal is not toward harmonious living
side by side, but *integration*!

It is interesting to note that one of the most common
topics for research in the previous stage of cultural relativism
was prejudice. For instance, in one of the best-known books
of this era, *Action for Unity* by Goodwin Watson,[W3] the author
summarizes the major action patterns for reducing prejudice,
none of which includes a direct attack on the deficit of intellectual functioning of slum children.

At present the topic of prejudice is not the major area of
focus. A recent research summary, *Compensatory Education
for Cultural Deprivation*,[B7] includes very few studies on prejudice, and those included deal primarily with the impact of
prejudice on achievement. The main emphasis of the summary
is on learning and intellectual achievement. Again we see that
while the previous stage stressed the acceptance of differences
and the diminishing of prejudice, the present emphasis is on
rehabilitation through learning.

re-examination of research on lower-class
personality and intelligence

In view of the "realist's position" with its emphasis on
change, learning, and integration, it will be interesting to re-
examine some of the major research contributions of the stage
of "cultural relativism" to the lower-class problem.

With regard to the social-class differences in child-rearing
practices,[D3] the observations that more lower-class babies are
breast fed, are fed at will, are taught bowel and bladder training later, etc., are valid facts.

In view of the present-day knowledge of the living conditions of the lower class, one may interpret such patterns of
parental behavior not as "permissive" but rather as an indi-

cators that lower-class parents are so preoccupied with survival that their emotional and intellectual energies are consumed by the struggle of daily existence and that little power is left to direct the lives of their own children. What was called "permissive" is in essence lack of power to guide. It underlies all the observed differences in child-rearing practices between the lower class and the middle class, such as an insufficient ability to guide children to go to sleep on time or the difficulty of implementing bottle feeding to supplement or substitute for breast feeding.

The interpretation of the behavior of the middle-class parent as producing "frustration and anxiety" and as "renouncing gratification" takes an overpessimistic view of human development, assuming that only the negative dynamics of anxiety and frustration lead to progress. A more optimistic view may postulate that the motivation to achieve is an inherently healthy drive and an integral part of the need to grow and become independent. (See, for instance, Marlow's[M2] conceptualization of human development as a continuous struggle between defense and growth.) In other words, the child-rearing practices of the middle-class parent can be interpreted as evidence of the ability to guide his children toward independence and instill in them the desire for continuous personal growth.

The point that the commonly used intelligence tests are unfair to the lower-class child must also be questioned. An attempt was made to develop a test which was not culturally loaded in favor of middle-class children.[E1] The Davis-Eells Game Test (developed on the basis of the above theoretical postulation) is made up of pictures of real life situations and commonsense questions about them. Even on this new test, lower-class children still average lower than middle-class children. In addition, the Game Test does not stress verbal ability as a component of intelligence. Perhaps this deletion explains the test's limited correlation with academic success in comparison with other intelligence tests.

Teachers' perceptions of intelligence tests are in the process of change and are becoming more realistic. It is recognized that we do not know how to measure native potential intelligence. What is measured is rather learned behavior, that is, the product of the interaction between life experience and native intelligence. Teachers recognize that the present intelligence tests are of limited range. For instance, they fail to tap the abilities which enter into creative functioning. Nevertheless, the majority of novice teachers question the decision of the New York City Board of Education to abolish intelligence testing and see it as a suppression of valuable information. Teachers do realize the brutal fact that the student from an intellectually impoverished surrounding is handicapped; the test merely tells how much. We do not solve malnourishment by throwing away the scale (despite its limitations) ; the solution is in a rich nutrition.

In contrast to previously implied assumptions, intelligence does not grow and unfold on its own. Its growth is not a predetermined curve. It is the educational impact of the environment on the child's inherent potential which results in the abilities called intelligence. Maternal, sensory, and school, deprivation may cause slowing of the growth of intelligence. A rich environmental stimulation may facilitate growth. The raising of the intellectual abilities of the disadvantaged child, and especially his verbal intelligence, is a major challenge confronting the teacher.

the impact on
the novice teacher

Research on urban mobility of the classroom teacher suggests the occurrence of horizontal mobility in one direction, from lower- to middle-class communities.[H8] Despite this evidence, it is at least partly incorrect to say that the novice is reluctant to work with the disadvantaged. It is more accurate to suggest that the young teacher has ambivalent feelings about this assignment. The discussion will attempt to explore the teacher's perceptions of the reward and threat inherent in teaching disadvantaged learners.

the dedicated teacher

As reported by various investigators,[F4] the most important factor influencing the career choice of prospective teachers is their desire to work with children. They love children and they want to be loved by them. Research[D1] points out that children's reaction is the most significant source of satisfaction or stress in the work of teachers. They are pleased, or even excited, when they see that the children are responding to their presentation and grasp the idea. They are rewarded when children show signs of affection: "We like you," "You are the best teacher we ever had; please don't leave us."

The significance of the reward of teaching children is clearly seen in the responses of the group to a test composed of incomplete sentences. The following are some illustrations:

It is most rewarding to see . . . children anxious to respond.

. . . . . . children's eyes light up because of something you showed them.

A good teacher wants . . . children to learn well and like her.

The most fascinating thing about teaching is . . . the response you get from children.

Not one of the novice teachers said: "The most fascinating thing about teaching is . . . the opportunity to develop new ideas and methodology." No one spoke about the reward of teaching as an opportunity to get more knowledge, to be challenged by colleagues, or about possible economic advantages for women. The emphasis was rather on the interaction between the teacher and the child, with specific emphasis on the child as he responds to the teacher as a person. As perceived by this group of beginning teachers, "responding" and "liking" are synonymous terms, which mean: "They learn because they like me."

The same primary concern can be seen in the logs written

by the teachers. The stress is on the need to serve, give, and love.

Children are children everywhere! Intelligence, the color of one's skin, religion, or sex have never been separated into defined categories. My inner emotions of interest, warmth, love, understanding, and the need to do something valuable for children has always been part of me in preparation for my teaching career.

It is not the kind of youngster you are dealing with which is the determining factor. It is more than this. It is what is in *you* which either builds or shatters the rapport that is most essential when dealing with any child.

It can be said that on the professed verbal level at least, the major characteristic of this group cannot be defined in terms of a social cause or a dedication to a specific discipline of knowledge, but rather in terms of devotion to children. The desire to give to children and be appreciated by children is a dynamic force which tends to motivate the novice teacher to work many hours into the night, to be experimental, and to attempt to be creative.

In their attempt to reach children, the majority of teachers report many successful ventures in individualizing instruction.

Then there is Michael who never had much to look forward to as far as school was concerned. All it took on my part was some extra encouragement in individual work and an interest in him that made him become part of the group. I am all the richer when I see his eyes shine, his face light up, and his hand wave—only too eager to participate in a class lesson.

Their attempts in reaching individual children are often successful, even with deprived lower-class children. The underprivileged child belonging to a minority ethnic group often develops a shell of toughness, aloofness, and non-involvement. This shell creates a barrier between the child and the education agent of the dominant white and middle-class society.

It is these victims of the clash of cultures and ethnic conflict whom these young teachers attempt to reach (in the psychological sense).

I know these children are underprivileged. I learned that the children are given beatings at home frequently and brutally. They are small and helpless in a big, cold, harsh world. I wanted to make these children feel happy and secure. I wanted to ease their suffering as much as I could.

The following incomplete sentences portray a teacher who stresses the importance of understanding lower-class children and their value system:

Classes of children of lower-class origins . . . need extra understanding.

. . . should be taught by the middle-class teacher who must always remember their somewhat different values.

A prevalent response to the same item is that the one who reaches these children is highly rewarded:

Classes of children of lower-class origin . . . admire the teacher greatly, sometimes even more than middle-class children.

. . . can be a rewarding experience to the successful teacher.

The descriptions in the logs of the teachers' experiences reveal that in many cases the individual attention and readiness to accept and provide individualized work help penetrate the ethnic barrier. Under these conditions, the child of a minority group may be ready for the first time to come out of his shell and stretch his hand toward the creation of contact.

Little Debbie (a Negro child), who was always passive and nondemonstrative, kissed me, presented the class letters to me and said, 'I'll miss you when you leave.' Pat's enthusiasm in reading was brought to my attention every morning when she would run to me and say: 'Don't you want to hear me read today?—I finished another book.' She had previously been a nonreader.

This mission to love and give generates not only individualized work with children, but also a sincere attempt to *know* children and understand the dynamics of their behavior.

Both the logs and the incomplete sentences demonstrate that the professional ego ideal of the novice teacher is a psychologically-oriented practitioner who is sensitive to mental health problems. Unstructured logs, where the young teachers are free to discuss topics of interest to them, are full of case studies and anecdotal records which describe the dynamics of children's behavior in the classroom and which attempt to analyze their home and community background. These writings indicate a strong interest in the psychological analysis of the dynamics underlying the behavior of children with emotional and learning difficulties. The interest is not only in the degree of subject-matter proficiency gained, but also in the total emotional and social adjustment of the child.

It is interesting to note that in responding to an item which deals with the predicted difficulties in the first year on the job, a prevalent reaction is the inability to reach all the children:

The thing I will have to struggle with most in my first year of teaching . . . is the realization that there are some children I'll never be able to reach.

The overemphasis on, "I like these children and therefore I want to teach them," also has a negative corollary: "I don't like these children and therefore I don't feel like teaching them." They often overlook the possibility that the act of teaching can be done in a less favorable climate of interrelationships. Teaching must continue regardless of subjective negative feelings toward a certain pupil and regardless of occasional failure to maintain emotional communication with children. The teacher must go on teaching even when the rewards of emotional closeness and warmth are occasionally absent. It is suspected that children's sensitivity to teachers' feelings for them and their dependency on affection as a condition for learning are probably related to teachers' inability sometimes to keep the functions of love and work somewhat separate in their own attitudes.[N1]

Teachers' need to like children and be liked by them is particularly strong with beginning teachers. They need to be more realistic and objective in their goals and attitudes and to recognize that one cannot always like a class or like every single child in the class. The teacher cannot expect to create a personal contact with every pupil or give of her own person incessantly. In spite of this less-than-perfect rapport, the teaching process must go on.

the impact of the slow learner

There is research evidence to suggest that a major cause for dissatisfaction of teachers in lower-class communities is the academic performance of pupils.[H8] As seen by teachers, working with the disadvantaged generally means teaching slow learners. Why do so many teachers tend to be reluctant to work with the slow learner?

Examine the following reactions:

Slow learners . . . need special attention.

. . . have to be studied for possible causes.

. . . are difficult to work with.

The young teacher recognizes the difficulty in working with the slow learner, and notes his special educational needs. However, almost nowhere do the responses to the incomplete sentences indicate that the slow learner is a pleasure or a challenge to the intellectual curiosity and ingenuity of the teacher. In contrast, look at the reactions toward the bright child:

Bright students . . . are a challenge to the teacher.

. . . stimulate my thinking.

. . . are a pleasure to teach.

The novice teachers accept the values of the educational culture, which call for study and understanding of the slow learner. However, their "real love" is the academically-minded bright child. It is evident that the slow learner is a source of frustration in the life of the novice.

I noticed in my own college class that when a teacher

relates her experience to the group by saying, "I work with a fourth grade; they are slow learners," too often the reaction is short laughter. I stopped many times to ask for the reasons underlying this laughter. After some evasive remarks, many teachers admitted that the laughter was an expression of their identification with the frustrations, or even futility, their colleagues must be experiencing in working with slow learners. They perceive the work with the slow learner as a hindrance to the teaching process. As one group member presented it:

With slow learners, you cannot concentrate on teaching, but rather *flit* around.

Despite their psychological orientation, despite their verbal acceptance of the concept of individual differences, and despite many successful attempts in providing for individual differences, the novice teacher finds it difficult to fully accept those individuals who deviate from the average in their academic ability. It seems that the teaching of the slow child is at variance with some of the basic motivation which brings teachers into the profession: the desire to teach, that is, to transmit knowledge. The basic dimension of the teacher's role is to communicate information. The successful fulfillment of this role is easier, and progress is more evident, in working with the bright rather than the slow learner.

The logs show that the involvement of teachers with the transmission of knowledge is only second in its importance to their involvement with children. The incomplete sentences point out that the novice finds it "most rewarding to see children anxious to learn and respond." On the other hand, "The most exasperating aspect of teaching . . . is to teach a lesson and find that no one has gotten anything out of it." It is evident that it is the bright rather than the slow child who more fully satisfies the teacher's need to transmit knowledge. It is the slow child who tends to frustrate this need.

To illustrate, when I went to observe a class of slow learners, a young teacher said to me: "They are the slowest group, 5-6. I want you to understand and have *sympathy*. . . ." In other words, this teacher does not expect "to shine" in being able to teach much subject matter, and therefore, does not think she will be a "success." She feels defeated and looks for sympathy.

In discussing the bright child in their logs, some teachers mention the resemblance of this type of pupil to their own classroom behavior as students. They see themselves before their own eyes in observing children follow the route toward success that they have followed in earlier years, when they derived their status and sense of success mainly from their academic ability. They ranked in the upper quartile of the student population. They now find it difficult to teach and relate to the lower quartile. With slow learners they often lack "their own kind" and sometimes refer to the slow learners, in their logs, as "those children."

Some educators[C2] speak about the *"self-fulfilling proph-ecy"*—a major cause of low achievement among learners of disadvantaged groups is the low expectations of teachers. Children seldom exceed the teacher's expectation.

The Higher Horizons Project in New York City[M14] is one of the best-known demonstrations that the school can make progress in helping the deprived pupil. The title of the project "Higher Horizons" symbolizes the secret of its relative success. It is not the enrichment itself which can change the pattern of resignation and apathy and its corollary—limited academic functioning—but rather the ideology of faith. Any attempt to copy the curricular and administrative approach of the project without adopting its basic ideology of faith in the power of the deprived to move ahead intellectually will not achieve similar results.

Some writers on the problem of deprivation and academic retardation suggest that one expression of the faith of the teacher in the academic abilities of the disadvantaged learner should be a *single standard of achievement*.[C2] They criticize the known educational principles of "meeting the learner where he is" or "adjusting the curriculum to his needs and interest" as leading to discriminatory treatment of lower-class children. They are critical of curriculum modifications in the direction of the more functional and the less academic.

In my judgment the slogan of "a single standard of

achievement" is a naive conception of the educational process and a misleading principle to guide the young teacher. It is correct that lack of trust and respect on behalf of teachers is a source of academic failure; it is, however, also correct that the confrontation with a too difficult or meaningless academic task is a source of alienation and failure. In the language of illustrations, to teach reading to a six-year old retarded in verbal ability or to teach Shakespearean drama to a child who reads on a fourth grade level is a futile teaching behavior, which is going to alienate both child and teacher.

A recognition of the academic deficiencies of a learner who has a history of cultural deprivation is not undemocratic or class-biased. The adjustment of the curriculum to his needs and abilities does not mean a soft and patronizing approach or lack of trust in the educability of lower-class children. It means rather an insightful and realistic approach which attempts to build on the present and move toward a more hopeful and dynamic future.

the impact of the aggressive child

As seen by the novice teacher, working with disadvantaged children means having to cope with incidence of aggressive behavior. The young teacher is afraid of being trapped in a blackboard jungle, of being a policeman rather than a teacher.

The group of teachers under discussion is composed of young women. In the role definition assigned to the sexes by our culture, aggression is usually associated with males. Femininity is at variance with direct aggression. (This point accentuates the great need for male teachers to balance the female-centered school.) Illustrations can be brought from some responses to the incomplete sentences:

The best kind of student is . . . one who pays attention and does his work.

Compared with boys, girls are . . . easier to control.

The kind of boy I like best . . . is the one who is a good student, well-behaved, may be a little mischievous, but never out of hand. The kind of girl I like best . . . is the one who pays attention and does her work.

. . . is a neat girl, who has good manners and pays attention and does her work.

. . . is the girl who behaves like a little lady.

The picture of the ideal child portrayed in the responses to the above items is well-delineated. The adjectives used are relatively limited in number and variety, and point to an emphasis on attentiveness to the teacher, and compliance with work assigned, as the main characteristics of good behavior. The teachers sense that this role is too docile for the boy and, therefore, permit him to be "a little mischievous" sometimes.

Whether the child is earthy and real, whether the child is creative and energetic, whether the learner relates intrinsically to subject matter, whether the student has deep feelings and convictions, does not seem to play a major role in the teacher's thinking. The emphasis is rather on the external manifestations of compliance to the teacher, that is, the eradication of aggressive elements of behavior.

The image of the ideal child has a direct impact on the teaching behavior of the novice teacher; it dictates the norms of behavior which the teacher fosters in the classroom. Two illustrations will be brought out here. In one fourth grade, the following chart hangs on the wall:

Manners

> We say thank you.
> We say please.
> We don't interrupt or tease.
> We don't argue.
> We don't fuss.
> We listen when folks talk to us.

In another fourth grade, a teacher developed a chart enumerating values of good behavior:

I Am a Good Student

1. I raise my hand before I speak.
2. I do not leave my seat without permission.
3. I do not speak out.
4. I walk quietly.
5. I do my work quietly.
6. I am always on time.

The inexperienced and insecure beginning teacher is subverted by his perception of the basic need of his profession—control and compliance, by his desire for oiled and lubricated relations with children, and by his fear of conflict. These dynamics contribute toward a limited conception of what a child should be and, in the long run, contribute toward a narrow conception of what a person should be.

The logs reveal that some of the teachers feel so hurt and angry by the actions of the aggressive child that they find it difficult to attempt to come close to him. Rather than move in the direction of close contact, the reaction of some young teachers is to withdraw into formal relations of group teaching, aloofness, and commanding behavior. A vicious circle is created here. A fearful child who may be craving for acceptance strikes at the teacher, and a fearful teacher, who wants to share, withdraws or even strikes back.

the impact of discipline problems

A comparison of the data collected by the use of the incomplete sentences, and the data found in the logs, suggests that a discrepancy exists between the professional ego ideals and some of the real classroom behavior of this group of young teachers. The professional ego ideals of an understanding and non-punitive teacher-psychologist do not stand the trial they are subjected to by the aggressive child. This is especially correct when the behavior of the aggressive child is contagious and the whole class becomes a *discipline problem*.

The desire to give to children and to be appreciated by children, the ideal of being an understanding teacher, motivates the novice teacher to work many long hours, to be experimental, and to attempt to be creative. The fear of the aggressive child, or broadly speaking, the fear of discipline problems in the classroom, presents a threat which tends to push the young teacher in a direction which is completely opposed to where she is trying to go. She turns to overstructured teaching and seeks the "safe" *A* orientation of repetitive teaching.

The relatedness of the novice teacher to the child in terms of attitudes and behavior is a product of the two opposing forces: the desire to love, give, come close to and reach, and the fear of being rejected and having discipline problems. This conflict of being torn between these two poles is revealed in many of the comments they make and questions they raise:

Should we start off very strict and then lighten up? In this way pupils will respect our authority.

Should we win the friendship of pupils first, so that later they will be glad to accept our demands and assignments?

Billy is a difficult child. I work with him individually with some success. Today he sent me a note asking me to be his mother. How *close* should I come to children?

The best advice for the young teacher—at the beginning—is, sit on them.

It is evident that a basic factor which determines whether the novice will move in the direction of the *C* orientation of creativity or toward the *A* overemphasis on specificity and routinized teaching is the resolution of the conflict of discipline.

The teachers under discussion here have grown up and lived in relatively sheltered middle-class environments. They experienced some rude awakenings through teaching in lower-class communities. The contact, and sometimes even the clash, with these children became a source of strain and challenge to them, and the attainment of good discipline became the major criterion of success and adequacy in teaching. The criterion

of discipline characterizes the responses to the incomplete
sentences:

It is often easy to lose sight of . . . your main objectives because of
discipline problems.

The most exasperating aspect of teaching . . . is to lose control of
the class.

The thing I'll have to struggle with most in my first year of teaching . . . is to have complete control in the classroom.

The most valuable thing I learned from my cooperating teacher . . .
is her approach to discipline.

It is easiest to teach when . . . the class is quiet.

Compared with boys, girls . . . are easier to control.

As seen from these typical illustrations, the criterion of
discipline is the major category of response and the most
frequent one. It overshadows the novice's interest in other
basic values of education—understanding children, transmit-
ting knowledge, developing thinking. As the incomplete sentences show, the preoccupation with discipline is often a
deterrent to experimentation:

When given freedom, children . . . tend to respond positively. However, this freedom must be guided so that bedlam does not result.

Changing classroom routines . . . may lead to trouble, in some cases
even chaos.

Introducing new ideas while being a student teacher in a class . . .
will often upset the routines and is therefore dangerous.

The literature on the topic of discipline discusses different levels of interpretation of the meaning of discipline, from
the more punitive and authoritarian approaches to the more
self-directive and democratic practices.[H17] However, when the
novice teacher speaks about discipline, his interest is not only
in how he should approach children, but also in the impact
of this approach on himself as a person.

When beginning teachers freely open up and discuss their

perceptions and experiences with discipline, the discussion tends to be charged with fear and anxiety. The cause of this particular emotional response does not have to do with methodology or logic; it stems from a much deeper level. It involves what the participants feel is a major threat to their self-concepts. The teacher is fully aware that when the class is not responding or is unruly, his feelings of adequacy as a teacher and as a person are damaged. He feels hurt, depressed, and antagonistic. His bitterness and disillusionment may cause him to have one or more of the following thoughts:

What I have learned is of no use. It does not work.

It is academic and theoretical and would not work in my neighborhood.

The only thing these children understand is punishment.

You must develop routines and never break them.

Don't smile and don't try to be friendly in the first few weeks.

Novice teachers are confused about the nature of discipline. This confusion affects their cognitive awareness of disciplinary incidents, their actual behavior in the classroom, and their self-concepts as teachers. Young teachers are under the strong impact of a teacher-education culture which fosters the image of the ideal teacher. They identify with the ego ideal and aspire to reach it; that is, they want to become friendly, permissive, warm teachers, who have excellent relations with children. The need to live up to this roseate expectation becomes a source of strain and confusion, some of the manifestations of which are evasion of, and inconsistency in, the treatment of disciplinary incidents:

I lost control of the class. Nothing helped. I was very angry and I broke the ruler on the desk. They became quiet, but I felt like a heel.

I wanted to be their friend, to be nice, not authoritarian. After a rich experience, I asked: "Now children, do you want to write a story?" They yelled "No!" and became wild.

Both anecdotes deal with the difficulty the novice teachers have had in asserting authority. In other words, in the teacher's mind the assertion of authority is made synonomous with authoritarianism.

Underlying the guilt and self-deprecation experienced by the teacher in the first anecdote is the variance between her image of the ideal teacher who has "nice" relations with children and the bitter reality of having to assert her authority. Perhaps if the novice teacher were sure of her right to *demand* "discipline," the class relations would not have deteriorated. Perhaps if the novice teacher were sure of her right to be angry, her anger would not have exploded to the point of breaking a ruler.

In the second incident, it seems that on the surface the young teacher wanted to be democratic and let children make choices. However, the children sensed that underlying the informal, friendly, and democratic behavior was a reluctance and fear to assert authority.

In their anxiety to copy the image of the ideal teacher, the teachers fail to realize that there are two types of friendly relations with children, one stemming from strength and the other stemming from weakness and a need for "chumminess." The first fosters healthy relations, but the latter leads to unruly behavior.

The beginning teacher may need to develop a more realistic expectation of the problems involved in relating to children. The ego ideal of a democratic, warm, informal, and permissive teacher is an oversimplification of the picture. As Ruth Cunningham[C6] points out, teachers whom observers agree are most effective use the widest range of patterns of leadership—adult rule to group-centered management. It is an oversimplification to assume that any teacher is always democratic in his approach to children, or that it is always desirable to be so. The teacher has a right to assert her authority, to demand respect, attention, and accomplishment.

Injured and harassed by a disciplinary crisis, the novice teacher becomes professionally, and sometimes personally, rigid. This rigidity is expressed in a reverse pattern: from a loving to a punitive attitude; from democratic to authoritarian behavior; and, perhaps most important, from an experimental approach of readiness and eagerness for new ideas to a dogmatic, disillusioned attitude that what counts is only fear, routine, and "busywork."

Curriculum improvement is dependent primarily on the growth of teachers, that is, on their enthusiasm and readiness to pioneer and experiment. If, too early in their careers, "occupational sclerosis" occurs in many of the novice teachers, the goal of a richer educational program will be very difficult to reach.

dedication to a social cause

In an interview a young teacher remarked:

The teacher today is the scapegoat; she is blamed for most of the school's and many of society's ills. She is accused of being incompetent, prejudiced, expecting less from the disadvantaged, being harsh and lacking sympathy.

Some writers[C2] on the problem of the disadvantaged learner identify the school and the teacher as the basic cause. As the discussion in this chapter shows, this is an oversimplification of the picture. A more realistic approach is to examine the multitudinal factors which interact and impinge on each other; to examine what happens to the teacher in the process of attempting to teach the disadvantaged learner. This analysis of the dynamics of teacher-disadvantaged learner interaction has direct implications for the improvement of teaching behavior. It is a challenge to the novice teacher to examine the impact of her contact with the disadvantaged learner not only on the child but also on herself.

A novice teacher practicing in a kindergarten located in a slum area writes:

I am the only white teacher in the school. The children look at my clothes, my jewelry and my hair in awe. How can I, an individual who never experienced the life that they have, hope to teach them successfully? I realize that I myself am not going to solve the problem, but with compassion, with understanding and patience, I must give it a try.

The preparation of teachers for disadvantaged learners should be improved; new curriculum patterns and teaching styles must be explored, new educational materials must be developed. Despite all these expected improvements, it should be said clearly that teaching in the slum will remain a taxing and often frustrating job, much more difficult than teaching in suburbia.[G5]

The major positive characteristic of the young teacher, the desire to give to children, is a dynamic force which motivates teachers to be dedicated and help. It seems, however, that the dedication to the individual child and the desire to transmit knowledge are not enough. What is also needed is idealism, that is, a dedication to a social cause, the commitment to the mission of the teacher as a leader in the war on poverty.

selected bibliography

BLOOM, BENJAMIN, DAVIS, ALLISON, and HESS, ROBERT, *Compensatory Education for Cultural Deprivation*. New York: Holt, Rinehart and Winston, Inc., 1965. A summary of research studies.

CLARK, KENNETH B., *Dark Ghetto*. New York: Harper & Row, Publishers, 1965. An insightful discussion of the Negro community. Chapter 6 "Ghetto Schools" is very critical of the defeatist attitudes of the teacher.

DAVIS, ALLISON, *Social Class Influences Upon Learning*. Cambridge: Harvard University Press, 1951. A study which had a great impact on educational thinking and practice.

PASSOW, A. HARRY (Editor), *Education in Depressed Areas*. New York: Bureau of Publications, Teachers College, Columbia University, 1963. Scholarly presentations of some of the educational leaders in this field.

RIESSMAN, FRANK, *The Culturally Deprived Child*. New York: Harper & Row, Publishers, 1962. A stimulating discussion.

STROM, ROBERT (Editor), *The Inner City Classroom: Teacher Behaviors*. Columbus, Ohio: Charles E. Merrill Books, Inc., 1966. A discussion of the role of the teacher.

8

the disadvantaged: in search of teaching style

Some teachers are reluctant to use the expression "the culturally-deprived child." They stress that the child growing in a slum community is not deprived of a culture; he only has a different culture. For insight into the strengths and weaknesses of the slum society, the reader is referred to books such as *La Vida* by Oscar Lewis.[L6] Here the discussion is going to be limited to the understanding of the deprivation aspects of the slum culture as they impede academic learning. The use of the expression "culturally deprived" is a way of stating the observed detrimental impact of slum living on schooling.

The tendency in this country is to associate cultural deprivation with the "dark ghetto" and the disadvantaged learner with the Negro child. In essence the dynamics of deprivation which impede learning do not stem from being a Negro, but rather from being of lower-class origin. The tragic fact is that the majority of Negro people in the U.S.A. have been relegated to lower-class position. To understand the impact of deprivation on learning and to understand that it is not related to racial-ethnic but rather to lower-class origin, I will present a brief survey of research conducted in different countries. There is no common racial origin among the populations to be described; the common denominator is rather lower-class belonging.

a cross-cultural analysis

the disadvantaged: Casablanca

Interesting studies were conducted on the nature of the educational retardation of Jewish children living in the slum ghetto of Casablanca (called Mellah).[F1] Their use of language lacked accuracy and differentiation. For instance, the same word—*car*, was used to mean car, ship, train and plane. In defining a term they referred primarily to its use rather than its characteristics, e.g., "a table is for eating," or "flowers are for putting on the table." The children were found to be concrete-minded, finding it difficult to think in relative terms and utilize language suggesting a hypothetical situation. For instance, when asked "If you had done something else what would have happened?" the typical response was: "But I did not do something else."

The tendency of the children was to use exaggerated language. Being angry, they impulsively yelled "I'll kill you!" —an expression of an undifferentiated language. The poverty of language contributed toward a *motoric* style of communication. Often, children were seen holding their partner by his hand or shirt in order to explain a point. They used gestures to the same extent that they used words. It seems that the "motoric expression" came to compensate for lack of words.

On the Rorschach Test, the Mellah children spoke about the picture as a whole less frequently than European youngsters of the same age. Their tendency was to enumerate the parts as discrete and aggregate elements. In drawing a picture of a child behind a house, they drew the child in a transparent position (the whole child is seen behind the house). In other words, the linguistic difficulties were an integral part of limitation in the abilities of intellectual functioning.

the disadvantaged: England

George Bernard Shaw says that the line that separates man from beast is the language line; the line that separates

middle class from lower class is the language line; and the line
that separates the intellectually advantaged from the disadvantaged is the language line. The story *Pygmalion* is a dra-
matic presentation of the point that language separates people
into social classes. Let the one who grew up in the slum—
beautiful Eliza—only change her accent and dialect; let her
learn to say "correctly" " 'The rain in Spain falls mainly in
the plain,' " and she is ready to move upward and marry the
noble man, Professor Higgins. The prerequisite to social
mobility is seen as a change in speech patterns.

Bernstein, studying the relationship between social class
and linguistic development in England,[B5] suggests that the
problem is much more complicated than differences in dialects.
Social-class differences in language represent two contrasting
modes of thinking, perceiving, and learning. The language of
the lower class, the "public-restrictive" is concrete, lacking in
differentiation and accuracy. It is a language of implicit
meaning which is easy to understand. In contrast, the language of the middle class tends to be "formal and elaborate."
It is a language which encourages preciseness, differentiation,
and the expression of variety of thought.

Bernstein stresses that language is not only a product of
class belonging, but also a factor which perpetuates class
belonging. The correlate of the restrictive public language is
a relatively low level of conceptualization and a way of responding primarily to the immediate rather than to the implications of the matrix of the relationships. The quality of the
language spoken determines what and how the child learns.
Language and speech are a product of the thinking processes
of an individual and his group. To improve language and
speech, the approach is primarily the enrichment of the
thinking processes of the learner.

the disadvantaged: the U.S.A.

Hess[H9] illustrates how maternal styles affect the contrasting class language and cognitive development. A child is playing and making noise. In one home the mother says "be quiet"
and answers the phone. In another home the mother says

"would you be quiet so that I can hear the other party?" In the first instance the child is called-on to obey without any explanations. In the second illustration the child is encouraged to think about the relationship between his making noise and the need for the two parties to communicate. He learns to perceive facts and stimuli in terms of their interrelationship.

The differences in the verbal exchange between the mother and child of the two social classes can be further illustrated by the following example brought by Hess. Two mothers instruct their children to play with a puzzle. The middle-class mother says to her child: "This is a puzzle. You have never seen one before; take out the pieces and put them back together. First see where all the pieces are, look at the colors, look at the shapes so you'll know where they go." The lower-class mother dumps the puzzle and tells the child. "Now you do it." The only guidance she gives is by repeatedly instructing him to "turn it around." The discouraged boy finally yells, "You do it!" and leaves.

Assuming that these illustrations are a representative sample of maternal teaching styles in the two homes, it can be said that they have a fundamental impact on the nature of the cognitive development of the child. The middle-class child learns that it is exciting to solve puzzling problems, that it is possible to do it by looking for clues and interrelationships, and that the adult is a supporting source for learning. The lower-class child, in being exposed to failure, learns not to search for clues and interrelations, not to see the adult as a source of learning, to refrain from searching and trying.

the disadvantaged: Israel

Adaia Shumsky and the author studied the impact of social deprivation on a group of lower-class Middle Eastern children in Israel and found limitations in intellectual functioning. The group was limited in areas of thinking which, unlike retention and recall, require the learner to move beyond the obvious and the immediate. They had difficulty in developing generalizations and in making interpretations.

For instance, in answer to the proverb, "A drowning

man clutches at a straw," the tendency of the lower-class child was to give a literal and concrete explanation: "A man who drowns tries to catch at a straw to save himself," whereas the typical answer of the middle-class child was an abstract interpretation: "People in trouble attempt all solutions regardless of how foolish they may be." In other words, the middle-class child was more able to move from the literal and obvious to the less obvious, to shift from a concrete level of interpretation to a more abstract and less bound form of behavior.

a theory of the
psychological meaning of poverty

The discussion above presented a brief survey of difficulties in intellectual functioning of children of various lower-class groups in several countries. One can give further demonstration of the problem in New Zealand, Australia, Japan, etc. The common denominator for all the groups studied is not ethnic or geographic; it is, rather, the lower-class and minority-group status. The common denominator between the Negro in the "dark ghetto,"[C2] the child living in the Mellah of Casablanca,[F1] the lower-class Middle Easterner in Israel,[S7] and the Maori in New Zealand[A4] is poverty and its psychological corollary—helplessness. For them, there is nowhere to go and not much they can do about the situation. When a group of people lives for centuries in poverty and despair, when they feel that it is not within their power to improve their lives, they tend to become *passive* in their total life orientation. Difficulties in intellectual functioning are an integral aspect of this *passive personal orientation*.

Adaia Shumsky and the author, in the previously mentioned study, examined the relationship between the psychological experience of poverty, that is, the sense that it is not within one's power to improve one's life, and the ability to learn. We suggest that children with an assertive personal attitude toward reality will have a greater tendency to succeed on tasks of intellectual functioning than children who have a passive personal attitude.

People who live in socially and economically depressed conditions develop a degree of immediacy about their approach to life problems which is associated with a similar approach in their intellectual behavior. When life conditions bind the individual to immediate problems and needs, when the view of the future is dimmed or narrowed due to limited possibilities, when little change can be expected in life conditions, and when the individual feels at a loss in doing something about his life conditions, he will develop an outlook on life characterized by *passivity* and *immediacy*. When such an outlook predominates there will be a greater tendency on the part of the individual to approach intellectual tasks with concreteness, rigidity, and boundedness.

What is an outlook on life characterized by passivity and immediacy, and how can it be recognized in children? In order to measure the "passive personal orientation," three tests were administered to several groups of eighth graders in Israel:

(A) A personal opinion questionnaire;
(B) A sentence completion; and
(C) A projective story about the future.

(A) *The personal-opinion questionnaire* was a "true-false" test consisting of statements dealing with the accidental or external nature of matters in the world and the individual's readiness to react to them in a positive, active manner. Examples: "The best things in life only happen to a small group of lucky people"; "Money and good family connections are the most important conditions for success"; "One's future is not determined by his place of birth"; and "The world situation is such that there is no point in getting excited about it or trying to do something to change it."

The results of the test show that whereas the middle-class child is confident in his power in dealing with the external world, the tendency of the lower-class child is to de-emphasize his own active role in determining his life chances.

(B) *The sentence-completion test* consisted of stubs designed to obtain children's perceptions of the role of the

individual as passive or assertive. It attempted to deal with
the following questions:

(1) Does the child interpret social phenomena as
caused by accidental and external forces, or does he conceive
of the active role which the individual can play in molding his
own life? Examples: To the stub "Some people never reach
happiness because . . ." a typical reaction of lower-class
children was "they have no luck," whereas a characteristic
middle-class reaction was, "they don't try hard enough."

(2) Does the child view the world in immediate-
personal or broader objective terms? Is the child concerned
with problems which have an immediate personal connection
to him, or can he extend himself beyond the most personal
and immediate? Example: to the stub "The thing which worries me most" typical worries of lower-class children had to
do with immediate concerns in terms of the immediate environment ("that I would not have enough money to buy
a bicycle") or the immediate future ("that I would not pass
the test"). In contrast more worries of middle-class children
had to do with less immediate concerns, for instance, "the
possibility of war" or a failure to achieve self-fulfillment,
"that I will not be able to go to college."

(3) Does the child value work and learning merely
as means of obtaining external and immediate gratification,
or is he able to perceive the inherent value in work and study,
that is, the sense of growth and self-fulfillment inherent in
work? For instance, to the stub "The best kind of work" a
larger proportion of lower-class children indicated preference
toward work which is easy, secure, steady, or untaxing, while
more middle-class children seemed to prefer work which is
satisfying, interesting, challenging, or in short, the kind of
work which promises "self-realization" and individual growth.

(C) Similar variations between the two groups were
found in a *projective story* where children had to describe
themselves as young adults. The tendency of lower-class children was to stress themes of concrete, practical, material,
and immediate concerns, whereas the middle-class child tended
to respond with themes describing achievement, mobility, and
excellence.

The lower-class child in the story seemed to center his view of the future around the solution of daily practical situations, around what he would or would not have. The middle-class child seemed to be more concerned with more abstract goals, such as what he would become or what he would do to reach toward his desired personal achievement. In brief, the difference is between the attitude of *"what will I have"* and *"what will I be."*

As a conclusion of our research in Israel and the research reported here conducted by other investigators in different parts of the world, a theoretical formulation about the relationship between poverty and learning is suggested:

When one finds himself stuck in the hampering aspects of poverty, where the lack of education and skill leads to further poverty, and where the chances to shape one's future are rather limited, the individual comes to see himself as a victim. He sees himself as a passive recipient of conditions which he cannot control and out of which he cannot move. Where the question of daily survival becomes a major life effort, there is little chance for the individual to be concerned with long-range planning, self-fulfillment, or broad social responsibilities.

The degrading poverty of slum existence causes the individual to become bound to himself; respond primarily to the immediate, the concrete; and experience difficulty in planning beyond the most immediate. He is preoccupied with what he will have rather than with what he will be.

Higher learning processes such as abstraction, generalization, differentiation, concept formation, organization, planning, approaching a problem from more than one point of view, making hypotheses, interpreting, plunging inquisitively into the unknown, all require the active participation of the individual in the process of learning. They all require the conscious investment of intellectual energy, and call for a learner who does not passively repeat but, rather, actively reacts and creates.

In contradistinction to these prerequisites, the task of learning is approached by the disadvantaged with the same relatively passive personal outlook with which he tends to approach reality in general. This passive orientation is a way of learning which tends to be confined to the concrete and the immediate, to specific bits of information that are drilled and memorized. What is absent in this mode of approach is that which the individual as an *intervening factor* makes out of the apprehended material.

The passive learner does not get involved in the material as a person; he only repeats and accepts it as given. He does not feel that he has the power to *act* on the presented subject matter, to control and direct it. Metaphorically, he is afraid to fly from the concrete to the abstract, not being sure that in coming back he will find the security of the concrete!

the conventional approach to the disadvantaged problem

The previous section discussed the psychological meaning of poverty as a passive personal orientation toward life and stressed that children with a passive personal attitude toward reality would tend to have more difficulties with tasks which require intellectual functioning than children who have an assertive personal attitude.

What are the implications for education of this theory of the psychological impact of poverty? There are several answers to the question.

subsidy to the poor

One answer is that the theory has no implications for education. Our society is plagued by discrimination, segregation, lack of economic opportunities to the lower-class stratum, and disintegration of the lower-class Negro family. Children come out of wild, disruptive slum life which makes them almost impervious to formal education. The school cannot change the social order; it can only mirror society, its strengths and its ills.

Moynihan, author of a challenging study on the Negro family,[M16] says:[M15:72]

We have received an awful lot of data recently that pouring money into slum schools makes very little difference whatsoever. The fact of the slum is the fact of the concentration of lower class children. What do you accomplish by doubling the expenditure on pupils? You double the expenditure on school teachers. Not a penny of it goes to the parents of the children . . . The whole point about the conventional strategy of providing more services to the poor is that the money invariably goes to well paid, over-employed middle class professionals . . .

I am afraid that we have simply got to acknowledge that simple extensions of our present educational efforts . . . probably will not work. We already doubled and redoubled and it hasn't done much.

Moynihan's position is that there has been too much concentration on doing things for the poor, such as teaching, and not enough concentration on giving them money. He questions whether increased educational activities are effective without the previous elimination of the basic factor—poverty.

integration

A second answer to the question is that the theory implies the need for integration. The pathology of the slum-ghetto community strengthens the sense of powerlessness, the despair, hostility, and apathy of its dwellers. To come out from the ghetto and live in an integrated community means, to the disadvantaged, a hope, a chance for real equality and entrance into the mainstream of American life.

The Supreme Court decision on school desegregation recognized the devastating human cost of segregation.[C2:76]

To separate them [the Negro children] from others of similar age and qualifications solely because of their race generates a feeling of inferiority as to their status in the community that may affect their hearts and minds in a way unlikely ever to be undone.

One of the findings of a most comprehensive research study by Coleman on *Equality of Educational Opportunity* is that[C3:22]

. . . if a minority pupil from a home without much educational
strength is put with schoolmates, with strong educational background, his achievement is likely to increase.

The school integration movement is in the forefront of
social reform. Under its banner many projects were and are
attempted: free enrollment programs, bussing of children,
rezoning of school districts, reorganizing the structure of the
elementary school into primary and intermediate (the first
to be a neighborhood school and the latter to serve a wider
district), pairing schools, planning educational parks, etc.

The belief is that integration is an essential factor in
developing self-respect, an atmosphere of hope, and a positive
attitude toward intellectual achievement among lower-class
Negro children.

compensatory education

A third implication of the psychological impact of poverty and cultural deprivation is the need for compensatory
education. If the family and the neighborhood of the lower-
class child too often find it difficult to fulfill their educational
roles, let the school take over. As a research summary dealing
with compensatory education suggests:[B7:6]

What is now required is not equality of access to education. What is
needed to solve our current as well as future crises in education is a
system of compensatory education which can prevent or overcome
earlier deficiencies in the development of each individual.

Recognizing the growing need for compensatory education, schools all over the country have moved energetically to
inaugurate a variety of projects.

The Head Start program is an attempt to prepare the
disadvantaged learner to cope with the school curriculum. It
started as a free summer program prior to first grade and is
developing into a free system of nursery schools for lower-
class children.

The Higher Horizon Project in New York City has
literally swept the country as a model of compensatory edu-

cation to be emulated. It stresses an enriched educational program, cultural activities, increased educational and psychological services, and parent involvement. And it has had a great impact on various projects such as The Great City Improvement Project, Special Service Schools, and More Effective Schools.[R4]

"Task force" groups, consisting of laymen and educators, both Negro and white, were organized in many communities to study the educational needs of the disadvantaged and suggest educational improvements. The end result was generally more services, more special teachers, smaller classes, more materials, a longer school day, and special courses.

The Federal government, whose direct aid to education has been traditionally a hotly debated issue, is deeply involved in supporting the educational war on poverty. This involvement is resulting in a higher expenditure per child and more educational services to disadvantaged children.

The hope is that the increasing efforts in compensatory education will help overcome the intellectual deficit caused by the psychological impact of poverty.

quantity versus quality

The three approaches under discussion (direct help to the poor in the form of money, housing, etc.; integration, and compensatory education) express the vision of the social and educational engineers of this country and their determination to overcome the deficit of social deprivation. These three significant approaches are an expression of a commitment to a healthier democratic society, and they should definitely be further pursued and improved.

At the same time, however, it is difficult not to observe the limitations of these approaches.

(1) Subsidy of the poor by itself, may raise the income of the disadvantaged person above the poverty level but is not sufficient in bridging the gap between the continuously rising prosperity of the affluent society and himself. Comparatively, he will still remain poor. He still needs more educational equipment to be able to compete in the economic market. In

this "automated era" schooling has become an indicator predicting economic success and undoubtedly determines the level of success.

(2) Integration is a powerful and challenging ideal, but in practice it runs into some serious difficulties. In addition to direct opposition by some sections of the community, integration in urban centers resulted in what is generally called "flight" or "exodus" of white populations. As the Allen Commission report said:[C2:115]

It should be obvious . . . that integration is impossible without white pupils. No plan can be acceptable, therefore, which increases the movement of white pupils out of the public schools.

Havighurst[P2] developed a mathematical formula which defines the "status ratio" of the school. To the extent that the ratio of the lower-class pupils increases, the status of the school decreases and its "holding power" for the middle-class population diminishes. The sad commentary is that in the large urban communities school integration did not make much headway and, in some cases, even lost ground.

Another difficulty confronting the integration approach is the administrative pattern of homogeneous groups. Observation of integrated schools shows that the lower-class Negro child generally attends the below-average classes, whereas the middle-class pupil tends to be in the above-average groups. In essence this setup is only "pseudo-integration" and is limited in its promise of changing the self-concept and releasing the potential of the deprived learner.

(3) The approach of compensatory education in the school as it is generally interpreted at present is primarily an "additive formula." More teachers, more services, more materials, are provided. The school day is extended. The school year may be lengthened. Although these practices may constitute part of the answer to the compensatory need, the formula of "let's have more of the same" is quantitative rather than qualitative in nature. To put it somewhat extremely, if a specific group of children feels alienated toward and is psychologically deaf to school teaching, why should one expect that being exposed to a dose of eight rather than six hours of schooling per day, this group will then open up and

get involved? Can quantity compensate for limitations in quality?

Deutsch[P2] states that about 80 per cent of the school day in classes of disadvantaged children observed by his team is used for organizational detail and discipline, only 20 per cent for academic work. Therefore, the difficult problem is not mainly that of getting more teachers and extending the school day. The main issue is, rather, that of having better teachers and of making better use of present time allotment.

The resolution of the problem of cultural deprivation does not lie merely in increasing school services, but rather in raising the professional competence of the present teachers as they try to cope with the cultural and social disadvantages. Education for productive thinking does not merely call for more hours at school but rather for a teaching style which helps children move from the concrete to the abstract. The main need underlying the planning of educational change for the deprived is to be occupied with more than quantitative, additive, and administrative solutions. The focus should be on the *quality* of the teaching-learning experience.

What is the quality of teaching which will help the deprived child overcome his basic limitation—the passive orientation toward reality and toward intellectual functioning?

It is usually easier to agree on observed facts than to agree on their implications for action. The search for a teaching style for the disadvantaged may lead the educator in two opposing directions. The first approach is that of adjusting to the limitations in intellectual functioning of the deprived learner. The second is an orientation which continuously attempts to alter the learning style of the disadvantaged child and promote an active involvement with reality and the act of learning.

adjusting to the learning style of the disadvantaged

The first direction is in essence the most prevalent approach to the education of the deprived child. A prevailing belief is that a realistic education must accept the intellectual limitations of the learner and operate in terms of these limitations. It advocates that the teacher focus on concrete and utilitarian subject matter and stress specificity of information and skill. It reminds the teacher that he faces the reality of a short attention span and thus must present to the students only short-range tasks. The classroom climate must be teacher-centered, and the learning process should be guided by specific and continuous instruction. The motto of this approach is that of controlling every activity to avoid any confusion (confusion leads to insecurity) ; organizing teaching by stressing routines in classroom management and learning habits.

The following examples of curricular practices may illustrate the approach under discussion:

The language arts program is skill-oriented, stressing patterns of language, phonetic analysis, grammar, vocabulary, and correct speech and language usage. In writing, the main emphasis is on spelling and short responses to workbook-type exercises. In reading, the focus is on the basal reader and the workbooks. Much time is spent on oral reading and recitation. Individualized reading is not attempted as it is feared that in working on his own the child may flounder and reinforce his errors. The child is continuously prodded by the teacher to review the material and practice the skills.

The focus of science teaching is primarily on transmission of information. There is much use of concrete materials, and demonstrations are guided by "step-by-step" instructions, or specific questions to guide observations. The culminating assignment generally consists of copying the experiment from the blackboard.

The arithmetic program stresses the most economic way of solving a computation problem. The emphasis is on practicing the correct response. Children are taught "one way" of doing things, in order to avoid confusion. The practice material is usually in the form of exercises rather than problem situations.

This school of thought tends to welcome programmed instruction and teaching machines as a most promising approach in meeting the learning limitations of the disadvantaged child. Programmed instruction is valued as very structured and graded material which moves the learner directly from one step (frame) to another. Immediate reward is built into the program so that the learner knows whether he is right or wrong at each step along the way. Teaching machines are seen as the ultimate in the use of programming and as meeting the needs of the "motoric style of learning" of the disadvantaged child.

The position under discussion stresses the importance of a resourceful teacher; a teacher who is inventive in the use of a variety of audio-visual materials, who is very orderly and systematic, and one who utilizes concrete materials and introduces many activities. Most important, this approach values a strong teacher who is continuously able to motivate children to move from one activity to the other.

Perhaps, this position can be best summarized by a statement of one of its advocates, speaking about the desired approach to working with the disadvantaged child. "You must have your groundwork laid before you are ready to spread your wings." The focus is definitely on the "groundwork."

altering the learning style

In contrast to the previous emphasis on the "groundwork," the second teaching style is dedicated to "spreading your wings," that is, the development of the learner's power to think. The intellectual limitations of the disadvantaged are not seen as a fixed entity nor as a *fait accompli*. Therefore, rather than adjusting to the relatively passive orientation of the disadvantaged toward reality and toward learning, the second position attempts to *alter his orientation and his learning style*.

According to this approach the desired teaching style for the disadvantaged is that of providing a climate which gives the learner continuous experiences of practicing his power of being less passive and more active; less powerless and more powerful; less of an object and more a subject, and most important, less of a recipient of predigested material and more a participant in perpetually emerging new learning and experiences. How can this goal be translated into teaching? An examination of some curricular practices and issues may be helpful in throwing light on this question.

reading: a thinking process

The unfortunate position is often stated that the objective in the primary school grades is "learning to read" rather than "reading to learn." This position overlooks the role of reading as an instrument for developing thinking. Whether the reader is a child or man, the book is as good as its effect on him. The teaching of the disadvantaged, too, calls for an approach which continuously explores the personal meaning of the reading content to the reader.

Issues on mechanistic problems, such as the introduction of the Initial Training Alphabet, the controversy of sight vocabulary versus phonics, or the role of reading machines, are only secondary in importance. What counts is the development of an active reader who "controls" the reading matter, that is, reacts, generalizes, criticizes, compares, interprets, chooses, and in various ways relates to what he reads in a meaningful, personal manner.

In the primary grades, helping the reader explore the main idea of the story should already be started. Exploring the motivation and behavior of the characters, the moral of the story in terms of human values or its relationship to experiences observed by the reader, need to be dealt with.

As an example, here is a story generally taught to third graders. It is a story portraying a fisherman who deserts his village, which is situated on a mountain, to live by himself on the seashore in order to be able to spend his time fishing. He makes much more money than he did before. However, he also becomes an unhappy and isolated person.

In reading this story, even young children can explore the conflict of values between the desire for material success and the need for human communication. The message in the story is not stated explicity. It is portrayed in concrete terms. One has to move from the concrete to the abstract in order to achieve comprehension and compassion.

I have seen, many times, Haiku poems taught to children. The preoccupation with the formal features of the poem (such as non-rhyming or the 5:7:5 syllable setting) tends to subvert the teacher from focusing on interpretation. In a recent visit to a disadvantaged group this was not the case. Here is part of the record. The teacher reads a poem from the blackboard:

> O, moon, why must you
> inspire my neighbor to chirp
> all night on a flute!

Teacher: What do you think of this poem?
Child A: Well, the man is angry and he wants to go to sleep but he can't because his neighbor is playing the flute.
Child B: It's not a man. It's a bird.
Child A: No, it's a man.
Child C: It's a bird because it chirps.
Child A: But it can't be a bird because a bird can't play a flute.
Teacher: What do you think, class. Is it a bird or a man?
Child D: Really, the poem does not say. It is so short.
Child E: It's up to you to decide. The poem does not say.
Child A: This man is tired and it's late and he is trying to sleep.
Teacher: How do you know he is tired?
Child F: Maybe he is not tired. I think he is jealous that the other musician plays so well. He would like to play all night.

This is a down-to-earth illustration of how a teacher's encouragement of interpretation and divergent thinking helps a group of children experience the power of moving away from boundedness to the model and realize that they have an active role to play in creating meaning. With such encouragement, the child may gradually learn that subject matter is not only the domain of the powerful people—the author and the teacher; it is also the domain of the potentially powerful reader.

Riessman says that[R4:70]

. . . deprived children for the most part are not introspective, nor are they greatly concerned with the self. They respond much more to the external, to the outside. . . . They are rather more likely to see the cause of their problems in external forces.

There is an urgent need for reading material for children which focuses on the psychological problems confronting people, their difficulty in deciding what is right and what is wrong, their conflict between expediency and justice, between utilitarianism on one hand, and ethics and aesthetics on the other; there is a need for children's literature which centers on the conflicts of morality.

In discussing the problem of moving from learning to thinking, Bruner says:[B10:186]

The Pablum School readers, stripped of rich imagery in the interest of readability, stripped of passion in the erroneous belief that the deeper human conditions will not interest the child—these are no more the vehicles of getting over the barrier to thinking than are the methods of teaching mathematics by a rote parroting at the blackboard.

In one century, education has moved from the moralism and adult-centeredness of the McGuffey[M5] readers toward the too often childish basal reader material. The first stresses the adult morality of a certain era, ignoring readability and children's interest. The second is preoccupied with controlled vocabulary and the childish aspects of the youngster's life, sacrificing literary quality.[G7]

Perhaps reading material for children should draw on the positive aspects of the two extremes under discussion: the stress on human values and moral issues (as they are perceived *today*), along with stress on readability and child experience characterizing the modern basal reader. There is a crucial need for children's literature which helps the relatively concrete-minded, ethnocentric learner of disadvantaged origin to feel compassion, to weigh issues, to experience the sense of power of the one who evaluates, and to become more flexible in his mode of thinking.

from the concrete to the abstract

Dewey[D8] criticized the rigidity and formalistic nature of the curriculum and stressed the importance of the activity, the concrete materials and the first-hand experience. Today, says

Bruner,[B11] the central question is how to utilize experiences and activity as a springboard to a higher level of abstraction; how to move from empiricism to constructionism.

Mere participation in an activity may mean low-level learning. Some proponents of the "experience curriculum" emphasized physical activity, but made little effort to generalize activities and discover their meaning. In some cases the curriculum was composed mainly of "doing experiences" for the sake of doing. As one writer puts it:[S4:294]

Thus a teacher who has faithfully learned to guide children through the life processes of the Pueblo Indians helps children to grind corn with a mortar and pestle, but is not sure why she does this, except that "the Indians did it."

On the other hand, lack of attention to the experience, the concrete data, or the activity often leads to difficulty in reaching meaningful generalizations. The following record of a teaching behavior may illustrate this point.

The teacher reads a poem "My Shadow" by Stevenson, describing its relation to the child. The class, composed of Puerto Rican children, listens carefully. The poem is enjoyable but I don't sense any reaction in their faces.
The teacher asks: "What does the poem say?" There is dead silence. The teacher calls on a bright girl: "Angela, what does the poem say?" No reply. It seems that the images in the poem did not arouse much in the children. They did not see the play between the shadow and the child.
The teacher calls Angela to come and stand in front of a projector. She starts the projector. The girl's shadow is seen on the wall. I sense that the class starts to understand the relationship. The teacher shuts the projector—no shadow; opens it—the shadow appears again. Angela moves toward the wall, away from the projector and the shadow becomes smaller. She moves back towards the projector; the shadow becomes bigger.
The class is excited. The children are ready to move toward the abstract and draw simple generalizations: The shadow of an object is made by the interruption of light that falls on it. If you move the object closer to the light, the shadow increases. If you move it further away, the shadow becomes smaller.

Once again, the teacher reads the poem "My Shadow." The children react to it and speak about the generalizations made before as they are expressed in the poem.

I have described this episode in some detail to illustrate how the concrete can be used to moved toward the far-reaching abstract. It is mainly in the area of science where the teaching style is commonly viewed by teachers as movement from the concrete to the abstract and where concept formation is viewed as being as significant as the factual subject matter itself. The major factor responsible for this relative success is the emphasis on experimentation and on inductive and deductive processes of thinking.

In social studies where the main goal should be the development of concepts about relationships between men and between man and his environment, one often observes the unfortunate tendency to operate on the level of specificity of information and aggregated facts. In many respects it is more difficult to demonstrate and develop social studies than science concepts. The teacher must be aware of these difficulties and continuously ask himself the question: Is my teaching limited to the transmission of information, or am I engaged in the development of concept formation?

Similar questions may be raised with regard to reading material. Because stories tend to have an exciting plot, raise tension and suspense or may be humorous, they may often serve as entertainment and may thus subvert the reader (and the teacher) from raising the question—What is the abstract idea that the concrete description attempts to convey? For instance, a Chinese story tells about a tiger who devours a boy. The boy's mother is *angry* at losing her supporting son, and she demands that the tiger be killed. However, when the tiger is caught, the suggestion is made that rather than being killed, the tiger will substitute for the dead son and will support the mother.

Children tend to read the story with excitement; they pay attention to the plot and sometimes fail to consider the concept of punishment conveyed by the legend, or the expectations of the mother from a son, which are so different than the expectations in this country.

Movement from the concrete to the abstract is central in altering the learning style of the disadvantaged learner. This movement calls primarily for two approaches: (1) Present concrete data and ask for generalizations, and (2) present generalizations and ask for specific and concrete illustrations. Any attempt to deal with concrete data without moving to the abstract may result in an additive approach to learning —storage of discrete facts. Any attempt to deal with the abstract without using the concrete, may lead to formalistic learning and glib generalizations. The movement from the concrete to the abstract should be perceived as an interactive process of the two factors.

the activation of the learner

In his study entitled *Equality of Educational Opportunity*, Coleman says:[C3:23]

A pupil attitude factor which appears to have a stronger relationship to achievement than do all the school factors together, is the extent to which an individual feels that he has some control over his own destiny . . .

Minority pupils, except for Orientals, have far less conviction than whites that they can affect their own environment and future. When they do however, their achievement is higher than that of whites who lack conviction.

What can be done to activate the disadvantaged child; to promote his self-image as the one who can influence his future, initiate, be enterprising, and be in control? A major answer, I believe, is in a school climate which provides the child with continuous opportunities to initiate ideas, to make plans, to make mistakes and revise his plans in the light of the mistakes, to work independently toward a long-range goal; in brief, to experience the opportunity to lead and be in control. These ideas were developed in previous chapters of this book. I will present only several examples to illustrate these points.

Examine the following instructions given by a primary teacher.

We are going to find out what wind does to the sailboat. [Puts the objective on the blackboard.] Take out the bottom of the milk container that I gave you. It has a hole. Put it down on your desk. Now watch carefully that you do not make a mistake. Take your paper first. Take a pencil and draw the sail. [Shows on the blackboard.] Do not make the sail too big because it will not fit the boat. [Waits until the children finish cutting the sail.] Now, make two holes in the paper, one here and one there . . .

This not atypical episode is an integral part of a style of teaching which perceives the learner as incapable of thinking and planning independently and lacking in intellectual resources and initiative. It is a clear-cut issue of "follow the leader." The only leader is the teacher. Children cannot be leaders, only followers. What counts is the achievement of the goal—making a sailboat. The activation of the child's potential and resourcefulness is entirely overlooked.

A more constructive approach to the solution of the same problem would be to ask pupils to make suggestions on how to construct the needed sailboat. Main points of discussion could be the design of the sailboat, the needed materials, the sequence of activities, and the expected difficulties. Let the disadvantaged child learn to follow instructions, but let him have the same opportunity *to plan ahead*. The school tends to overemphasize the first and neglect the second.

A novice teacher who tried a "planning ahead" approach to the above problem reported that the children made many mistakes. They designed a sail which did not fit the boat. They blew wind on a sail when its wide surface was not opposite the blowing source. The fact that the pupils encountered difficulties only enriched the lesson. They learned to cope with difficulties. They learned that they have to try to predict and plan for possible obstacles.

Examine the following episode of a teacher guiding observation of seeds in a science lesson.

Teacher:	What do you see?
Child:	Little brown seeds.
Teacher:	How are they different?
Child:	They are different colors and shapes.

Teacher:	[Distributes some lima beans that have been soaked in water.] Are the wet beans larger?
Child:	They are larger than the dry ones.
Teacher:	How is the skin?
Child:	Softer.
Teacher:	Try to peel it off.
Child:	It is easy to do it.
Teacher:	What is inside?
Child:	A baby plant.

There is no attempt here to underestimate the strength of this approach to observation. It is experiential in nature and leads to meaningful concepts about seeds. It generally arouses the enthusiasm of primary school children. However, despite this positive contribution, the example illustrates the spoon-feeding of step-by-step structuring. In reply to a question, the child's function is limited to one act: "Are the wet beans larger than the dry beans? Are they softer? Where is the baby plant?"

In developing this lesson, it is possible to replace the scores of minute questions with one major task: "Observe the various seeds (apple, dry and wet lima beans), 'manipulate' them, and be ready to present a report." Under this setup the child has to work independently or in small groups for a certain period, putting things together and creating his own sense of order. The teacher's function is to guide the discussion and further observation on the basis of the presented reports.

Despite the fact that in both approaches children may come out with similar information, in terms of the activation of the learner they travel through different routes. In the first route a "powerful person" moves others by his continuous questions. With each question the learner moves a step ahead and waits for the second command to move. His field of vision, his power of aspiration, are limited to one-step distance. The second route is triggered by the teacher, but from here on the learner is free to move on his own. He takes many steps. Only the sense of his resourcefulness and the nature of the observed objects limit his exploration. He learns to create order on his own and to prepare himself for the challenge of further questions and information to come from the teacher and his peers.

The activation of the learner does not only mean that a teacher should be "nice," accepting, supporting, and interesting. It calls for a teacher to structure learning tasks which provide the learner with a field to stretch and a guidepost to use while he moves in his exploration and planning ahead.

The reader is invited to examine some typical activities conducted by teachers in terms of the principle of the activation of the learner. Here are some questions which may be asked:

Do children plan the science experiment, or is it a pseudo-experiment dictated by the teacher?

Do children plan the dramatization by discussing the nature of the characters and the major ideas they want to convey, or is it wholly directed by the teacher?

What is the nature of planning and initiation of new ideas which occurs in committee work?

Do all children have to do the same thing at the same time, or are there sometimes provisions for children to make choices, to suggest a sense of direction, or to work on their own project?

What is the number of choices made by children, as opposed to the number of choices made by the teacher in a specific lesson? Can the first be increased?

The trend to extend the school day in disadvantaged communities brings the principle of the activation of the learner into sharper focus. What will be the nature of the curriculum of the extended school day? It seems that the educational practitioner was quick to demand financial support for the extended-day organizational structure, but was relatively slow to develop the principles guiding instruction. Are we going to move from a six-hour day to an eight-hour day and merely change the time extension?

There is a need to examine the educational philosophy

underlying all these projects and plan research to evaluate the ways in which the extended school time is used by different communities. In the light of the discussion on the activation of the learner, it is possible to suggest that this principle become the major guideline in deciding the curriculum of the new organization. In contrast to the secondary school, and in contrast to elementary schools in some other countries, the American elementary school tends to lack extracurricular activities.

The extended school day may be devoted primarily to the pursuit of individual and group projects. The time may be used to develop clubs for literature and writing, publishing newspapers, art, dramatization, science, community affairs, etc. In these clubs the emphasis should be on the learner as he individually or collectively plans and decides on the nature of his activities and as he evaluates his own or his group process.

In brief, in order to alter the relatively passive learning style of the disadvantaged, he must continuously practice the role of an "active learner." He should experience daily, in the most simple school activities, the feeling of being in control of his actions. He should become less an object that is moved and more a force which moves on his own initiative.

curiosity: from the known to the unknown

An integral aspect of the relative passivity, boundedness, and concrete thinking of the disadvantaged learner is a deficiency in curiosity, in the desire to move from the known to the unknown. Metaphorically speaking, the disadvantaged feels secure only in his own native territory. He does not dare to emerge and explore new horizons.

Altering the learning style of the disadvantaged learner implies helping him to "spread his wings" and venture out from his own sheltered nest. It means helping him become intellectually curious and daring enough to move from the known to the unknown. How can this principle permeate teaching?

In my observation of teachers in classrooms, I often spend a full day in a school without hearing one question raised by children. I am not referring to questions such as "May I go to the bathroom?" or "Should I start on a new page?" but rather, questions which express an intrinsic desire for knowledge.

Encouraging children to raise questions is a function which is seriously neglected in the schools. The school is often referred to as a strange institution where the one who knows, the teacher, raises all the questions, and those who do not know, the pupils, give all the answers.

Both Getzels[G2] and Torrance[T4] assess the ability to raise questions and identify problems as one of the indices of produtive thinking. To raise a question may often mean to be open to an experience and the desire to pursue knowledge. The ability to raise questions is as important as the ability to find the answers.

The disadvantaged learner should be taught to raise questions. Here are a few examples of how this can be done:

Show a diagram of a plant and ask the children to raise as many questions as possible about it. Build the lesson around the questions.

After completing a science lesson about the poles of the magnet, assign as seatwork the task of raising three questions related to the conclusions. In the next lesson summarize and categorize all the questions and base the lesson on some of the reported questions.

Have a permanent bulletin board devoted to the questions raised by children. Encourage children to pursue individually or in small groups some of these questions.

Encourage children to raise questions about their readings, fiction and non-fiction. You may find the newspaper as very useful data for this purpose.

Present children with arithmetical data or "stories," but *without* indicating the question. Ask them to identify the problem, or problems.

Play the game "Twenty Questions."

Another approach to the promotion of curiosity is through

encouraging children to develop an interest of their own, a hobby, or a taste for a specific activity. A balanced curriculum calls for a core of subject matter required of all children and interest areas of learning which are left to the choice and the taste of the individual learner.

It is my observation that a constructive balance between the required core and the aspect of the individual's choice is reached primarily in classes of bright children. When it comes to the disadvantaged learner, the tendency is to stress the core of uniformity and to neglect the individual interest. For instance, individualized reading is generally a much more prevalent practice in classes of affluent rather than deprived children.

The motto of the individualized reading movement is seeking, self-selection, and pacing.[M10] In the past, attention was given primarily to "pacing." The need to develop curiosity and desire to move from the known to the unknown calls for giving equal stress to the values inherent in "seeking" (the importance of the child's desire to look for a book) and in "self-selection" (the importance of the child's choosing a book in terms of his interest).

People who do not care, who are lukewarm about things, find it difficult to learn. A school curriculum stressing uniformity is not conducive to the development of curious learners. In teaching the disadvantaged, the curricular aspect of individual interest and choice should be enhanced. This can be encouraged by a library-centered reading program, individual projects, the development of hobbies, and the development of clubs devoted to the pursuit of learning.

One of the tragic aspects in the lives of many deprived children is that they fail to learn to be intellectually curious. Very early in life their curiosity is not rewarded by the parents. The adult rarely listens to them, does not enjoy their questions, does not try to answer, or does not encourage them to explore.[D5] The end result is that their intellectual curiosity does not blossom. The changing of the passive orientation of the disadvantaged child toward intellectual functioning calls for a concentrated effort on releasing and promoting curiosity.

the quality of
the educational experience

The first chapter of the book *Dark Ghetto* (entitled "The Cry of the Ghetto") consists of data from interviews with Harlem residents. Most of them speak about their despair and only very few about their hopes.[C2:1-10]

A lot of times, when I'm working, I become as despondent as hell and I feel like crying. I'm not a man, none of us are men! I don't own anything. I'm not a man enough to own a store, none of us are.

No one with a mop can expect respect from a banker, or an attorney, or men who create jobs, and all you have is a mop. Are you crazy? Whoever heard of integration between a mop and a banker?

I would like to be the first Negro President!

As the most deprived group in the U.S.A. is demanding its rights for equality of opportunity and equality of results, it is difficult to foresee where the Negro revolution is going. Is it going to be taken over by extremists, or is it going to be led by responsible leaders devoted to constructive social action? As one Negro minister put it: "Will despair explode into 'Burn Baby Burn,' or will progress promote 'Learn Baby Learn' and the healthy integration of the Negro group into the mainstream of American life?"

The responsible leadership in this country, both white and Negro, is convinced that the answer to this question depends to a great extent on the school. Perhaps more than ever before formalized education is seen as the major channel for progress and the resolution of internal social strife.

The ideal is noble and the challenge is great. But the time has come to raise certain questions: Is the school moving toward the ideal, and is there evidence of progress in meeting the challenge? Is our trust in what education can do justifiable?

The United States Commission on Civil Rights in a recent study[H6] presents information related to this question. It states that academic performance of Negroes is higher when classes are integrated. For instance, the grade-level performance of disadvantaged twelfth grade Negroes (in a study based on a northeastern metropolitan community) is grade level seven where no white students are in class. It is at the eight and a half grade level where more than half the class consists of disadvantaged whites.

The above progress suggests that school integration has a positive impact on disadvantaged Negro children in terms of achievement. However, this positive impact is not sufficient to equalize the achievement of Negro and white children. In other words, even if by some miraculous act school integration should be fully achieved, the average disadvantaged Negro child would still tend to lag in his performance.

Integration is a helpful measure toward upgrading intellectual functioning, aspiration, and self-confidence of the disadvantaged Negro child. However, it does not seem to be sufficient. There is an urgent need, in addition, for *compensatory education.*

Spurred by the hopes invested in compensatory education, vigorous attempts are being made all over the country to inaugurate programs to bridge the gap of scholastic achievement between the disadvantaged and affluent learner. But again, we must face a question as to the success of these efforts.

The answer to this question, as suggested in recent evaluation studies, is not encouraging. For instance, the abovementioned study of the United States Commission on Civil Rights,[H6] and the Coleman report on *Equality of Educational Opportunity,*[C3] conclude that the efforts to upgrade the education of children in ghetto schools through compensatory education have been of *limited effectiveness.* Similar conclusions were reached by other teams of researchers in evaluation studies which were never published.

Why is compensatory education limited in its effectiveness? Why isn't the progress made much quicker? The basic answer, I believe, can be understood in the light of the discussion in this chapter. It seems that compensatory education is based on the belief in the miraculous healing power of quantitative, additive, and administrative solutions. What is often lacking is sufficient *thinking through* of the educational philosophy underlying new projects. The thinking is quantitative and additive rather than *qualitative*.[G5]

An excellent illustration of preoccupation with quantity and de-emphasis of quality is the best-publicized Head Start program. This program provides children with educational experiences during the summer to prepare them for first grade. I had several opportunities to discuss this project with college students who served in the capacity of teachers in various parts of New York City. The picture portrayed suggests that the only common denominator denoting the program is the existence of children, teachers, shelter, and equipment. In terms of the *quality* of the educational experience, the programs ranged on a continuum from babysitting setups to rich and meaningful climates.

An attempt to evaluate the effectiveness of the above Head Start project may find "limited progress." When the statistics are computed for the *total* city, the scores of the successful and the poor programs will cancel each other and the average will tend to show "limited effectiveness."

The comprehensive research project entitled *Equality of Educational Opportunity*,[C3] suggests that enriching school facilities, such as school libraries or science laboratories, shows *small* relationship to the achievement of disadvantaged children. Why is the relationship "small"? Is the implication for action that school libraries and science laboratories are of little value?

Again, I believe the above research study has failed to distinguish between quantity and quality. It is very possible that if one measures the general impact of the existence of school libraries on disadvantaged children the result will be "small gains." School libraries differ tremendously in their educational climate. Libraries range from mere physical facilities for storing books, to a setup of consultative relationship between librarian and reader. Science laboratories range in their *use* from poorly or well-equipped rooms where a teacher presents a science lecture, to a laboratory where children conduct meaningful experiments.

Any attempt to evaluate the scholastic gains achieved by the initiation of a new educational facility should take into consideration that the existence of a facility or a program, and its proper use, are not identical. There is an urgent need for a new research approach to evaluation which will attempt to tap the neglected factor of *quality*.

These studies should not only stress the effectiveness of a certain innovation in terms of its impact on the disadvantaged learner, but should also delve into the question of whether the same innovation is effective in some schools and fails in others. There is an urgent need for research which attempts to identify the characteristics of a specific program (for instance, language laboratories) in terms of the ways it is put into practice. The emphasis should be on the operative qualities of successful versus non-successful attempts to implement the same educational innovation.

I believe a research approach of this nature will give further impetus to the movement of compensatory education and will channel the energy of the innovators into a continuous search for improving the *quality* of the educational climate.

The discussion in this chapter attempted to conceptualize a theoretical model of teaching style for the disadvantaged learner as an integral part of an educational philosophy which views curriculum change and learning as primarily qualitative rather than quantitative processes.

selected bibliography

COLEMAN, JAMES, *Equality of Educational Opportunity*. Washington, D.C.: Office of Education, 1966. A most comprehensive study dealing with the comparative educational status of the disadvantaged learner.

FRANKENSTEIN, CARL, "The School Without Parents," in Dushkin A. and Frankenstein C. (Editors) *Studies in Education*. Jerusalem: The Magness Press, 1963. A psychoanalytically oriented discussion dealing with the personality development of the disadvantaged learner and the role of the school.

GOLDBERG, MIRIAM, *Methods and Materials for Educationally Disadvantaged Youth.* H.M.L.I., Teachers College, Columbia University, 1963. A critical analysis of the major approaches to the education of the disadvantaged learner.

foreign countries

AUSUBEL, DAVID, *Maori Youth.* New York: Holt, Rinehart and Winston, Inc., 1965. A study of the problem of disadvantaged youth in New Zealand.

BERNSTEIN, BASIL, "Social Class and Linguistic Development," in Halsey, A. H. (Editor), *Education, Economy and Society.* New York: The Free Press of Glencoe, 1961. A research study conducted in England.

FEUERSTEIN, R. and RICHELLE, M., *Children of the Mellah.* Jerusalem: The Szold Foundation, 1963 (In Hebrew). A study of children in the ghetto of Casablanca.

SHUMSKY, ABRAHAM, *The Clash of Cultures in Israel.* New York: Bureau of Publications, Teachers College, Columbia University, 1955. A discussion of the disadvantaged child in Israel.

epilogue:

son of man, stand upon thy feet and I will speak unto thee

The observer, who spends some time in schools, listens to teachers questioning pupils, examines assignments, tests, workbooks and teachers' guides, cannot but he be impressed by the repetitive orientation of many of our schools. Foshay, in his presidential address to an educational convention, makes the point which undoubtedly expresses the critique of many toward prevalent educational practice:[F3:15]

We pedagogues have brought up a whole population that does not know the difference between grammar and composition because we taught the one in the name of the other. Similarly we have taught prosody in the name of poetry, thus killing poetry in our culture.

The problem confronting the educator is how to change the lack of balance at school—how to move from over accentuation on specificity, retention, and repetition, to a balanced curriculum which gives equal stress to productive thinking. What is needed is a change in the total intellectual atmosphere of the school. To quote from *Creativity and Intelligence*:[G3:127]

Are there certain areas of instruction in which opportunities are promoted for "discovering" as well as for "remembering?" Is there provision in the curriculum for playing with facts and ideas as well as for repeating them? Can we teach students to be more sensitive to the nature of problems? Can we teach them that a problem may have several different interpretations and solutions? Even if there is only one right answer, as in mathematics problems, can the student solve the problem in a number of different ways?

This book attempts to conceptualize and illustrate the teaching style which aims at the promotion of intellectual functioning. It attempts to look at intellectual functioning as an integral aspect of personality development.

The common position stressed in the educational and the psychological literature is that mental hygiene has an important role to play in learning. For instance, when emotional problems interfere with learning reading, the prerequisite to the improvement of reading should be the treatment of the emotional problems. The attempt, here, was to go a step further and suggest that while psychological well-being does have an impact on thinking, the promotion of thinking has no lesser effect on the emotional growth of the learner.

This study brought evidence to support the existence of a direct relationship between an assertive personal orientation toward reality and success in intellectual functioning. It is the person who looks at life with confidence, who feels that it is within his power to aspire toward a goal and achieve it, who will tend also to be successful in his learning ability. And inversely, the individual who experiences helplessness, who feels that he is a cog in an impersonal machine, tends to feel that he cannot control his destiny or intellectual problems.

A typical orientation of the educational practitioner is that working on the lack of confidence is conducive to the growth of intellectual functioning. This study is adding another dimension to the above common educational approach. The hypothesis is that improvement of intellectual functioning is conducive to a more positive attitude of confidence and assertiveness toward reality.[F5]

Teaching toward productive thinking is seen as a climate which provides the learner with continuous opportunities of being less passive and more active, less powerless and more powerful, less an object and more a self-directed subject, less bound to the concrete and more mobile and able to fly toward the abstract.

The prophet Ezekiel says:

I fell upon my face and I heard a voice of one that spake. And he said unto me, son of man, stand upon thy feet, and I will speak unto thee.

And the spirit entered into me when he spake unto me, and set me upon my feet, that I heard him that spake unto me.

In the symbolic language of the Bible the point is made that one cannot learn in a passive position and state of mind; he must rather, "stand on his feet!"

bibliography

A1 AMIDON, EDMUND and HUNTER, ELIZABETH, *Improving Teaching*. New York: Holt, Rinehart and Winston, Inc., 1966.

A2 AUSTIN, MARY, *The First R*. New York: The Macmillan Company, 1963.

A3 ————, *The Torch Lighters*. Cambridge: Harvard University Press, 1961.

A4 AUSUBEL, DAVID, *Maori Youth*. New York: Holt, Rinehart and Winston, Inc., 1965.

A5 AXLINE, VIRGINIA, *Play Therapy*. Boston: Houghton Mifflin Company, 1947.

B1 BALDWIN, JAMES, *The Fire Next Time*. New York: The Dial Press, Inc., 1963.

B2 BARRON, FRANK, "The Psychology of Imagination." *Scientific American*, Vol. 199 (September, 1958), No. 3.

B3 BARTLETT, FREDERIC, *Thinking*. New York: Basic Books, Inc., Publishers, 1958.

B4 BELLACK, ARNO (Editor), *Theory and Research in Teaching*. New York: Bureau of Publications, Teachers College, Columbia University, 1963.

B5 BERNSTEIN, BASIL, "Social Class and Linguistic Development," in Halsey, A. H. (Editor), *Education, Economy and Society*. New York: The Free Press of Glencoe, 1961.

B6 BIBER, BARBARA, *Premature Structuring as a Deterrent to Creativity*. New York: Bank Street College of Education, 1959.

B7 BLOOM, BENJAMIN, DAVIS, ALLISON, and HESS, ROBERT, *Compensatory Education for Cultural Deprivation*. New York: Holt, Rinehart and Winston, Inc., 1965.

B8 BLOOM, BENJAMIN (Editor), *Taxonomy of Educational Objectives*. New York: Longmans, Green & Co., Inc., 1956.

B9 BROWN, THOMAS and BANICH, SERAFINA, *Student Teaching in the Elementary School*. New York: Harper & Row, Publishers, 1962.

B10 BRUNER, JEROME S., "Learning and Thinking." *Harvard Education Review*, Vol. 29 (1959).

B11   ——, *On Knowing*. Cambridge: Harvard University Press, 1962.

B12   ——, *The Process of Education*. Cambridge: Harvard University Press, 1960.

B13   ——, GOODNOW, JACQUELINE, and AUSTIN, GEORGE, *A Study of Thinking*. New York: John Wiley & Sons, Inc., 1956.

B14   BURTON, WILLIAM H., "Education and Social Class in the United States." *Harvard Education Review*, Vol. 23 (Fall, 1953), No. 4.

B15   ——, *The Guidance of Learning Activities*. New York: Appleton-Century-Crofts, 1962.

C1   CHESS, STELLA, *Your Child is a Person*. New York: The Viking Press, Inc., 1965.

C2   CLARK, KENNETH B., *Dark Ghetto*. New York: Harper & Row, Publishers, 1965.

C3   COLEMAN, JAMES, *Equality of Educational Opportunity*. Washington, D.C.: Office of Education, 1966.

C4   CONANT, JAMES, *The Education of American Teachers*. New York: McGraw-Hill Book Company, Inc., 1963.

C5   CREMIN, LAWRENCE, *The Transformation of the School*. New York: Alfred A. Knopf, Inc., 1961.

C6   CUNNINGHAM, RUTH, *Understanding Group Behavior of Boys and Girls*. New York: Bureau of Publications, Teachers College, Columbia University, 1951.

D1   DAVIDSON, HELEN, *Satisfying and Stressful Experiences of Student Teachers*. New York: Office of Education Research, The City College, 1960. Mimeographed.

D2   —— and LANG, GERHALD, "Children's Perceptions of Their Teachers' Feelings Towards Them Related to Self Perception, School Achievement and Behavior." *The Journal of Experimental Education*, Vol. 29 (1960).

D3   DAVIS, ALLISON, *Social Class Influences Upon Learning*. Cambridge: Harvard University Press, 1951.

D4   DEANS, EDWINA, *Elementary School Mathematics: New Directions*. Washington, D.C.: U.S. Department of Health, Education, and Welfare, 1963.

D5   DEUTSCH, MARTIN, *Minority Group Class Status as Related to Social and Personality Factors in Scholastic Achievement*. Society for Applied Anthropology, Monograph No. 2 (1960).

D6   ——, "The Disadvantaged Child and the Learning Process," in Passow, A. Harry, *Education in Depressed Areas*. New York: Bureau of Publications, Teachers College, Columbia University, 1962.

D7   D'EVELYN, KATHERINE E., *Meeting Children's Emotional Needs*. Englewood Cliffs, N.J.: Prentice-Hall, Inc., 1959.

D8   DEWEY, JOHN, *The Child and the Curriculum*. Chicago: University of Chicago Press, 1902.

D9   DUKER, SAM, "Basics in Critical Listening." *The English Journal*, (November, 1962).

D10   DUNFEE, MAXINE and GREENLEE, JULIAN, *Elementary School Science: Research, Theory and Practice*. Washington, D.C.: ASCD, 1957.

E1   EELLS, KENNETH, *Intelligence and Cultural Differences*. Chicago: University of Chicago Press, 1951.

F1   FEUERSTEIN, R. and RICHELLE, M., *Children of the Mellah*. Jerusalem: The Szold Foundation, 1963 (In Hebrew).

F2   FLEMING, ROBERT S. (Editor), *Curriculum for Today's Boys and Girls*. Columbus, Ohio: Charles E. Merrill Books, Inc., 1963.

F3   FOSHAY, ARTHUR, *A Modest Proposal for the Improvement of Education*. New York: Teachers College, Bureau of Publications, Columbia University, March, 1961. Mimeographed.

F4   FOX, RAYMOND, "Factors Influencing the Career Choice of Prospective Teachers." *The Journal of Teacher Education* (December, 1961).

F5   FRANKENSTEIN, CARL, "The School Without Parents," in Dushkin, A. and Frankenstein, C. (Editors), *Studies in Education*. Jerusalem: The Magness Press, 1963.

F6   FROMM, ERICH, *Escape from Freedom*. New York: Holt, Rinehart and Winston, Inc., 1941.

G1   GAGE, N. L., *Handbook of Research on Teaching*. Chicago: Rand McNally & Company, 1962.

G2   GETZELS, JACOB and JACKSON, PHILIP, "A Study of Giftedness," in *The Gifted Student*. U.S. Office of Education, Cooperative Research Monograph OE-35916 (1960).

G3   ———, *Creativity and Intelligence*. New York: John Wiley & Sons, Inc., 1962.

G4   GLAZER, NATHAN and MOYNIHAN, DANIEL, *Beyond the Melting Pot*. Cambridge: The M.I.T. Press, 1963.

G5   GOLDBERG, MIRIAM, *Methods and Materials for Educationally Disadvantaged Youth*. H.M.L.I., Teachers College, Columbia University, 1963 (Mimeographed).

G6   GRAY, S. WILLIAM (Editor), *Before We Read*. Chicago: Scott, Foresman and Company, 1951.

G7   ———, *The New Friends and Neighbors*. Chicago: Scott, Foresman and Company, 1952.

G8   GUILFORD, J. P., *A Revised Structure of Intellect.* Los An-
           geles: Reports from the Psychological Laboratory, No.
           19, University of Southern California, April 1957.

H1   HANNA, LAVONE, POTTER, GLADYS, and HAGAMAN, NEVA,
           Unit Teaching in the Elementary School. New York:
           Holt, Rinehart and Winston, Inc., 1963.

H2   HARGRAVE, ROWENA, *Building Reading Skills.* Wichita, Kan-
           sas: McCormick-Mathers Publishing Company, Inc.,
           1960.

H3   HARRINGTON, MICHAEL, *The Other America.* New York: The
           Macmillan Company, 1962.

H4   HAVIGHURST, ROBERT and NEUGARTEN, BERNICE, *Society and
           Education.* Boston: Allyn and Bacon, Inc., 1957.

H5   HEATON, MARGARET, *Feelings are Facts.* New York: National
           Conference of Christians and Jews, 1952.

H6   HECHINGER, FRED M., "Integrated Versus Compensated."
           The New York Times, February 26, 1967.

H7   HEIL, M. LOUIS, POWELL, MARION, and FEIFER, IRWIN, *Char-
           acteristics of Teacher Behavior Related to the Achieve-
           ment of Children in Several Elementary Grades.* New
           York: Brooklyn College, 1960.

H8   HERRIOT, ROBERT E., *Social Class and the Urban School.* New
           York: John Wiley & Sons, Inc., 1966.

H9   HESS, ROBERT, "Maternal Teaching Styles and Educational
           Retardation," in Torrance, E. Paul and Strom, Robert
           (Editors), *Mental Health and Achievement.* New York:
           John Wiley & Sons, Inc., 1965.

H10   HILDRETH, GERTRUDE, "Learning to Read with McGuffey."
           Elementary School Journal, Vol. LXII (April, 1962).

H11   HILGARD, ERNEST, *Theories of Learning.* New York: Apple-
           ton-Century-Crofts, 1948.

H12   HOFFMAN, BANESH, "The Tyranny of Multiple-Choice Tests."
           Harper's Magazine, March, 1961.

H13   HOLLINGSHEAD, AUGUST, *Elmtown's Youth.* New York: John
           Wiley & Sons, Inc., 1949.

H14   HOLT, JOHN, *How Children Fail.* New York: Dell Publishing
           Company, Inc., 1965.

H15   HUGHES, MARIE, *Assessment of the Quality of Teaching in
           Elementary Schools.* Salt Lake City, Utah: University of
           Utah Press, 1959.

H16   HUNTER, ELIZABETH and AMIDON, EDMUND, *Student Teach-
           ing: Cases and Comments.* New York: Holt, Rinehart and
           Winston, Inc., 1964.

H17   HYMES, JAMES, *Discipline*. New York: Bureau of Publications, Teachers College, Columbia University, 1962.

J1   JENNING, HELEN HALL, *Sociometry in Group Relations*. Washington, D.C.: American Council on Education, 1959.

K1   KELLEY, EARL, *Education for What is Real*. New York: Harper & Row, Publishers, 1947.

K2   ————, *The Workshop Way of Learning*. New York: Harper & Row, Publishers, 1951.

K3   KENWORTHY, LEONARD, "Ferment in the Social Studies." *Phi Delta Kappan*, October, 1962.

K4   KIEL, NORMAN, "The Myth of Fun." *The Journal of Educational Sociology*. (September, 1961).

L1   LANSDOWN, BRENDA, "Creating Mathematics." *Mathematics Teachers Journal*, Vol. X (June, 1960), No. 3.

L2   ————, "Orbiting a Science Program." *Science Education* (March, 1962).

L3   LEWIN, KURT, "Field Theory and Learning." *Forty-first Yearbook*, Part II, National Society for the Study of Education, 1942.

L4   ————, "Principles of Re-Education," in Benne, Kenneth, *Human Relations in Curriculum Change*. New York: The Dryden Press, Inc., 1951.

L5   ———— and LIPPIT, RONALD, "Patterns of Aggressive Behavior in Experimentally Created Social Climates." *Journal of Social Psychology* (May, 1939).

L6   LEWIS, OSCAR, *La Vida*. New York: Random House, Inc., 1967.

L7   LINDQUIST, E. F. and HIERONYMUS, A. N., *Iowa Tests of Basic Skills*. Grades 3-9, Form 1. Boston: Houghton Mifflin Company, 1955.

L8   LIPPIT, RONALD, *Training in Community Relations*. New York: Harper & Row, Publishers, 1949.

M1   MACKINNON, D. W., "Identifying and Developing Creativity." Berkeley: University of California Press, May 1959. Mimeographed.

M2   MASLOW, A. H., "Defense and Growth." *Merrill Palmer Quarterly*, Vol. 3 (1956).

M3   MAYER, MARTIN, *The Schools*. New York: Doubleday & Company, Inc., 1963.

M4   MCCRACKEN, GLENN and WALCUT, CHARLES, *Basic Reading*. Philadelphia: J. B. Lippincott Co., 1962.

M5   MCGUFFEY, WILLIAM HOLMES, *McGuffey's Fifth Eclectic Reader*. 1879 Edition. New York: New American Library of World Literature, Inc., 1962.

M6   MEAD, MARGARET, *The Schools in American Culture*. Cambridge: Harvard University Press, 1951.

M7   MEARNS, HUGHES, *Creative Power*. New York: Dover Publications, Inc., 1958.

M8   MICHAELIS, JOHN, *Social Studies for Children in a Democracy*. Englewood Cliffs, N.J.: Prentice-Hall, Inc., 1963.

M9   MIEL, ALICE, *Changing the Curriculum*. New York: Appleton-Century-Crofts, 1946.

M10   ——, (Editor), *Individualized Reading Practices*. New York: Bureau of Publications, Teachers College, Columbia University, 1958.

M11   —— and BROGAN, PEGGY, *More Than Social Studies: A View of Social Learning in the Elementary School*. Englewood Cliffs, N.J.: Prentice-Hall, Inc., 1957.

M12   MILNER, ERNST, *You and Your Student Teacher*. New York: Bureau of Publications, Teachers College, Columbia University, 1961.

M13   MILNER, ESTHER, "A Study of the Relationships Between Reading Readiness in Grade 1 School Children and Patterns of Parent-Child Interaction." *Child Development*, Vol. 22 (1951).

M14   MORSE, ARTHUR, *Schools of Tomorrow Today*. New York: Doubleday & Company, Inc., 1960.

M15   MOYNIHAN, DANIEL, "The Moynihan Report and Its Critics." *Commentary*, February 1967.

M16   ——, *The Negro Family*. Washington, D.C.: U.S. Department of Labor, 1965.

N1   NASS, MARTIN, "Characteristics of a Psychotherapeutically Oriented Group for Beginning Teachers." *Mental Hygiene*, Vol. 43 (October, 1959), No. 4.

N2   NATIONAL COUNCIL FOR THE SOCIAL STUDIES, *A Guide to Contents in the Social Studies*. Washington, D.C.: National Education Association, 1957.

N3   NAVARRA, J. GABRIEL and ZAFFORONI, JOSEPH, *Science Today for the Elementary School Teacher*. New York: Harper & Row, Publishers, 1963.

O1   O'DONNEL, MABEL, *Guidebook for Runaway Home*. Basic Sixth Reader, The Alice and Jerry Basic Reading Program. Illinois: Harper & Row, Publishers, 1957.

O2   OLSEN, G. EDWARD, *School and Community*. Englewood Cliffs, N.J.: Prentice-Hall, Inc., 1945.

P1   PACKARD, VANCE, *The Wastemakers*. New York: Pocket Books, Inc., 1963.

P2   PASSOW, A. HARRY (Editor), *Education in Depressed Areas.*
      New York: Bureau of Publications, Teachers College,
      Columbia University, 1963.

P3   PUGH, GRIFFITH, *Guide to Research Writing.* Boston: Hough-
      ton Mifflin Company, 1963.

R1   RATHS, LOUIS E., HARRIMAN, MERRILL, and SIMON, B. SIDNEY,
      Values and Teaching. Columbus, Ohio: Charles E. Mer-
      rill Books, Inc., 1966.

R2   REDL, FRITZ and WATTENBERG, WILLIAM, *Mental Hygiene in
      Teaching.* New York: Harcourt, Brace & World, Inc.,
      1951.

R3   RIESMAN, DAVID, *The Lonely Crowd.* New York: Doubleday
      & Company, Inc., 1953.

R4   RIESSMAN, FRANK, *The Culturally Deprived Child.* New
      York: Harper & Row, Publishers, 1962.

R5   ROSENZWEIG, E. LOUIS, *On Teachers and Teaching.* New
      York: Brooklyn College, January, 1964. Mimeographed.

R6   ———, *The Slow Learner.* New York: Brooklyn College,
      March, 1964. Mimeographed.

S1   SANDERS, NORRIS, *Classroom Questions.* New York: Harper &
      Row, Publishers, 1966.

S2   SARASON, SEYMOUR, DAVIDSON, KENNETH, and BLATT, BUR-
      TON, *The Preparation of Teachers.* New York: John
      Wiley & Sons, Inc., 1962.

S3   SCHACHTEL, ERNEST, *Metamorphosis.* New York: Basic
      Books, Inc., Publishers, 1959.

S4   SHAFTEL, FANNIE, "Evaluation for Today and for the Fu-
      ture." *Educational Leadership,* February, 1957.

S5   SHUMSKY, ABRAHAM, *Creative Teaching in the Elementary
      School.* New York: Appleton-Century-Crofts, 1965.

S6   ———, *The Action Research Way of Learning.* New York:
      Bureau of Publications, Teachers College, Columbia Uni-
      versity, 1958.

S7   ———, *The Clash of Cultures in Israel.* New York: Bureau
      of Publications, Teachers College, Columbia University,
      1955.

S8   ———, "The Personal Significance of an Action Research
      Problem to Teachers." *The Journal of Teacher Educa-
      tion* (June, 1958).

S9   ——— and MURRAY, WALTER, "Student Teachers Explore
      Discipline." *The Journal of Teacher Education.* Vol.
      . . . (December, 1961), No. . . . .

S10 SHUMSKY, ADAIA, *Social Orientation and Intellectual Approach.* New York: The Great Neck School System, 1964. Mimeographed.

S11 SMITH, NILA, *Reading Instruction for Today's Children.* Englewood Cliffs, N.J.: Prentice-Hall, Inc., 1963.

S12 SMITH, OTHANEL, STANLEY, WILLIAM, and SHORES, HARLAN, *Fundamentals of Curriculum Development.* New York: Harcourt, Brace & World, Inc., 1950.

S13 STAHL, STANLEY, "Methods in Teaching." *The Journal of Teacher Education* (December, 1961).

S14 STENDLER, CELIA, *Teaching in the Elementary School.* New York: Harcourt, Brace & World, Inc., 1958.

S15 STERLING, EDNA, *English is Our Language.* Boston: D. C. Heath & Company, 1957.

S16 STOFFER, G. A., "Behavior Problems of Children as Viewed by Teachers and Mental Hygienists." *Mental Hygiene*, Vol. 36 (. . . . ., 1952), No. . . . .

S17 STRATEMEYER, FLORENCE and LINDSEY, MARGARET, *Working with Student Teachers.* New York: Bureau of Publications, Teachers College, Columbia University, 1958.

S18 STROM, ROBERT (Editor), *The Inner City Classroom: Teacher Behaviors.* Columbus, Ohio: Charles E. Merrill Books, Inc., 1966.

S19 SUZUKI, D. T., *Zen Buddhism.* New York: Doubleday & Company, Inc., 1956.

T1 TABA, HILDA, *Reading Ladders for Human Relations.* Washington, D.C.: American Council on Education, 1947.

T2 TAYLOR, CALVIN, "A Tentative Description of the Creative Individual," in *Human Variability and Learning,* ASCD, 1961.

T3 TERMAN, LEWIS and MERRILL, MAUD, *Measuring Intelligence.* Boston: Houghton Mifflin Company, 1937.

T4 TORRANCE, E. PAUL, *Education and the Creative Potential.* Minneapolis: The University of Minnesota Press, 1963.

T5 ———, *Guiding Creative Talent.* Englewood Cliffs, N.J.: Prentice-Hall, Inc., 1962.

T6 ——— and STROM, ROBERT (Editors), *Mental Health and Achievement.* New York: John Wiley & Sons, Inc., 1965.

T7 TRAVERS, R. and RABINOWITZ, W., *Exploratory Studies in Teacher Personality.* New York: Division of Teacher Education, The City College of New York, 1953.

T8   TROW, WILLIAM CLARK, *Teacher and Technology.* New York: Appleton-Century-Crofts, 1963.

T9   TULARE COUNTY SOCIAL STUDIES, *A Study in Comparative Communities.* Visalia, California: Tulare County Schools.

V1   VAN TIL, WILLIAM, "Better Curriculum—Better Discipline." *N.E.A. Journal* (September, 1956).

V2   ———, "Is Progressive Education Obsolete?" *Saturday Review,* February 17, 1962.

W1   WANN, D. KENNETH, DORN, MIRIAM, and LIDDLE, ELIZABETH, *Fostering Intellectual Development in Young Children.* New York: Bureau of Publications, Teachers College, Columbia University, 1962.

W2   WARNER, W. LLOYD, HAVIGHURST, ROBERT, and LOEB, MARTIN, *Who shall be Educated?* New York: Harper & Row, Publishers, 1944.

W3   WATSON, GOODWIN, *Action for Unity.* New York: Harper & Row, Publishers, 1948.

W4   WICKMAN, E. K., *Children's Behavior and Teachers' Attitudes.* New York: Commonwealth Fund, 1928.

index